CRUCIBLE *of*
FIRE

Related Titles from Potomac Books:

The Money Trail: How Elmer Irey and His T-Men Brought Down America's Criminal Elite by Robert G. Folsom

CRUCIBLE *of* FIRE

NINETEENTH–CENTURY *Urban Fires and the* *Making of the* MODERN FIRE SERVICE

BRUCE HENSLER

Potomac Books

Washington, D.C.

Library of Congress Cataloging-in-Publication Data

Hensler, Bruce, 1953-
Crucible of fire : nineteenth-century urban fires and the making of the modern fire service / Bruce Hensler.
    p. cm.
Includes bibliographical references and index.
ISBN 978-1-59797-684-8 (hardcover : alk. paper)
1. Fire prevention—United States—History—19th century. 2. Fires—United States—History—19th century. 3. Cities and towns—United States—History—19th century. 4. City and town life—United States—History—19th century. 5. Fire extinction—United States—History—19th century. 6. Fire departments—United States—History—19th century. 7. Fire fighters—United States—History—19th century. 8. Fire prevention—Social aspects—United States—History—19th century. 9. Fires—Social aspects—United States—History—19th century. I. Title.
TH9503.H45 2011
628.9'2097309034—dc22

2011007448

Printed in the United States of America on acid-free paper that meets the American National Standards Institute Z39-48 Standard.

Potomac Books, Inc.
22841 Quicksilver Drive
Dulles, Virginia 20166

First Edition

10 9 8 7 6 5 4 3 2 1

In memory of E.H., M.H., and M.S.

Contents

Preface

The history of the development of the modern fire service in the United States is thin. There are many books about the various fire departments, as well as some excellent firefighter memoirs. There are books about fire engines and fire stations. Only a few books, most out of print now, capture the development of firefighting in the United States over the past two centuries. This book approaches the subject differently. It attempts to explore the lesser known cultural, social, and technological aspects of the war waged against fire in the combustible cities of the nineteenth century. As U.S. cities rapidly expanded in the wake of industrialization in the 1800s, they burned with regularity, requiring a massive response in firefighting capacity. Paid fire departments and steam-powered fire engines became popular thanks to civic-mindedness and the necessity of economic preservation. Cities had to be safe from fires to protect the financial investments of the private sector. The effort to preserve economic wealth resulted in the organized fire service we know today. These great urban fires changed the face of the U.S. cityscape as new buildings replaced old ones. The fires and conflagrations provided a crucible of learning for firefighters, builders, architects, engineers, insurance underwriters, developers, and civic leaders. From these times grew new methods of building construction, new building materials, high-capacity public water systems, building codes, and a body of knowledge in fire protection. Out of this era grew the modern fire department.

Writing a history implies a responsibility for an honest analysis. In this book my experience as a firefighter provides a certain additional perspective.

If I could name everyone I spoke with about these matters over the years, however informal the conversation, that list itself would fill a book. The Internet provided a rich source of contemporary and historical information. The Google Books Library Project provided access to many works I could not have located without travel to major research libraries. I read many fire service blogs and related websites to understand better the contemporary modes of thinking about firefighting. I also read many fire service books, histories, journal articles, and magazine stories. "Firefighter" is the standard term for describing a man or woman whose duty is extinguishing fires, although, like many others, I frequently use "fireman" and do so frequently in this book simply as a matter of habit.

I am indebted to Deborah Hensler for reading and commenting on many versions of the early text and Ed Marks for reading later versions, as well as for numerous and lengthy conversations about firefighting. Special thanks to the Portland Veteran Firemen's Association for access to their photographic collection of the 1866 Great Fire of Portland, Maine. Susan Berlowitz was invaluable for her diligent photo research. She located rare photographs of the Fire Department of New York (FDNY) from the Frederick Smythe Collection at the New York Historical Society and another source of rare FDNY photographs, the Dreyfous Collection held by the Connecticut Firemen's Historical Society. Gary Pinkham, a fire historian with that organization, assisted by providing background information on the collection and offering several images for inclusion in this book. Special thanks to Anne Holmes for creating the index. Finally, I would like to acknowledge my many firefighting associates, most notably my mentors, the late Dan Aston and Bruce Woodward, and Fred Bray, a veteran city firefighter who went on to be chief of department. Fred worked alongside me in my early years and listened enthusiastically to my sometimes nontraditional ideas about modern firefighting on those long shifts at Engine 3.

—*BH*

Abbreviations

AIA – American Insurance Association

ANSI – American National Standards Institute

BTU – British Thermal Unit

DOT – Department of Transportation

EMS – emergency medical services

EMT – emergency medical technician

EPA – Environmental Protection Agency

FDNY – Fire Department of New York

GIS – geographic information system

GPS – global positioning system

hazmat – hazardous materials

IAFC – International Association of Fire Chiefs

IAFF – International Association of Fire Fighters

ISO – Insurance Services Office

NBFU – National Board of Fire Underwriters

NFIRS – National Fire Incident Reporting System

NFPA – National Fire Protection Association

NIOSH – National Institute for Occupational Safety and Health

OSHA – Occupational Safety and Health Administration

PPC – Public Protection Classification

PPE – personal protective equipment

SCBA – self-contained breathing apparatus

SOG – standard operating guideline

SOP – standard operating procedure

TIC – thermal imaging camera

USFA – U.S. Fire Administration

Introduction

Firefighters study fire protection science, which encompasses the chemistry and physics of combustion, building construction, and fluid hydraulics, among other technical subjects. They also study first aid, emergency medicine, leadership, and risk management. Successful firefighting involves application of technical knowledge under frequently hazardous conditions. The ability to exercise essential skills is achievable not through classroom learning but through continued hands-on practice. Flawless execution of these skills must be second nature. In addition, to be fully competent in firefighting, one must actually participate in fighting a fire at some level. Live-fire training has value, but it cannot replace real-world experience. How the modern fire service learned to fight fires effectively and efficiently came at a great cost over hundreds of years.

While ancient Rome can lay claim to the first organized firefighting force, the methods of organized public fire protection as we know them today have their origins in Amsterdam. By 1700 the city of Amsterdam employed relatively advanced methods of fighting fires. As the world's center of commerce, it faced a complex fire problem. The city saw the solution in the invention of improved fire pumps and fire hose by Jan van der Heyden, a talented Dutch artist. His ideas were not limited to technology alone but also covered the administration of firefighting resources. A century or so later, the industrial age elevated the threat of fire beyond anything realized to that time. Fires in urban-industrial areas threatened lives and property, requiring highly organized firefighting efforts. In 1820 James Braidwood became the fire chief of Edinburgh's firefighting force, and he rightly deserves credit, along with Jan van der Heyden, as one of the founders of the modern fire service. Braidwood would later do for London what he did for Edinburgh. He died in 1861 at a warehouse fire in London. In 1866 an army officer and former fire chief of Belfast, Eyre Massey Shaw, took over the leadership of London's firefighting forces during the transition to a metropolitan fire brigade under government control. Under Shaw, firefighting and fire protection evolved into a professional occupation following principles of science. Shaw was the first modern fire chief who also acted as executive leader. At the same time, New York City's reorganized Metropolitan Fire Department developed along paramilitary lines roughly paralleling London's forces, but with some major differences. In the nineteenth century, circumstances in the United States, including its natural resources and particular national character, set the stage for a series of great urban fires. From that experience, the modern fire service took the form we know today and developed a unique occupational culture that remains powerful to the present.

Many books on the history of particular great fires or about specific fire departments exist; fewer books take a broad view of the development of the modern fire service. The historical script of early firefighting in the United States follows a line that usually starts with Benjamin Franklin's volunteer fire company and tracks the mostly futile efforts of colonial bucket brigades and brawling, rowdy volunteer firemen. The traditional stories track the demise of the unruly volunteers through the introduction of steam fire engines and paid fire departments. Traditional firefighting histories have limited scope and perspective, focusing usually on a particular city and a few notable people. Many myths and half-truths have their origin in these works. The traditional story leaves the reader to think that volunteers no longer exist, or if they do exist, they are somehow inferior to paid firefighters and found only in rural communities. The reality of public fire protection in the United States is far different. The delivery of public fire services in the United States has become increasingly complex. To fix the problems and move forward, we must first understand the past, looking deeper into the cultural, sociological, and technological history of firefighting over the late nineteenth and early twentieth centuries. Through that lens, an honest picture emerges, one that reflects the U.S. fire service of the twenty-first century. This book explores the people, events, ideas, and technology that helped to forge the U.S. fire service into what it is today.

Large segments of U.S. cities burned in the late nineteenth century; in the first half of the twentieth century, fires burned city blocks and groups of buildings. By the late twentieth century, firefighters had learned to contain fires to floors and individual rooms. Block and group fires are rare today. They are rare because of what firefighters and the fire insurance industry learned in the nineteenth- and twentieth-century American city. Human capacity to control or manage fire is limited at best. Control of fire gives meaning to the phrase "eternal vigilance." Centuries of experience with fire have taught vital lessons, which prove disastrous when ignored. Fire, or the process of combustion, is an exothermic or heat-producing chemical reaction between a substance and oxygen. Fire is controlled by one of four means: separate the burning substance from the flame, remove or dilute the oxygen, reduce the temperature of the combustible or the flame, or introduce chemicals to modify the combustion process. Control of the combustion process is essential to the survival of humans and the viability of civilized society. Early humans settled in groups and built protective structures for shelter. They quickly learned that fire in an uncontrolled state is catastrophic and often deadly. Keeping fires kindled overnight created a need for someone to tend them. In the larger settlements, towns, and cities, fire watches and fire brigades met this need. Members of the Roman legion formed the first officially sanctioned fire brigade to protect Rome. The soldiers were well suited to the task, as they were already committed to protecting the citizens of Rome. When commerce took on everyday importance, the control of fire became even more critical in order to preserve wealth.

The first great city of the modern age to burn was London in the year 1666. The most significant outcomes of the Great Fire of London were rules for rebuilding the city. In the decades after, fire insurance and the formation of fire brigades paid for by insurance companies came into existence. This arrangement remained intact for many years before the government of London assumed full responsibility for the maintenance of these brigades. Public fire protection has always maintained close ties to the fire insurance industry. This fact is critical to understanding how the modern fire service developed.[1]

Those English who immigrated to America brought with them the fundamental concept of fire protection for the public good. This protection proved essential in colonial settlements where wood was used in the construction of buildings in the midst of very combustible wilderness. In America the earliest public fire protection measures regulated chimney construction and roofing materials, but the settlers often ignored these simple rules. Native Americans of the Northeast routinely burned the undergrowth of forests to facilitate hunting. Farmers adopted the practice to clear land, as did hunters for killing game. The practice evolved as a tool for various purposes. Europeans had similar practices; however, to avoid disaster governments banned the use of fire to clear land. Governments in the American colonies eventually outlawed the practice as well, but as with other fire prevention and control regulations, they failed to enforce the law.

With some exceptions, such as in Amsterdam, measures to control fire remained primitive until the industrial age. The earliest urban-industrial fires occurred in England, where the mix of materials, processes, people, and ignition sources in factories and warehouses merged, often with volatile results. Efforts to control and manage fire concentrated on the materials and construction methods used for factory buildings. The new knowledge of fire protection thus developed in England and Scotland. Decades later the practices migrated to the United States as industry there began to develop. New England factory owners formed mutual pacts for the strict purpose of underwriting their own insurance. These agreements laid the foundation for mutual insurance companies specializing in factory and warehouse risks. The managers of the factory mutual insurance companies took an especially strong stand on preventing fires.

In early nineteenth-century America, laws were enacted to control the storage and use of hazardous and volatile substances in the thickly settled areas and commercial districts of towns and cities. Later laws specifically addressed egress from buildings, especially schools. Despite early attempts at fire control, the urban fire problem steadily grew worse from mid-century onward. In the rush to economic expansion and industrialization, Americans created combustible, densely built urban areas, the right mixture of features for conflagrations. Very large urban conflagrations of that era were often called great fires. We tend to use the term "conflagration" to describe those fires we imagine as larger than normal, most often involving several buildings. Americans once accepted the inevitability of unwanted fires in buildings that could and would burn whole towns and cities. We have learned to prevent and control fires to the degree that we accept building fires as commonplace but no longer expect them to consume adjacent buildings or blocks.

Accepting the fact that buildings will catch fire, the most basic method to prevent building-to-building spread over a wide area, aside from having an excellent fire department, is to construct fire-separation walls or limit the spread by isolating the buildings into groups separated by open space. Understanding the inherent hazard, or fire susceptibility, is critical to understanding the urban conflagration problem of the nineteenth century. Beyond ignition, it is the form, placement, construction, and condition of nearby buildings that influence any subsequent spreading of fire beyond the building of origin. Taken together, these features determine the relative fire susceptibility of an area. Variance in wind, moisture level, and temperature affect the climate and play a role in fire susceptibility in all regions of the world and, to some extent, between areas within individual countries.[2]

Determining the overall conflagration hazard involves an assessment of the aggregate fire susceptibility of the individual buildings, as well as the density of the structures and their degree of division and/or separation. Density has three components: percentage of land built upon, pattern of the built structures, and intensity of development as it relates to building height (i.e., the volume of building per square foot). The pattern of buildings affects the potential for fire from one building igniting another, creating an exposure problem. Fire-separation walls (if high enough and built properly) and open areas (such as parks) may impede the spread of fire. Urban fires spread among combustible materials and structures via radiant heat and direct contact with flames.[3] Thus, unchecked combustion is simply a process of transferring heat energy from one object to another. Noncombustible fire-separation walls and open areas serve to defeat the process of heat energy transfer. Fire-separation walls and open spaces are often compromised by brands and embers carried aloft on superheated convection currents and on the wind into unburned areas downwind, where they ignite spot fires. In some large conflagrations, powerful flame fronts have jumped open spaces thought to have been sufficient to prevent fire spread. Fighting an urban conflagration successfully requires that firefighters utilize fire walls, separations, and open space to their advantage. This means they use these features to make a defensive stand, usually at the flanks (sides) of the advancing fire front, and bring the fire under control by protecting exposures (unburned buildings) and applying water to the less severe fires at the margins. They must operate on the periphery of the conflagration, where the fire is relatively cooler and where their hose streams will be more effective in quenching the cooling the flames. Many conflagrations continue consuming combustibles only until slowed by rain or snow or geography, allowing firefighters to then move in on their centers and kill them.

Elected public officials failed miserably to address the urban fire problem into the last decade of the nineteenth century until pressure mounted from the private-sector fire insurance industry. New York City saw its share of major fires, and it is likely that only the heroic efforts, diligence, and experience of the city's volunteer firemen prevented major conflagrations of significant proportions. For the cities that experienced large-scale fire disasters, contributing factors were likely the inexperience of poorly equipped volunteer fire brigades. In 1835 New York City experienced a great fire that lasted several days, destroying the New York Stock Exchange and many nearby buildings. Ten years later, one-third of Pittsburgh burned in a fast-moving fire that did most of its damage in about three hours but lasted nearly seven. In both fires, roughly the same size area of developed urban land burned, approximately sixty acres. The pace with which American cities of that era grew influenced their susceptibility to fire, and fire insurance and firefighting capacity could not keep up. The facts became evident after the New York and Pittsburgh fires, but increasingly so in the great urban fires following the Civil War.

The New York and Pittsburgh fires were notable, yet they did not capture the attention and interest of the fire insurance industry as did a conflagration in Portland, Maine, on July 4, 1866. The city was a significant seaport with high-value commercial interests, and the losses of the fire insurance companies were so great that fire insurance underwriters feared a financial disaster. Underwriters from insurance companies in other states went so far as to provide financial backing to their competitors for fear the public would lose faith in fire insurance altogether. The threat of urban conflagration steadily grew as the United States' densely packed urban-industrial centers rapidly expanded. The elements of this formula for disaster included hazardous substances, open flames, wood-frame construction, and too many people. The Great Fire of Chicago occurred on October 8, 1871, and gave impetus for the recognition of Fire Prevention Week in future Octobers. Conflagrations in Boston (1872), Baltimore (1904), and San Francisco (1906) were notable for their individually distinct influence on the development of municipal fire services, public water supply systems, architecture, building codes, and fire protection technology. Through the late nineteenth and early twentieth centuries, larger cities and towns replaced their volunteer firemen with paid personnel. They also replaced antiquated fire equipment with horse-drawn apparatus, including steam-powered pumpers, hose wagons, and ladder trucks. Improvements to public water supply infrastructure featured increased capacity, larger mains, grid distribution systems, and fire hydrants.

The devil is in the details, and water system engineers failed to standardize the thread size for fire hydrant hose connections. This little fact spelled disaster in fire after fire. Fire companies coming to the aid of another city to help control a conflagration were unable to connect their fire hoses to the hydrants in that city because the thread size of the hose connections was different. Unbelievably, in the twenty-first century, this problem remains. A few years ago, a government study by the National Institute of Standards revealed that forty-eight major American cities had yet to adopt the national standard for fire hydrant threads.[4] Just as appalling is the fact that many neighboring fire departments still use different hose threads, making the problem of working together ever difficult.

The Portland fire prompted the fledgling insurance industry to organize local boards of fire insurance underwriters in the largest cities. These boards eventually recognized the need for a concerted effort at the national level. The National Board of Fire Underwriters (NBFU) formed in the late nineteenth century. Its first effort involved collecting data on the threat that fire posed. Armed with information on the causes of fires, it subsequently proposed regulations and improvements. Unfortunately, the influence of the NBFU was not widely embraced. The NBFU also developed an evaluation system for grading municipal fire departments, building departments, and water supply systems, although not all communities followed the recommendations. It would take the lessons from the disaster of the Baltimore fire in 1904 for the NBFU municipal-fire-grading system to take hold. The new NBFU grading system intended to push cities to develop the means to defend against conflagrations, and the effort worked. By the mid-twentieth century, urban fires were better controlled; fires that at one time might have leveled a city were being contained to city block areas.

By the 1950s and '60s, fires were routinely contained to single blocks, single buildings, and even to several floors of a building. Although American fire departments experimented with supplied breathing air beginning in the early twentieth century, not until the 1970s did firefighters begin to accept self-contained breathing apparatus (SCBA), which let them enter burning buildings with a supply of breathable air. Once perfected, SCBA technology allowed fire crews to penetrate deep into hot, toxic, smoke-filled environments to extinguish even large fires inside enclosed structures. Fires were now routinely contained to the floor or even the room of origin. SCBA was accepted only because the contents of modern buildings were increasingly composed of plastic and synthetic materials that emit toxic gases when burned. By the 1990s, with the introduction of fire-resistant protective gear, firefighters had some personal protection from toxic smoke, high heat, and flashovers, thus allowing them to work a bit longer within burning structures. At this point, controlling a fire meant stopping it in or close to the room of origin.

The NBFU grading system, motorized fire apparatus, paid firefighters, building codes, fire safety regulations, self-contained breathing apparatus, and automatic sprinkler system protection were factors in the near total conquest of urban-industrial fire. As the twentieth century unfolded, firefighters started to embrace technology and adopt new fire-control tactics. The fire insurance industry, working through NBFU inspectors and local insurance agents, began a simultaneous effort to promote basic fire prevention. Building codes and fire-prevention regulations were part of a campaign against urban fire. The firefighting lessons learned from the age of urban conflagration and knowledge of the elements necessary to create a fire-safe environment came about through systematic data collection and the application of scientific principles. It was not hard to make a case that thickly populated, densely built cities of wooden structures were an open invitation to disaster. Experience proved, in fire after fire, that cities with brick buildings were inherently safer. Even better were brick buildings with fire-resistive window frames and doors with no wooden ornamentation. Increasing the width of streets and the distance between structures, as well as adding parapet fire walls to buildings with common walls, further reduced the hazard of fire. The addition of automatic sprinkler systems and full-time fire departments meant that firefighters could now keep fires to the floor or room of origin.

The NBFU is gone, but their work continues under the auspices of the Insurance Services Office (ISO). In a 1965 merger, the NBFU, along with other insurance trade entities, became the American Insurance Association (AIA). In 1971 AIA spun off what is today the ISO. The ISO publishes their Fire Suppression Rating Schedule (known as the ISO rating schedule or the FSRS).

The new rating schedule replaced the NBFU's Standard Grading Schedule for Grading Cities and Towns of the United States with Reference to Their Fire Defenses and Physical Conditions. The United States paid a heavy price over a hundred-year period to learn how to control urban fire, and it is a lesson we cannot afford to neglect or forget. That period was a crucible of learning and is the focus of this book. Without the influence of the NBFU, municipal fire departments in the United States would likely look and act differently. Whether they would be better in some manner than they are now without the NBFU is debatable. Given the entrenchment of tradition and past practice in our departments today, it is reasonable to guess that things would be a lot worse.

In the coming chapters this book will define the extent of the fire problem in the United States, examine the forces of change that keep U.S. firefighters scrambling, illustrate how we learned to fight the great city and block fires, and consider the influence of collective experience in our ongoing struggle to control fire.

I

THE CONTEXT OF THE MODERN FIRE SERVICE

CHAPTER I

Origins of Organized Fire Service

At the dawn of the twenty-first century, the fire service in the United States appears to stand firm with one boot in the nineteenth century and the other in the twentieth. More precisely, one boot represents cultural traditions while the other represents technological change. The well-worn idea that the fire service represents 250 years of tradition untouched by progress is a half truth. The United States' firefighting resources—stations, apparatus, and personnel—are mostly deployed in a nineteenth-century pattern. Great urban fires overwhelmed the firefighters of that era. They were simply no match for uncontrollable fire racing through combustible blocks of buildings, and they knew it. The great urban fires and conflagrations showed us the necessity of planning urban areas, limiting combustible materials in buildings, installing high-capacity public water systems, and creating a model for delivering municipal fire services. As those concepts fell into place during the last decade of the nineteenth century and the first decade of the twentieth century, the fire service gained the ability to attack great fires with some chance of success. From there, fire chiefs and firefighters set about building a foundation for the new occupation of firefighting.

Politics, opinion, opportunity, and personality greatly influence the acquisition and use of resources. History, tradition, and occupational culture control firefighter behavior. Too frequently, local politicians practice cronyism when appointing senior fire officials, allowing self-interest to guide them in making decisions affecting the safety of the public and the firefighters. Despite any negative perceptions, the fire service collectively does a commendable job, and Americans widely admire and trust firefighters. Working or volunteering as a firefighter in this country is generally very rewarding, resulting in a feeling of doing something important and making a contribution to society. However, there is cause for concern for the volunteer fire service as it struggles to exist in a complex world while still maintaining those elements of its nature that have sustained it as a form of fire protection for over two hundred years.

The twenty-first century will see the end of the second era in the history of volunteer firefighting in the United States. In the second half of the nineteenth century, the first era of volunteer firefighting ended as cities created paid fire departments to provide stable and efficient municipal fire protection. In the initial phase of development, those early paid fire departments mirrored their volunteer brethren for the most part. The end of the nineteenth century and the beginning of the twentieth century marks a transition for firefighters, fire engineers, and fire underwriters. The challenge of combating conflagrations in cities and towns built of wood and brick set into motion evolutionary forces that transformed those first paid departments into truly professional organizations. This second era witnessed the birth of the modern fire department through the combined influence of the fire insurance industry, a few notable fire chiefs, and advances in technology. Another remarkable outcome was the remolding of the remaining volunteer departments in the likeness of the paid departments, just as the first paid forces had mimicked the volunteer system. This is an important distinction to recognize and acknowledge.

In the act of attacking and extinguishing a fire, one cannot (and should not) perceive any difference between a volunteer and a paid or career firefighter. Firefighter unions have long attempted to attach "professional" to their title, as if receiving a paycheck made a notable difference in the ability to attack and extinguish a fire. The real difference, however, is functional. It is the difference between firefighters being on duty (in the firehouse) and being on call (carrying a pager and going about their daily chores). The volunteer fire system in the United States is in a transformative mode precipitated by social, demographic, and economic forces. Thousands of small town and suburban volunteer fire departments struggle to staff fire apparatus and ambulances in response to an ever-increasing volume of emergency calls. Certainly the volunteer fire service across the United States responds to fire and emergency medical calls every day, thus meeting the demand, but the system is under stress and on the verge of breakdown. In some areas, outright collapse of the volunteer system is at hand, while in others the prospect is for transformation rather than elimination.

The factors in the decline vary from community to community, but a study of volunteer fire services in Pennsylvania provides a basis for beginning to understand the volunteer problem. The Pennsylvania study issued in 2006 confirms the findings of other studies: the volunteer system is failing nationwide. Two critical issues are department funding and quality of leadership. If volunteers must devote their limited free time to raising funds and meeting critical training needs, their morale and motivation to be an active member will suffer. Time also plays a part in leadership. If fire company officers must devote time to increasing demands for recordkeeping and filing reports, they have less time to devote to meeting critical leadership and supervisory needs. Other issues include safety concerns and training requirements. Volunteers have a strong desire to serve their community, and receiving direct compensation in the form of pay is not a significant incentive. Incentives that do attract the attention of volunteers, at least in Pennsylvania, include having state-of-the-art equipment available, income tax credits, college tuition credits, health insurance coverage, and pension benefits.[1]

There is no accurate count of active volunteer firefighters in the United States. There are various informed estimates, but safely speaking the number is around 750,000. What makes this problem so difficult to address is that the factors influencing change vary among individual volunteer firefighters and among volunteer fire departments. The decisions we make today regarding volunteer fire departments will determine whether the volunteer system survives. This decision is important because the small U.S. cities and towns cannot afford the financial cost of creating full-time fire departments; the taxes necessary to replace volunteers can cripple local economies.

The National Fire Protection Association (NFPA) report *Fire Department Profile through 2007* classifies U.S. fire departments by staffing arrangement (whether the firefighter is paid or a volunteer). A career department is one in which all members are full-time, paid; mostly career is 51 to 99 percent full-time, paid; mostly volunteer is 1 to 50 percent nonpaid; and volunteer is 100 percent nonpaid. The NFPA determined through the 2007 National Fire Experience Survey that there were approximately 1,148,800 structural (i.e., non-wildland) firefighters in the United States in 2007. Of that number, 28 percent were career firefighters and 72 percent were volunteers. Most of the career firefighters (74 percent) protected communities of 25,000 or more people. The majority of volunteers (95 percent) served in departments protecting fewer than 2,500 people. The NFPA estimated 30,185 fire departments in the United States, with 2,263 being all career; 1,765 mostly career; 4,989 mostly volunteer; and 21,168 all volunteer. Forty-four percent of U.S. fire departments provide emergency medical services (EMS). By those statistics, the potential consequence of the demise or collapse of the volunteer fire system has a direct financial impact on a significant portion of the U.S. population.[2]

Our entire municipal fire protection system, whether the department is full-time or volunteer, depends on mutual assistance and automatic aid agreements to cover service demand over a region. In other words, for all but the very largest metropolitan-size fire department, mutual aid agreements are essential to bring nearby departments into neighboring cities and towns to cover major fires and disasters. Under such an agreement, whenever the incident scene commander determines that the local resources of the department cannot meet the challenge, a request to respond goes to member departments in the mutual aid system. With mutual aid, you get help only if you ask for it. However, as the number of volunteers has fallen, getting enough volunteer firefighters to respond for basic house fires is a problem in many areas. There is now a trend for departments to go beyond mutual aid to automatic aid. Under an automatic aid agreement, departments respond per specific scenarios. For example, upon receipt of an E-911 call for a building fire, dispatchers notify the local fire department, as well as the neighboring departments to ensure adequate staffing is present at the fire. The pressure on staffing also affects combination fire departments (those composed of a mixture of paid and volunteer members), forcing many to resort to automatic aid to meet incident response needs.

Even if a community has a career fire department, there is no guarantee they have adequate staffing to meet even ordinary fire challenges. In fact, many so-called full-time departments are severely understaffed and may depend on volunteers from surrounding communities to help. If those volunteers are in short supply, the fire protection in that community may be in jeopardy. Most fire chiefs will say that they lack a sufficient force of on-duty firefighters. Rural communities are especially at risk of shortages. Wildland firefighting requires the movement of labor, tools, and water to a fire scene spread out over hundreds or thousands of acres in rough terrain. The larger the fire, the more resources are needed. The inability to amass an effective concentration of force (labor) and resources (tools, equipment, and water) exacerbates the challenge of wildland fire control. In urban areas, fire protection is located strategically and concentrated to meet the expected demand. In addition, water systems with strategically placed fire hydrants serve to support the effort.

Rural firefighting is not just fighting fires in woodland and grassland. The interstate highway system cuts through large swaths of rural land linking various urbanized cities and towns. Recent decades have seen the suburbanization of once-remote rural areas, as well as a proliferation of big box stores and retail centers to serve the residential population. Another part of this development is the placement of warehouses, transportation depots, feedlots, and megafarms along rural stretches of the interstate highway system. These features serve the needs of a modern economy that functions 24/7. The fire protection needs of these features are beyond that of most rural volunteer fire companies. Thus small towns must upgrade fire stations to accommodate new fire apparatus and recruit, train, and equip volunteers at a significant cost. This recent development places increasing strain on rural and suburban firefighters and raises the cost of fire protection borne by the taxpayer.

There is a link between poverty, high-density living, and the potential for fire. Firefighters know this. The duty of firefighters to extinguish fire but also to protect life developed at the turn of the nineteenth and twentieth centuries, especially in the Fire Department of New York (FDNY). As the city grew vertically and buildings filled with people working and sleeping, the fire department faced the challenge of not only extinguishing fire but also assisting and removing occupants threatened by fire and smoke. This is where the modern public's trust in firefighters grew and sustained itself. Immigrants to the United States knew that pulling the handle of the fire alarm boxes found on street corners in the city brought assistance from the city's firemen; thus the people of New York knew that their firefighters would not let them die in a fire.[3]

The average person is unlikely to be able to discern the difference between a volunteer and a paid firefighter, especially in the performance of fighting a fire. The traditional U.S. firefighter in caricature is a burly man, with handlebar mustache, soot-smeared face, wearing a leather fire helmet. Reality is something altogether different. When someone dials 911 to report a fire, the nearest fire engines will quickly appear at their front door, but it is likely that the caller will have no clue whether the men and women who step off the truck are paid or volunteer. In difficult economic conditions, there is even an effort to utilize volunteer systems as opposed to the more costly paid or career system.[4]

Many local governments struggle to provide essential services, including fire protection. While the number of emergency response requests to fire departments increases, the actual number of fires is decreasing. This leaves many observers to question fire department expenditures and leaves fire administrators in the difficult position of justifying expenditures for services. In fact, some fire chiefs feel they need to offer additional services to justify department spending, and in some cases add services without planning, adequate staffing, or long-term financing.

In the late 1980s, occupational safety came to the fire service, along with a new focus on training and competency. It was not that safety and training were absent prior to this time, just that they began to receive attention for a few important reasons. This was about the time that the decline in actual fires was surfacing, but it was also when hazardous materials accidents were occurring with more frequency. The nation's rail lines were in bad shape, and more than a few times, trains passing through populated areas derailed. Some of these accidents resulted in spilled chemicals or the release of toxic gases. Explosions and fires were also common. Because firefighters and police officers are the first responders to land transportation accidents, they were coming in contact more frequently with chemicals and similar hazardous products at accident scenes.

The 1980s were also a time when we began to recognize the significance of environmental pollution. Transportation accidents involving hazardous cargoes and chemical-plant fires added to the concern, so the government began to regulate the use, handling, transportation, and storage of hazardous substances. At the national level, the Department of Transportation (DOT), Environmental Protection Agency (EPA), and Occupational Safety and Health Administration (OSHA) began taking steps to regulate hazardous materials in transportation and industry. The government agencies issued safety regulations requiring training and the use of personal protective equipment, recognizing that emergency first responders were in harm's way when dealing with hazardous-product accidents.

More than a few fire chiefs of the era saw an opportunity in the new focus on hazmat (hazardous materials) response to create revenue through federal safety program grants, as well as postaccident-cleanup and product-recovery fees. The lasting consequence of the federal regulations was that industry and transportation began to take steps to improve the storage and handling of hazardous substances. Within a few years, the situation improved, and there were fewer large-scale accidents. Another result was that the fire service ended up with a new task (hazmat response) but generally did not receive any significant funding to support the new responsibility.

One rarely recognized benefit from the Vietnam War was the knowledge gained in providing emergency medical care to wounded soldiers and the use of air transport to evacuate the critically injured. Advances in trauma care, as well as other advances in medicine, provided Americans with a new standard for medical care. The emergency medical system as we know it today began in the late 1970s under the guidance of trauma surgeons and the highway safety division of the DOT. As the country sprawled outward from the cities, travel by car became a necessity leading to more overall travel. Travel at higher speeds on new superhighways and substandard secondary roads led to more motor vehicle accidents and trauma victims.

Simple first aid was inadequate for victims of serious motor vehicle accidents. Survival of accident victims required immediate intervention with critical care provided by paramedics. The DOT, working with trauma surgeons, developed the EMS system based on intervention by trained emergency medical technicians combined with rapid transport to specialized medical trauma centers. Thus, EMS as we know it today was born. Americans quickly recognized the benefits of emergency care and were willing to support local EMS systems. Some EMS systems are hospital based, but local government and private firms dominate as providers. The potential for cost recovery for EMS systems is strong enough to make private sector and fire-based EMS appear attractive. Fire chiefs seeking to preserve basic fire protection capacity in the wake of declining fire calls often fund the fire response end of the operation by providing EMS. For cash-strapped local governments, any service with the potential to generate revenue is attractive, especially in a time of declining fires.

Organized societies are notable for their use of fire for survival, and industrialized societies are notable for their efforts to use and control fire for the creation of wealth. The more forward-thinking industrialized societies place an emphasis on fire prevention and control. Preventing unwanted fires is a better investment than fire suppression. Automatic fire suppression is far superior to manual fire suppression because it minimizes damages and is more cost-effective.

The United States invests heavily in manual fire suppression, suffers one of the highest fire loss records among industrialized countries, and ranks high in fire death rates.

The risk from fire varies but is always associated with certain conditions. The conditions that favor fire differ depending on the environment. In wildland areas, fire risk is associated with weather conditions, available fuels, terrain, and opportunity. Lightning strikes are a significant cause of remote wildland fires. Where people live and work, the conditions that favor fire are population density, building construction, socioeconomic characteristics, and opportunity. Firefighters often joke that the three causes of fires are people, people, and people.

There is a link between the development of cities and the formation of organized firefighting forces. As clustered farms and dwellings evolved into settlements, villages, towns, and cities, more and more people lived closer together. This trend persists as the number of people living in cities continues to increase. Today in the world's largest cities, the population density averages around 25,000 people per square mile. However, going backward in time, large cities likely had higher densities of people, in some cases thought to be about 150,000 individuals per square mile. Early cities used perimeter walls for protection and to mark the cities' boundaries. Analysis of archeological sites reveals population estimates through study of the density of dwellings and the known extent of the perimeter wall. At the start of the Christian era, there were approximately two hundred people per acre in the six square miles that made up the city of Rome. It is believed (and very likely) that the expense of constructing perimeter walls kept Rome's extent small.[5] Many people today have their home on a single acre and think the neighborhood is getting crowded. Combine people, business, trades, foul water, untreated sewage, fire, and disease, and you have a stewpot of urbanization. To the people of Rome, their walled city was the "urbis" and the area just outside the city wall was the "sub-urbis."

The timeline of organized public firefighting efforts includes the Roman vigils, Amsterdam's new fire engines and fire hose, the New Amsterdam (New York) rattle-watch, Boston's first paid on-call fire force, and Franklin's colonial volunteers. What is missing is recognition of what appears to be the birth of the modern fire service and the man who was the founding father of firefighting. This story opens in Edinburgh, Scotland, in 1824, then moves on to

London around 1860. Just as the system of policing in the United States followed the British system, our system of firefighting is organized on the British model.

U.S. cities experienced more severe fires than their European counterparts. With the advantage of forests, the United States was able to construct homes and buildings with wood, while larger structures (and building owners seeking something more permanent) used brick. The United States used oil as an energy source where England and Scotland used coal. Because of immigration, U.S. cities had higher population densities. When we add up these factors, we have a recipe for frequent urban fires and conflagrations.

Over the course of the nineteenth century in the United States, these factors influenced the growth and development of our cities and our fire service. The type of building construction that caused so much trouble goes by two names: quick-burning and ordinary construction. This type of construction is prevalent in older U.S. communities in which brick and wood commercial buildings exist. Its principal features are brick exterior walls, wood trim, wood furnishings, open vertical shafts, and void spaces. U.S. cities and towns featured block upon block of these mixed-use buildings. We will cover this construction method later, as it greatly influenced the development of the fire service in the United States.

The modern fire service began when several catastrophic fires befell the city of Edinburgh, Scotland. The fires prompted the city's leaders to reorganize the insurance fire brigades under one leader with the title of fire chief. Before this, the title "foreman" was used to designate the leader of a fire brigade. The funding for the new Edinburgh Fire Engine Establishment came from fire insurance companies and public funds. Twenty-three-year-old James Braidwood, a surveyor, received the appointment as the first fire chief. The new chief recruited men aged eighteen to twenty-five years (all with building trade experience) for the city's fire service. Since they retained their regular day jobs, they were part-time firemen.[6]

Braidwood's ideas were novel for the time, but so fundamental that firefighters today follow the basic precepts. He did not hold with the convention that thought it satisfactory to fight building fires from the street. He trained his men to enter the fire building at all costs and remain there until they successfully extinguished the fire or were ordered to withdraw from their position. Making an aggressive interior attack is fundamental to modern firefighting. The Edinburgh firemen earned a reputation for skill and daring and in the process achieved a level of professionalism hitherto unknown. Casualties were frequent, but fatalities were rare because of Braidwood's principle that no fireman should enter a building alone.[7] His rule, in effect, meant that any firefighter injured or overcome would have a comrade alongside to help. Working in teams of two is a fundamental safety rule in modern firefighting; it is noteworthy that the U.S. volunteer firefighters of the era typically operated from the relative safety of the exterior of fire buildings.

Braidwood's notoriety accelerated after 1830, when he published the first firefighting manual in English. (There was a Dutch manual detailing Amsterdam's firefighting system in 1690.) His book provided theory as well as detail. An example is his discussion on fire engines. He favored compromise in sizing the pump, looking for effectiveness balanced by weight and the reality of using muscle power. He stressed getting up close to the seat of the fire with a good steady stream of water and applying it directly. His concept required firemen to find middle ground in any decisions regarding the size of their pumping engines (a unit's size affects pumping capacity and ultimately total weight). Smaller pumps offered maneuverability and thus allowed getting closer to the fire, while larger pumps dictated a stance farther from the fire. He required servicing and maintenance of the fire engines (pumps) after each fire, as well as routine monthly testing. The engine design called for conveyance by four men, with horses rarely needed. Four-wheeled units were better than two-wheeled because the larger size meant more capacity to carry tools. Remarkably, the equipment on his list is similar to that carried today on motorized fire apparatus.[8]

Braidwood considered riveted fire hose more reliable than sewn hose and required that new fire hose undergo testing to ensure suitability for service (something that continues to this day). Before placing the riveted hose into service, it was subjected to a pressure of approximately 200 feet of head (roughly 87 pounds per square inch [psi]). A pressure head of 500 feet (approximately 217 psi) would cause riveted hose to rupture violently. The waterway diameter of the hose was 2 3/8 inches (very close to the 2 1/2-inch hose used in the United States for the past hundred-plus years).[9] He also recommended that fire stations be centrally located, preferably on a hilltop next to a police-watch station, thus allowing quicker notice of alarms of fires from the watchmen and permitting fire engines a rolling start downhill. The firehouse must be well ventilated and have a stove (important for drying wet hose).[10]

Braidwood's book and innovations in Edinburgh also influenced radical change in London. In 1833 Braidwood agreed to accept an offer for the position of chief fire officer of the London Fire Engine Establishment. London, with greater resources available, provided for full-time paid firemen. The new fire chief made a shrewd observation regarding the inherent differences between the part-time, on-call staff and the full-time staff. He recognized the need for structured discipline to maintain a sober staff of firemen around the clock. His recruiting efforts for the new department focused on former sailors of the Royal Navy because they readily accepted orders and had the discipline to stand day and night duty watches. The new firemen earned their high pay, demonstrating both courage and efficiency. Braidwood died in the line of duty in 1861 at a warehouse fire on London's Tooley Street by the Thames River. Although he has been long recognized by English and Scottish firefighters as a significant contributor in making the modern fire service, Braidwood's contributions are widely unknown among firefighters in the United States.

CHAPTER 2

Firefighter Culture

U.S. firefighters go all out to fight fires. They follow a high-risk, aggressive, move-forward approach with minimal to no tolerance for a defensive (i.e., safe) position outside the burning building. Their culture is one of taking the offensive position against fire, one that frequently leads them into trouble and even death. Why not take a safe defensive stance? Some of the reasons are tradition, peer pressure, and ignorance of scientific principles. The latter is attributable to poor training, but the first two purely relate to occupational culture. What is it about fire that prompts firefighters to react as they do, to go beyond the call of duty, to risk everything, including, for some, their very lives? To be a firefighter requires some level of acceptance of inordinate risk, but on top of that firefighting is rooted in a culture rich in brotherhood and heroic tradition.

Fire is a force of nature that, when out of control, appears to have a mind of its own. It is at the same time both awesome and threatening. Fires in nature will burn until the fuel source is exhausted or the weather intervenes. The same is true of large urban fires. When people formed settlements, villages, towns, and cities, they increasingly used fire for cooking and warmth. Under such conditions, fires will spread quickly among combustible shelters. As the level of risk increased, extinguishing fires took on greater significance. Fire spreading among a few dozen buildings was one thing, but a fire consuming the entire city could destroy the community's wealth and thereby everyone's well-being.

Rookie firefighters usually find that their best goal is to be competent— not necessarily great, but competent at the craft. Through competence, one earns the trust of fellow firefighters, which is singularly important in a team-based workforce. The goal is to save lives and protect property, which involves physical work, environmental extremes, coordinated action, disciplined thinking, elements of risk, and pure excitement. The firehouse becomes a second home, and once accepted, the rookie becomes a member of a larger family. Measures of acceptance are stamina, fidelity to duty, exhibiting a sixth sense about fire, and meeting all challenges that arise. The result is a building of trust among fellow firefighters. This is the essence of urban firefighting as described by Dennis Smith in *Report from Engine Co. 82.*[1]

Police officers are often the "finest," while firefighters are the "bravest." Bravery means having the courage and the resolve to do something extremely difficult. Courage plus boldness equals valor. Firefighters earned the description "bravest" because of the task of suppressing fires. Heroism is a distinction with a difference. In antiquity, heroes were mythic characters. Today, one may be a hero without being courageous simply through the accident of circumstance. Is a firefighter who simply shows up for work or answers a pager a hero? There is a good probability that some misguided individuals secretly fantasize about being the centerpiece of a firefighter funeral. Moreover, a firefighter, career or volunteer, might not respond to an emergency call, let alone a real working fire, for an extended period. The questions we need to ask are these: Are all firefighters heroes? Do some firefighters have a desire to die? There are experts who believe this may sometimes be the case, but they also believe these individuals are in the minority.[2]

To be a firefighter is to follow a calling. It takes dedication to do the job well under work conditions that are dangerous, deadly, and dirty. Police, firefighters, and paramedics see the dark side of life more frequently than other workers. Firefighting is a craft that blends applied skills with applied science to combat a force of nature. There is a movement today to make firefighting safe. It can be safer, but it cannot be safe. The movement could put civilians at risk. Overprotecting firefighters from the inherent dangers of the job may occasionally require allowing some buildings to burn and some trapped occupants to die. That runs against the nature of those for whom firefighting is a calling. Firefighters bring order to chaos. There is an inherent risk in the job. Firefighters accept that risk when they sign on. Their choice is no accident but rather a deliberate act. They essentially sign a contract that requires them to assume certain risks, which sometimes have consequences. This does not imply that they lack appreciation of the inherent risks, but simply that they act with measured judgment and use their best common sense. Each firefighter is a risk taker to one degree or another. However, a desire for taking risks is not necessarily the highest motivating factor in becoming a firefighter. In *Working Fire: The Making of an Accidental Fireman*, author Zac Unger relates how in his adolescent years he dreamed of being a rescuer and helping people.[3] In light of his dream, his choice of occupation was hardly an accident. The motivation to belong to the fire service, essentially to be a firefighter, is a combination of emotional needs in the form of a desire to take risks, help others, and be part of something special, such as a brotherhood. These same emotions motivate warriors and explain why many return to combat voluntarily.

Fire or combustion was and is essential to our survival. We accept living with certain risks, like fires, tornadoes, and hurricanes, and in doing so we mentally calculate, accurately or not, that the risk is tolerable because of the benefits of using fire or living in storm-prone areas. We can make such choices because of insurance and the best public safety system in the world.

Our idea of safety is relative in the respect that it is weighed against the level of effort or the cost entailed to achieve it. Safety has a price. U.S. firefighters now offer risk reduction and safety education programs, but the public has yet to embrace them. This is similar to the situation with residential fire sprinklers. While we acknowledge that automatic fire sprinkler systems save lives and reduce property loss, efforts to install them in new homes are resisted at every turn. Even though the technology has improved and the cost decreased, there is no rush among homebuilders to install these safety systems. Plus, insurance companies offer little incentive to install residential sprinklers but generally encourage sprinklers in commercial and industrial buildings. They do this because a fire in a commercial or industrial occupancy can be catastrophic whereas a fire in a residential dwelling is a relatively small concern from a standpoint of property loss. What they do not care to account for in that financial equation is the fact that most fires and fire deaths occur in residences, not in commercial and industrial properties.

U.S. homeowners, like fire insurers, seem content with smoke and heat detectors. In a country that loves its combustible wood-frame homes, one would think homeowners would demand residential fire sprinklers. People build homes in wildland-interface areas (i.e., those areas where undeveloped wildland abuts developed land) and ignore the threat of wildfire. If offered the choice, many homeowners might opt for a sprinkler system, but few home builders want to add another cost to the price of their wood structures.

It is not that we believe that fires only happen to others; it is that we calculate the probability of having a fire as one of low order based on personal experience. That logic works only if one has never actually had a fire in his or her house. Consider that most people in the United States have never witnessed more than a few building fires. How many have actually witnessed several contiguous, large buildings or even a block of buildings on fire? Even after those who build in wildland-interface areas experience a wildfire and lose their homes, many of them rebuild in the same place. Most of the Atlantic coast of the United States is susceptible to hurricanes, yet expensive residential and commercial resorts line that coast. In the Southeast, hurricanes are a part of life. Why do residents of these areas simply rebuild after a storm and move on with their lives? Just like living in fire-prone urban-wildland interface areas, it is part of the U.S. culture to take risks (or ignore reality).

Firefighters also take risks, but in a slightly different way. They seem to abide by a moral imperative that holds their personal actions (i.e., risks) as purposeful, and thus the outcome of their actions seem positive, even when the result is tragic. The result of this misconstrued logic is that the margin for being wrong is very small. It is not fair to project what the firefighters of the FDNY who entered Towers 1 and 2 of the World Trade Center on 9/11 were thinking that morning. If I had been in their place, I would have very likely acted within the framework of the occupational culture just as they did. The public expects firefighters to do their duty, and firefighters are hardwired to fulfill that expectation. Not only did the FDNY firefighters adhere to their training and on-the-job indoctrination, most probably did what they believed was right and died as a result. They did what they always do: they made a great effort to save as many lives as possible under dangerous conditions. It is the essence of the firefighting culture to take that risk.[4]

The cultural norms of a group are their behavior patterns. The same is true for individuals. We learn or assimilate these behaviors from leaders, parents, teachers, peers, coworkers, and others whose values, attitudes, beliefs, and behaviors shape the context of everyday life, as well as culture in groups and organizations. Some cultural norms are good because they contribute to our betterment. Some are detrimental because they promote risky behaviors that the mainstream would prefer to eliminate. Because cultural norms are central to our core beliefs, conflict and uncertainty arise when we are forced by circumstance to alter or change our behavior.[5]

We hold cultural norms so close that we are often unaware of their influence on behavior. Sometimes we have to have someone show us the difference between undesired behavior and desired behavior. Without this comparison of values, we cannot understand the result of our negative actions. This process of comparison intends to model behavior and is the foundation of intervention programs and prevention training. It is the reason some efforts to effect change succeed and some fail.

People need a good reason to change. If they cannot see a positive impact, they probably will not try to change. A safety campaign based solely on a slogan, such as "Remember the ABCs of safety, Always Be Careful!" is useless without corresponding training that explains why this is important to you as an individual. Even a reinforcing message may not work. Take, for example, a campaign to encourage automobile drivers and passengers to wear seat belts. Flooding the media with messages advocating seat belt use does not drive the point home to everyone. In the end the higher authority resorts to threat, using enforcement by police who issue fines. Good intent not withstanding, safety campaigns formed around slogans to change behavior fail miserably or take years of hard work to implement, often with unintended results. The apparent failure of or general disregard for well-intended public safety campaigns results in frustration for the angels of change who would save us from harming ourselves. Frustrated in their attempt to influence behavior through education, they lobby for increased safety through new laws or industry safety standards. All of this effort ignores the reality of human behavior. People become ambivalent about safety either because they rationalize the risks they take or grow complacent from overexposure or overprotection.

Like race car drivers, firefighters benefit from Nomex, a special flame-resistant material. Modern firefighters wear protective clothing made of Nomex and carry their own supply of air in a self-contained breathing apparatus (SCBA). Firefighters wear the Nomex hood to protect their neck, ears, and scalp from heat and flame. In the days before Nomex, a fireman's ears were exposed to the heat. Our ears are thin, and cold and heat affect them rapidly. Firemen used their ears to tell them when it was too hot (when the flesh of your ears starts to sting, it is time to exit or back away). A Nomex hood covering the earlobes dulls the sensation of heat. In addition, because they breathe supplied air rather than hot, toxic smoke, firefighters' lungs are protected from superheated gases. With his senses thus dulled, the firefighter relies on visual cues. However, where there is fire, there is smoke, and smoke reduces visibility. In a layered ensemble of flame-resistant Nomex and with a GORE-TEX vapor barrier and supplied air, the firefighter is in a protective cocoon, albeit a fragile one. Two things inherent to this protective ensemble challenge the firefighter's survival. First, the self-contained air supply is limited, and thus firefighters can remain inside the fire compartment only as long as their air supplies holds (from fifteen to fifty minutes or so). Second, the firefighter wearing Nomex lacks a margin of safety in terms of the ability to sense extreme heat through the ear's sensitive skin tissue. All too often, by the time the potential victim (the firefighter) senses that it is too hot, it is too late to get out unharmed. Thus, protective safety equipment—essential as it is—unfortunately also provides the firefighter with a false sense of security and invincibility. To compensate, firefighters must receive training in fire behavior and fire control techniques. Gaining experience is this regard is vital, but with fewer fires to fight, firefighters can lack experience.

We should acknowledge another aspect of firefighter line-of-duty deaths. Some safety proponents call for zero tolerance for firefighter deaths in the line of duty. A more realistic goal is a reduction in the ratio of firefighter deaths per year. Because the annual rate hovers at a hundred firefighter deaths, it seems to some experts that we have to ratchet up our safety efforts. Given the number of apparent preventable deaths, that goal is appropriate. If firefighters would simply buckle their seat belts, drive less aggressively, watch their diet, and exercise regularly, we could easily lower the rate of deaths.

Eliminating firefighter line-of-duty deaths in the United States is unlikely, given our levels of fire service staffing, building construction methods, fuel loads, lack of code enforcement, occupational culture, and public attitude toward fire. That said, we have to determine and then acknowledge a statistically valid annual death rate for firefighters; to fail to do so is to ignore reality and possibly expend our limited resources on poorly designed safety programs. There are simple, cost-effective means for reducing firefighter line-of-duty deaths, and that is where we should focus our safety efforts. In addition, we should determine the statistical annual ratio of firefighter deaths and use that as threshold for improvement.

Reuben Smeed, a British expert in operations research, was a professor of traffic studies at University College London. Professor Smeed applied operational research methodology to traffic problems worldwide. He designed such things as intelligent traffic-light control systems to optimize the flow of traffic through cities. Having done similar work for the Royal Air Force bomber command in World War II, he was not likely to be unrealistic about death. In fact, he probably held a fatalistic view of traffic. Smeed theorized that the average speed of traffic in central London would always be nine miles per hour because that is the minimum speed that people will tolerate. Intelligent use of traffic lights might increase the number of cars on the roads but would not increase their speed. As soon as the traffic flowed faster, more drivers would arrive to slow it down. He had a similarly fatalistic view of traffic-related vehicle collisions. Using traffic death statistics going back to the dawn of the age of automobiles, he posited that the number of traffic deaths in a country per year is found by a simple formula: the number of deaths equals .0003 times the two-thirds power of the number of people times the one-third power of the number of cars. Published in 1949, the formula is known as Smeed's law, and while not exactly accurate today owing to automobile and roadway engineering improvements, it stills holds within a factor of two for almost all countries at almost all times. The number of deaths is not strongly dependent on a given country's size, quality of the roads, traffic rules, or vehicle safety equipment. In the professor's opinion, human nature was at work in that the number of deaths was dependent principally upon psychological factors that in turn were independent of material circumstances. In simple terms, people drive as recklessly as they can rationalize it until the number of deaths reaches a number they cannot otherwise tolerate. To avoid exceeding that psychological tipping point, they will begin to take measures to drive more carefully. Thus, Smeed's law defines the number of deaths that we find psychologically tolerable.[6] Should we ask whether the firefighter has a similar psychological threshold? Have U.S. firefighters decided collectively (at the subconscious level) that a hundred firefighter deaths per year is acceptable?

Culture is an abstract concept visible only in its behavioral and attitudinal consequences. We can observe behavior, but identifying the internal forces behind it requires effort. Political leaders, teachers, family, neighbors, friends, peers, and coworkers influence individual development. This comes out in personality and character. Culture is to the group as personality is to the individual.

Culture is not absolute nor is it necessarily right or wrong or even visible to us in our consciousness. Because diverse influences shape our behaviors and beliefs, we all have slightly different cultural assumptions. Thus, when we interact with others or as part of a group, we must constantly reassess our own cultural assumptions and compare them against those of the group. This is why it is so difficult for individuals to change and to influence change within a group. Change for the sake of change is irrational. Collectively, the cultural assumptions of a nation, society, organization, family, or peer group are the customs and rituals wrapped up within the thoughts and practices of the group.

Whether a culture exists or not depends on the presence of common experiences and backgrounds among group members. To understand why people do things or why a group (e.g., firefighters) follows certain practices, you must look beyond individual personalities. Understanding group behavior requires that we identify the artifacts, values, and assumptions of the group. Artifacts are the so-called visible structures and processes of the organization; they are complex and difficult to decode. Values, in contrast, are usually stated and easy to identify; these include strategies, goals, and philosophies. Assumptions are the foundation of values and behavior and rise up from perceptions, thoughts, feelings, and everything that is taken for granted by the members. Because assumptions are rooted in the individual and group subconscious, they are very difficult to uncover. Identifying and understanding underlying assumptions is essential to implementing change in a group.[7]

We know that fire department A and fire department B both extinguish fires. However, we observe that A and B approach the task differently. The equipment, strategies, and behaviors are different, but they still put out fires. If we ask the members of the department about their methods, they will tell us that they are doing it the way they have always done it, the way they were taught. They are almost helpless to change their methods because they do not understand where they come from. All they know is that they are able to put out fires, and that is their job. They see no problem. We can observe that fire department A is very efficient, cost-effective, and safe, whereas fire department B has problems, but observation alone does not tell us why they are so different. To understand or help change department B, we have to explore its history, literally learn its story.

What we are interested in are the values, beliefs, and assumptions of the founders. If followers believe the founders were successful leaders, the followers will take on and accept those values, beliefs, and assumptions. In essence, through a process of accumulated learning, a group develops entrenched characteristics and behaviors. These characteristics and behaviors make up an invisible mental model of perceiving and dealing with the world that the group takes for granted. Neither the group collectively nor the individuals are consciously aware of the model; they simply do what they have always done. Thus, the culture itself is not right or wrong; the outcome of the culture's relationship to the outside world or operating environment makes it appropriate or inappropriate. Attempting to implement change forces members to evaluate the request for its inherent credibility, especially in terms of existing values and beliefs. The success of the request for change hinges on whether or not it has meaning in the context of the culture and validates underlying assumptions.[8]

Line-of-duty deaths among the 1.2 million firefighters in the United States may be so few that we are complacent about the potential for dying. Just as homeowners believe that fires happen only to other homeowners, firefighters mask the potential of dying on the job behind a shield of bravado cemented in place by an occupational culture that willingly accepts the inherent danger.

Attempts to make firefighting safer have a slim chance of success because the occupational culture values lifesaving, risk taking, and heroic effort. Changing these aspects of firefighter culture will require altering the mental hardwiring of current members and rescripting the training curriculum. If this effort is successful, it is unlikely that firefighters will retain their image and status with the public, they will become just another bureaucratic service bound by script and standard operating procedure. The only way to change the culture is to recast the firefighting model. Rather than a calling, it becomes simply a job. U.S. firefighters commonly wear their blue fire department t-shirts off duty. In another country, firefighters may not do the same. In Sweden, firefighters take their job as seriously as do Americans, but they leave the job (and their t-shirts) at the fire station when they are off duty.[9]

We know that wearing a seat belt improves the odds of surviving a motor vehicle crash. While firefighters know this firsthand, some still fail to buckle up. An accident investigation may show that the members of the crew never wore seat belts because department policy or their company officers did not specifically require it or failed to set an example by buckling their own seat belts. We could call this learned behavior. Firefighters in the United States are the recipients of a new message to "change the culture" of the fire service in order to reduce on-the-job injuries and line-of-duty deaths.

The theory goes that firefighters are taking risks that may lead to death or injury and that these risks are learned behavior. That the risky activity is learned behavior is almost certain, but the blame for the learned behaviors is not properly attributed. This campaign is unfortunately another product of the contemporary everyone-safe movement. Blaming risky actions on peer pressure and poor leadership is simplistic and misses the mark. Peer pressure is powerful among firefighters. Aggressive firefighters are by nature competitive. Is there anything wrong with that? No. Can it lead to problems? Yes. Is leadership the answer? Partially yes, but each firefighter must also share responsibility for reckless behavior. Also responsible are the countless training instructors who promote overaggressiveness and help to cultivate the image of the tough urban firefighter.

The argument for safety fails to assess in a meaningful way the connection between occupational risks and a specific behavior, how that behavior leads to injury, and how that behavior stems from culture. There is no proof of connection by scientific study because no one has yet contrived the experiment that will prove or disprove it. Statistics collected after the fact do not and cannot make the case for or against the effectiveness of any so-called safety culture. Once an accident or fatality occurs, the organization adapts, and you will not likely find any organization willing to remain unsafe for the purpose of a scientific study. If there is to be a safety culture, then it must be linked to the organization's culture. If organizational culture develops as a member response to meeting the challenges of the intended mission, then creating a faithful safety culture requires effort by all of the members, top to bottom. It would be better to take a new approach to the training and education of firefighters. Contemporary firefighter training programs reinforce the very culture we are trying to change and, worse, fail to include sufficient education in fire behavior.

Are occupational injuries and fatalities among U.S. firefighters extraordinarily high, too high, moderate, or about right according to statistical probability? Does the occupational culture expose U.S. firefighters to a higher level of risk than firefighters in other countries are exposed to? What are the consequences of changing firefighting's occupational culture? Some people would reinvent firefighting and remold firefighters to achieve some sort of safety nirvana. By what measure do we judge the safety record of firefighting in the United States? Both the NFPA and the U.S. Fire Administration (USFA) collect data on fires and the fire service. Their data constitute the only nationwide record of the fire service. Unfortunately, the data are incomplete, as not all fire departments participate in surveys and the national incident reporting system. The data collected are reliable (if we can use that word here at all) only back to about 1986. Earlier data provide only an estimate. The following analysis uses various NFPA data obtained from published reports produced through their annual surveys and U.S. census data. A review of data covering 1986 to 2006 reveals the following:

- The U.S. population increased by about 25 percent.
- The total number of fire calls per year more than doubled.
- The total number of actual fires per year decreased by about 30 percent.
- The total number of career and volunteer firefighters increased by 9 percent.
- The total number of firefighters killed per year in the line of duty decreased 25 percent.
- The total number of firefighters killed per year while fighting a fire decreased 21 percent.
- The total number of firefighters injured per year decreased 21 percent.
- During that period, 2,506 firefighters died of duty-related causes (including 343 FDNY deaths on 9/11).

There is no question that firefighting is hazardous. Given that safety and training received more emphasis beginning in the late 1980s, these statistics show improvement. While correctable problems exist (and their existence requires attention from a moral leadership standpoint), the record of occupational safety—given the hazards firefighters face—is almost remarkable. Some safety experts call for actions that would hamper firefighters and likely result in increased property loss and civilian casualties. There is no basis in the safety record for the wholesale reinvention of firefighting anymore than deaths on a battlefield are cause to change warfare. That is a blunt statement, but the reality is that in battles, warriors die. That fact notwithstanding, we need a new way to train, educate, and motivate firefighters to increase their situational awareness and model safer behaviors.

Firefighters need to become experts in the science of fire behavior. It is debatable whether U.S. firefighter training programs offer students all they need to know about fire behavior and ventilation tactics for enclosed or compartment fires. Reinventing the fire service at the expense of public safety compromises the ideals that have shaped the public's perception of firefighters. We can improve safety and change culture through a new training model. Initiatives to change or remodel firefighter behavior will fail without an understanding of the culture of firefighters and the occupational culture ingrained in fire fighter behavior, occupational training programs, and institutionalized culture in every fire department.

Simply calling for a change in the culture squanders valuable energy. If we want to stop killing firefighters needlessly, we will have to do something much more radical. When we have that discussion, we might want to include the taxpayers who pay firefighters' salaries because they also have expectations. The questions we should ask are these: Why has society passed on its responsibility for fire protection to firefighters? Should we expect firefighters to take the risks that they do when there are safer alternatives? What factors have influenced the development of the occupation so that risk taking is an expectation? There is certainly a culture of risk associated with the firefighting occupation, and we should want to know how that came to be.

CHAPTER 3

Contemporary Firefighting

Firefighters, past and present, have accepted risk as part of the job. That acceptance acknowledges that firefighters face inordinate levels of personal risk occasionally and, in some rare instances, may be expendable. Consider New York firefighters on 9/11 or Russian firefighters at Chernobyl. To exhibit bravery in the face of risk without question or regard for personal safety is expected. Many build reputations on this reality through public displays of courage at fires. So strong is this notion that it has become a hallmark of the fire service, although modern-day authorities increasingly frown upon and question the need for it.

I listened recently to a young firefighter lament that he was born fifty years too late. This statement came out during a discussion about the modern fire service and the belief that modern firefighting is really all about emergency medicine and avoiding risky behaviors. This young man is like so many firefighters today who joined the service for the action and found instead endless routine and attention to administrative details, punctuated mostly by ambulance calls. It is in this context of risk taking and bravery that the first chapter of *Euro Firefighter*, by Paul Grimwood, begins with a discussion of operational fatalities in both the UK and U.S. fire services. Make no mistake; this is all about culture and tradition.[1]

Grimwood, who has worked urban fires in both London and New York City, sees a different fire service emerging in the twenty-first century. He has a new view of the relationship between bravery and risk, one with respect for traditional values but with greater emphasis on the application of risk-management techniques. Firefighters today face fewer necessary and unnecessary risks.[2] This has created a new administrative and leadership role for fire service managers, including both the company officer and the chief fire officer. If firefighters cannot police their own risky behavior, then management will use enforcement techniques. If management fails to act on its moral responsibility, the occupational health and safety arm of the government will step in and levy fines.

In the simplest terms, though firefighters may be willing to risk all, even death, they must be constrained by fire department policy, procedure, leadership, and management. In the old days, captains or chiefs might have planted size-ten boots on your backside for motivation in the face of danger. Today their job is to keep firefighters from hurting themselves. This statement is not meant to be amusing. In my early training, we heard, usually whispered, that an aggressive fire attack sometimes requires, figuratively speaking usually, the swift application of an officer's boot onto a firefighter's backside to get it up and moving in on a fire. Not all firefighters have the desire to make an aggressive attack on a fire or get in harm's way to make a rescue. To be certain, at the individual level, firefighters mentally calculate potential risk from the hazards present. If the firefighter is not making mental calculations of potential risk, those around may want to avoid following him or her. An understanding of fire behavior and the dynamics of fire and smoke in a building is essential to a successful career.

Firefighters must receive training commensurate with their duties and responsibilities; they must also be properly equipped for the job, and the apparatus (i.e., engines and ladder trucks) staffed for expected workload. Modern firefighting is in a transitory phase, adapting its internal decision-making models from a "git'er done" frame of mind to one of risk management. To understand and appreciate the new fire service requires a thorough understanding and appreciation of risk management techniques, as well as a new way of doing things. Management of people and things means dealing with problems and finding solutions. Managing problems effectively requires that you know something about the problems. Knowledge of the problem requires information.

If the fire service lacks anything, it is information—or at least readily accessible information—about itself and the environment in which it must work. The one difference between law enforcement and the fire service is the institutional mind-set toward collecting data about its own operations. While

law enforcement thrives on data about crime and crime control, the fire service resists and even denigrates efforts to collect data about the fire problem
and firefighting efforts. Law enforcement agencies are relatively more successful than fire agencies in securing funding and grants because they worship data
and collaborate with higher authorities. In stark contrast, the fire service enthusiastically avoids paperwork, even brags about avoiding paperwork, and then
suffers as a result from a lack of funding and the difficulty of winning grants.
The fire problem exists much as it has, and we keep dealing with it, expend-
ing resources to attack a problem, rather than trying to eliminate it. We are
U.S. heroes, the bravest, and we avoid paperwork!

Paperwork here means anything related to collecting data about fires,
resource deployment, and occupational safety issues related to fire control.
Without this data, real improvement through risk management is next to
impossible. Risk management depends on data because managing risk involves
calculating probabilities of an event and tracking related losses to determine
what is an acceptable level of risk.[3] This is the key to firefighting at the tactical and strategic levels.

The problem is with the individual firefighter who must reconcile the influences of firefighting tradition, occupational culture, and peer pressure with their
personal perception of their role. A healthy level of risk acceptance is essential
to being a good firefighter, but any desire to "give the full measure" is without
question unacceptable. The belief that firefighting is first a calling and second
a job is rampant within the U.S. fire service. Occupational pride runs high in
U.S. fire departments. The question to ask is, does that attitude do more harm
than good? Determining an acceptable level of risk must consider firefighting's
strategic goals of lifesaving and property conservation (i.e., saving civilian lives
and minimizing civilian property damage). Exposure to greater risk to save a life
is acceptable, whereas exposing oneself to great risk for an abandoned building
is unacceptable. Aggressive, highly motivated firefighters want to practice their
skills all the time, even in abandoned buildings; some, whether paid or volunteer, consider this fun. Their supervisor's job is to control that tendency without quashing motivation. That is infinitely more difficult than applying a size
ten to someone's backside. Being a modern fire officer requires a new set of leadership skills, and of course, there is the paperwork. Using abandoned buildings
for live-fire training is quite appropriate and even essential, as long as the environment is controlled with appropriate measures for managing risk.

The fire officer must evaluate the probability of success for a given situation and determine an acceptable level of risk. Like the military, the fire service has developed rules of engagement to guide decisions in potentially risky situations. In the format of a matrix, the rules of engagement rate life risk as low, medium, and high, and probability as low, marginal, and high. Thus, a high risk to firefighter safety and a low probability of success requires a defensive stand by fire crews, whereas a low risk to firefighter safety and a high probability of success calls for offensive (aggressive) action. Risk analysis of a building fire encompasses the important characteristics of the building (size, type of construction, condition, occupancy); fire conditions (location, extent, behavior, length of time burning); smoke conditions; risk to occupants and assessment of survival; assessment of firefighting capabilities present; and available firefighting resources.[4]

The rules of engagement for structural firefighting look at the acceptability of risk through assessment of the risk. The model accepts that firefighting in buildings has inherent risk but that no building is worth the life of a firefighter. It also holds that firefighting efforts for severe fires in abandoned and derelict buildings should be defensive in scope rather than offensive. Every firefighter must make risk assessments, but the incident commander must assess risk continuously throughout the incident, limiting or avoiding it as necessary. Maintaining situational awareness throughout the incident is critical because if conditions change, thereby increasing the risk, the incident strategy and the tactics must change accordingly. Operations are typically either offensive or defensive, and mixing the two is very risky. An example of an undesirable mixed strategy has crews operating on the building's exterior, potentially compromising or endangering crews operating on the inside. Incident commanders avoid mixing strategies. No building or property is worth the life of a firefighter. At the transition from offensive to defensive operations, the incident commander orders the firefighters to withdraw to the outside, and the building is essentially written off as a loss.

Fire service managers today face a dilemma, as the following story illustrates. In cities and towns where the government operates on a shoestring budget, fire chiefs face the difficult task of balancing services and the safety of both firefighters and civilians. In 2008 a paid firefighter in a small city in New England protested his assignment to a backup ladder truck. The truck in question was one of the city's reserve apparatus, intended to fill in for the city's primary unit, which was out of service that day. Reserve apparatus are typically units that have already seen frontline service and are now maintained for use only when a frontline piece is out for repair or when another unit is required, as in the event of a large fire.

A reserve apparatus should be functional and have the necessary equipment. This particular truck, however, had a serious problem in that its aerial ladder did not function. In most cities, this condition would mean that the truck was not suitable even as a reserve piece. Incredibly, in this cash-strapped city, the administrators thought they could use the truck, broken ladder and all, because the truck's complement of ground ladders was still usable. They also felt that they could safely rely on outside help (mutual aid) from a neighboring fire department. A paid or volunteer firefighter willing to make a stand for safety, especially when a stand brings punitive action, is commendable. Years ago, refusing an assignment meant dismissal. The president of the firefighter's union in that city said that while mutual aid is a good thing and having ladder trucks respond from nearby departments helps, the physics of fire does not change. That statement is definitely true.

An enclosed fire may roughly double in size and intensity every 30 seconds, depending on the fuel load, compartment size, and degree of ventilation in the room. An additional ladder truck may or may not be available to support ventilation of the building when needed, thus endangering any occupants who may be trapped, as well as any firefighters in the building. Speaking as a true politician, the mayor of this city claimed the fire was not a crisis and stated that many communities have only one working ladder truck. The mayor initiated an effort to work with mayors of the region's other cities to find answers and alternatives.[5]

In June 2007, in Charleston, South Carolina, nine firefighters died in the line of duty in the Super Sofa Store fire. Located on West Savannah Highway, the business was a combination store and warehouse. At the time, the City of Charleston Fire Department held an ISO Class 1 Public Protection Classification. Class 1 is the highest of ten classes, and it is held by only forty-two fire departments in the United States. Despite that distinction, the Charleston department made some horrible mistakes both before and during the fire. The nine deaths were preventable, and the failure was one of leadership and management at the top. An extensive post-incident analysis conducted by an independent investigative team of experts identified numerous factors contributing to the tragedy.

Among these factors was the failure of the store's owner to meet building code requirements. The violations involved allowing the storage of combustibles and flammable liquids near an employee smoking area located by the loading dock. Also, the owner had not obtained city permits that would have required installation of a fire sprinkler system or, in lieu of that, firewalls to separate the interior spaces within the building. The report also noted that the fire department was proud of its reputation for conducting aggressive interior fire attacks using small-capacity hose lines, an approach to firefighting that stressed fast attacks based on independent initiative. In the words of the investigators, the fire department "was inadequately staffed, inadequately trained, insufficiently equipped, and organizationally unprepared to conduct an operation of this complexity in a large commercial occupancy." The members of the department took risks because they recognized that their resources were limited. Their pride in their collective ability overshadowed any potential for failure. They believed that by engaging in aggressive attacks (even when uncoordinated), they could take on any reasonable fire successfully.[6]

The state of South Carolina eventually fined Charleston $9,325 for various violations of industry safety regulations.[7] That's a modest penalty, considering that it represents just over a thousand dollars for each dead city firefighter lost through the alleged negligence of the city fire department. The failure in Charleston is not unlike that in other firefighter line-of-duty deaths, and the failure of the officer in charge, the fire chief, or both is only part of the problem—firefighters themselves are to blame because they often make choices with fatal consequences. Firefighter training is also to blame. Many fire departments also fail to regularly inspect buildings and collect data about risk. They essentially fail to appreciate the real risks involved with the buildings they protect.

In Worcester, Massachusetts, in 1999, six firefighters died in the failed search of an abandoned cold storage warehouse. Here, as in Charleston, the fire department failed to translate their collective appreciation for the potential and inherent risk that the buildings posed. It was and remains business as usual in the U.S. fire service. These were large structures with confusing interior layouts and unique fuel loads. Searching and firefighting in these buildings with due regard to firefighter safety would have required knowledge and full understanding of the hazards, assessment of risk on the basis of probability, a strategy for particular events occurring in the specific building, and operational concessions for what is normal in an aggressive fire attack. These are positive actions undertaken as part of a planning process, and they are essential in forming strategy during a fire attack. Advance planning for an incident (known as pre-incident or pre-action planning) in a specific building provides data that becomes useful when the officer in charge performs the size-up in a developing incident to formulate the strategy for the impending attack.

The processes of inspection, data collection, pre-incident planning, and situation assessment create the opportunity for situational awareness among the fire department's members. Firefighters must also maintain their own personal situational awareness, just as the incident commander maintains overall situational awareness for everything involved throughout the length of the operation.[8]

Thus situational awareness is a critical component of safety and risk management; it is the direct opposite of suffering tunnel vision. Full application of situational awareness includes communication with those around you. In both Worcester and Charleston, the failure of command officers and fire crews to maintain situational awareness, communicate effectively, and maintain accountability factored heavily in the outcome. Firefighters are all too often their own worst enemy; even the experienced ones can make incredibly stupid and fatal errors of judgment.

Today, new firefighters, whether volunteer or career, receive basic training. Such training typically follows a formal curriculum, often based on national performance standards. In other words, a successful graduate of the program will have learned to perform essential job-oriented tasks in a universally validated method. The outcome is a fully programmed, modular-like employee unit ready for placement—where needed, when needed—from a strategic standpoint. Though well trained to perform singular tasks, the newly minted firefighter unit lacks the ability to apply the learned tasks in a structured sequence through a range of tactical situations under high-risk emergency conditions. This means years of on-the-job coaching and mentoring will be necessary before the rookie firefighter is fully productive and less likely to get into a fatal situation. Supervising line officers and senior firefighters provide the coaching and mentoring. This is a critical element in developing effective fire services, and too many U.S. fire departments, especially those using volunteers, neglect on-the-job training, consequently limiting their ultimate effectiveness, jeopardizing public safety, and compromising the safety of firefighters.

Firefighters gain experience from going to fires, and that is partly why they like fires and why they answer alarms with a sense of excitement. In May

2007, in a small rural town in northern New England, a volunteer firefighter answered a call for assistance and lost his life as a result. His death fits a profile common to other firefighter deaths. Yet his intentions that day were unquestionable. His family did not and will not receive the federal and state death benefits available to fallen firefighters because no one in authority managed the aftermath of the fatality according to procedure. No autopsy was done, the funeral was austere, and the burial occurred in his backyard in a box made locally. A few dozen firefighters attended the small funeral with the family and some townspeople. The next month, June 2007, in Charleston, nine career firefighters died. Thousands of firefighters from across the country attended the funeral, which was covered by the national media. They buried the nine firefighters with full honors while a crowd of thousands watched. Their families will receive full benefits. In the aftermath came government reports and studies.

The contributing factors to the deaths in both events were obvious, had anybody bothered to look closely at the potential risk from the hazards. Both tragedies resulted from inexperience, poor training, inadequate equipment, lack of leadership, lack of accountability, failure to follow accepted practice, and lack of a command structure. In hindsight, these were two fires with very predictable results. If the deaths were unpredictable, then we need to learn more. If predictable, we need to do more to manage risk. If fire administrators recognize the risk, what should they do to minimize it? If someone acted to reduce the risk potential, would these ten firefighters and hundreds of others be alive today? What influences have played critical roles in shaping firefighting in the United States?

As a group, Americans have always been irresponsible when it comes to preventing fires. Fire insurance covers our mistakes today, as it has for hundreds of years. Principally two groups of people have waged the war on fire: fire insurance underwriters and firefighters. Both have contributed significantly and equally, but the firefighters have paid the cost of the battle more dearly. When buildings burn, the responsibility for putting out the fire lies with the fire department. It makes sense that the form and function of fire services reflect the type and characteristics of the buildings that are burning. Unfortunately we often end up with the fire department we can afford, not the fire department we need. As a result we get less than we really need, and firefighters try to make up for the difference with courage and dedication.

The fire service enjoys a short moment of collective glory after the big fire or big rescue, but notoriety quickly vanishes until the next big blaze or until another firefighter dies. Firefighters appear to be both essential and expendable. Someone once told me they thought we were the United States' first-class heroes during the fire, but second-class heroes after the fire fades from memory. What they implied was that we make heroic sacrifices only to be ignored when we later ask elected officials and taxpayers for essential resources. Change for the fire service (and public) frequently comes in the aftermath of tragedy. The best firefighters are not concerned with labels such as hero—for them firefighting represents a calling. Like the warriors who live to go to war, firefighters live to go to fires.

The institution of firefighting has a structural weakness that makes us our own worst enemies. We are enthusiastic in our service, and in the process we assume huge risks almost without question. We ask for essential resources and are told to do more with less. We pay the price with courage and dedication. Will we lose public esteem in the process as risk management replaces uncommon heroism?

The fire services of the United States are on the verge of change, incremental in some ways and radical in others. Social, economic, demographic, and political factors combined with new threats to U.S. security may soften up the barriers to change within the fire service ranks. No matter how it turns out, an understanding of the past gained through a look at the people and events that shaped firefighting in the United States is valuable. It is the heritage of firefighting in the United States.

2
THE FIRE PROBLEM DEFINED

CHAPTER 4

Great Fire in Pittsburgh

In 1845 Pittsburgh was the gateway for westward journeys. At the confluence of three rivers—Allegheny, Monongahela, and Ohio—the city provided access to a navigable waterway for steamboats down the Ohio to the Mississippi River and south to the Gulf of Mexico. Adding to its geographic advantage were abundant natural resources in the form of coal, natural gas, oil, and sandstone. As a center of trade, Pittsburgh was building boats, manufacturing glass, making iron, and warehousing essential products for the westward expansion. It had been home to Native Americans for sixteen thousand years, but by the mid-eighteenth century, the French and English recognized the strategic value of the location, built forts, and fought over control of the territory. Laid out in 1784, its street grid took on an almost vexing character owing to geography, an inaccurate surveyor's chain, and armed squatters in the center of undeveloped town. The plan featured two grids of parallel streets, each set at an angle—one to match the banks of the Monongahela River and the other the banks of the Allegheny River—and generally avoiding Grant's Hill, which was situated between the two grids.[1] Triangular-shaped blocks solved the problems encountered where the two angular grids met.

The industrial, coal-dust-stained region was hilly and possessed steep valleys along the rivers, which further its irregular shape. The smoky, low-hanging air in the valley may have influenced the naming of the town across the Monongahela—Birmingham, the same as England's own industrial center. Legally a borough, not a city, Pittsburgh had a mostly young population

47

numbering 10,033, according to the 1840 census, with most of its residents under the age of thirty. Ten years later, the seventh U.S. Census put the population at 46,601, over four times the number from 1840. The actual population in 1845 was anybody's guess and had to be somewhere between the two census counts, plus a large number of transients who worked on the Pennsylvania Canal. Looking at the greater urban area—taking in the boroughs of Birmingham across the Monongahela River and Allegheny across the Allegheny River—the official 1840 population of the small region was 21,115. The compact, urban area encompassing today's central business district was all of Pittsburgh in 1845. This roughly one square mile of land included almost all of the industrial, commercial, institutional, and residential properties. That makes the population density around the time of the conflagration no less than ten thousand and very likely double that number, or greater, because as many as six thousand were made homeless in the 1845 fire.[2]

Wooden bridges connected Pittsburgh to its cross-river neighbors. At the time of the fire, bridge engineer John A. Roebling was building a suspended aqueduct using wire rope to replace an existing wooden aqueduct that crossed from Allegheny to Pittsburgh. The aqueduct carried the Pittsburgh Canal. Pittsburgh's public water system included a steam-driven pump taking its supply from the Allegheny and feeding various reservoirs located on hills. The reservoirs used gravity to supply the distribution system; the water level and atmospheric pressure determined the static pressure of the system. In the built-up area, the main distribution lines consisted of two pipes, a six-inch and an eight-inch, feeding a network of two-inch pipe, as well as the fire hydrants. The high friction loss in the small pipes made static pressure in the system inadequate for supplying hose streams connected directly to hydrants, and so the fire engines had to be hand-pumped to supply the fire hoses with adequate pressure to throw a good stream. By 1845 Pittsburgh and Allegheny had ten volunteer fire companies between them. In the year of the fire, five of Pittsburgh's six fire engines were in less than full operational status. The situation with fire hose was just as bad, with most of it unfit for use. Even if the hose had been in top condition, drafting water from the rivers and pumping it in a relay operation was impractical; the total length of hose carried by the companies could not reach the center of the downtown from the river, and there was no extra hose for use as hand lines.[3] Taking river water via draft, or suction, and forcing it under pressure through many lengths of hose requires the use of at least one suction pump and several force pumps. The energy required to force the water through hose was supplied by firemen hand-pumping the engines, as steam-powered fire engines were still years away for Pittsburgh.

The wharf along the Monongahela River was active with steamboats and keelboats, and warehouses lined nearby streets all the way to the tip of land known as the Point (where the three rivers met). The densely built district, comprising the area from the old military forts—near the Point in an area called the Triangle—uptown to two hills (Herron and Grant), was a combustible mixture of wood and brick buildings housing business, commerce, culture, industry, institutions, manufacturing, and people. The brick buildings had structural members, window frames, and doors of wood and some cast-iron elements. The largest of these buildings were three to four stories in height. While most of the houses were wood, brick homes also offered fuel for a fire with their wood-shingled roofs. The weather in Pittsburgh in the spring of 1845 was relatively dry, especially in the weeks that preceded the fire. This resulted in two things: high potential for fire and low levels in the water system's open reservoirs.[4]

Around noon on April 10, 1845, a small fire (likely used for heating wash water) in the yard of a property located at the corner of Ferry and Second Streets went unattended long enough for the wind to whip up the flames and ignite nearby combustibles. The washerwoman's neglect of the fire lit among dried-out combustible buildings and in the face of strong wind was enough to fuel a conflagration of historic proportions. The hungry flames quickly jumped to a nearby icehouse located on Ferry and then over to frame buildings on Second (later renamed the Boulevard of the Allies). Entrenched on Second, the fire consumed a cotton factory and an adjacent brick building, despite the early efforts of the firemen. A valiant stand at the corner of Third and Ferry saved the Third Presbyterian Church. A wooden cornice surrounding the church's roof provided a shield for firefighters extinguishing spot fires on that structure. As the cornice began to smolder, a section of it was quickly chopped away using axes and tossed into the fire below; this action saved the church. The quick action on the church fire also saved an adjacent printing shop. Though the volunteers of the Eagle and Niagara Companies earned high praise for their work on that corner, they would eventually be outflanked. The fire moved beyond them, roughly eastward, toward Diamond Alley and down Fourth, funneling around Grant's Hill as the western wind pushed the fire eastward.

The powerful wind created a blowtorch effect so that the brick buildings on Second and Third Streets offered no resistance.[5]

Soon the larger brick structures on Third and Fourth ignited as their exterior woodwork (cornices, window frames, and doors), heated by radiant energy, first smoldered and then burst into flame; heated window glass fractured and allowed the fire entry to the interior space. While iron shutters protected a window opening, the building fell prey to its zinc roof, which melted as flames reached the interior. On the southern side, the sector closer to the Monongahela River, the fire raged through warehouses on Water Street, the wharf along the river, and the wooden bridge over the river. The heat, smoke, flames, and flying brands forced steamboats to move down the Monongahela as far as Saw Mill Run. On Third Street, the fire took a hotel, a church, and the Western University of Pennsylvania (now the University of Pittsburgh) but spared the Library of the Tilghman Literary Institute. In Kensington (also known as Pipe-town) fire consumed the ironworks and damaged the gasworks. In that same area, wood-frame houses situated at a lower elevation were spared while brick structures above them burned. The starting point of the fire, slight shifting of the wind direction, lack of fuel, actions of firemen, and availability of water (poor as it was) all likely contributed to the fire's progression being checked on the north flank along Diamond Way and Fourth Street. The presence of one of the city's largest water mains under Fifth Avenue also helped the firemen's efforts on that flank, even if the water pressure was unsatisfactory. The conflagration's forward momentum finally decreased or halted entirely when it ran out of potential fuel at a bluff on the south flank running along the river. It simply burned until all was consumed, leaving a scene of destruction over one mile in length, about one-third of a mile across, and covering twenty blocks or roughly fifty-five to sixty acres. More than a thousand buildings burned, and an estimated six thousand people were without a place to sleep. An observer from out of town offered an account of that day of destruction. He noted that the fire reached its peak within three hours, so by that time most of what could burn was already ablaze, and the conflagration had a wind-driven flame-front about three hundred yards wide. Still, it continued to burn for three more hours.[6]

In 1832 volunteers formed a fireman's association, but it was nothing more than a body of similarly interested people; it was hardly the requisite structure for a municipal fire department organized around discipline. The condition of the pumps and hose in Pittsburgh in 1845 was not an indicator of poor mechanical ability so much as poor leadership. The same is true of Pittsburgh's public water system at the time. These failures were caused by the men who controlled business and government. To have any chance of control of a large fire in its early stages requires a coordinated effort, a strategy, command and control measures executed by experienced firefighters with the right equipment, and a good water supply. What hampered firefighting the most in Pittsburgh that day was the lack of an adequate supply of pressurized water available from hydrants placed at strategic locations and the failure to establish a unified command and control structure. Without those basic measures, the firemen in Pittsburgh had no chance for quick control of the rapidly spreading fire. Even with water, equipment, and experience, though, effective firefighting still depends on weather conditions and the number of combustibles.

On April 10, 1845, many factors hampered the probability of success against a major fire in Pittsburgh. Much of the fire hose was unfit for use; the water level in the reservoirs was low, creating flow and pressure deficiencies; the moisture content of combustibles was low; the wind was up and blowing from the west, thus aiming for the built-up area; and the fire companies were not organized as a unit. Had their hose been fit for use, had the water supply from the fire hydrants been better, and had they been organized as a department, the volunteers might have held the fire to a smaller area. Pittsburgh was spared greater devastation and loss because of geography in the form of a steep bluff along the Monongahela, the division of the street pattern into two grids with several long dividing avenues, and the critical fact that the fire simply ran out of buildings to burn. The financial loss was estimated to be somewhere between six and twelve million dollars. The city's four fire insurance companies paid out only 22 to 80 percent on the insured losses; additional relief came from other U.S. cities, as well as Europe.[7]

In a fast-moving fire such as this one, the challenge for the firemen would have been figuring out the best open space for fire separation ahead of the fire front where they could set up for a defensive stand. Combine the deficiencies of hose, insufficient number of engines, poor water supply, lack of an operational command, and it is unlikely that they could have acted quickly enough to set up ahead of the fire. Given what they had, it makes sense that they utilized Fifth Avenue, as it likely provided a modest water supply, fed from the largest distribution main. The street also provided a possible firebreak (an open space allowing good separation between the fire and exposures) parallel to the wind direction, and it permitted movement of fire-fighting resources along the fire's flank. That Fifth Avenue met Grant Street at Grant's Hill also helped, as this is where the wind was probably deflected helping to keep the fire from spreading, thus turning the flank. The focus of any firefighting effort in this area would have been mostly defensive, meant to protect exposures and knock down spot fires resulting from burning brands carried aloft by the convection currents created from the fire's heat and then carried away on the wind. Fifth Avenue was also the place where any sane person would go to flee the fire, as it was in the only safe direction. As for the other possibilities, the burned-over area would have been too hot and dangerous, and heading toward the Monongahela River would have meant entrapment. Fifth Avenue also afforded ready access to Liberty Avenue, a street that could have served as a principal firebreak had the fire jumped Fifth Avenue and continued burning toward the Allegheny. If this fire had spread outward from Fourth and over Fifth toward Liberty, the added destruction could have crippled the young city. The firemen and at least a few thousand people would have found Fifth Avenue useful either to fight the fire or escape it. The rate of spread, size of the flame front, intense heat, choking smoke, falling brands, collapsing walls, and throngs of people simply gaping at the huge fire or else running from it all served to hinder the efforts of the fire companies. Finally, what the near lack of water did not do to make this day a disaster for all, the disorganization of the mostly autonomous volunteers did. In the years ahead, Pittsburgh quickly recovered from its great fire, improving its water system and organizing a municipal fire department, but the linchpin in its future success was bringing the Pennsylvania Railroad to the city.

The Pittsburgh fire serves as a useful example of societal and governmental failure to recognize and appreciate the potential for fire to destroy the wealth of a city. If the city's business and civic leaders recognized the potential for a major fire, they failed to act at the most basic level to protect their interests. In that case, their failure was a moral one and demonstrated a blatant disregard for common sense. Pittsburgh was not unique in this respect, for this neglect of fire safety was repeated throughout the nineteenth century in the United States. By 1900, after many great fires, we finally absorbed the lesson through the school of hard knocks and began to change our ways. The result was an equation for the protection of a city: good water supply plus an organized firefighting force plus fire-safe building construction yields a lower probability for significant urban conflagrations.

CHAPTER 5

Fire in the Built Environment

The United States has one of the worst fire records of any industrialized nation.[1] It is true that there are occupations that present higher risks if measured in terms of numbers of workers killed on the job—occupations such as commercial fishing, construction, and mining, for example. Though the firefighter's death may attract more publicity, the day after the funeral it is no different than if they had died in a farming accident. To a safety expert, it is another predictable occupational death. Risk and probability are intertwined and inescapable. We expect to see approximately a hundred U.S. firefighters die each year in the line of duty. A high percentage of this cohort dies of heart attacks responding to, during, and after returning from fires. Another large percentage dies in traffic-related events while responding to or returning from a fire. Those firefighters who succumb on the fireground are victims of burns, crushing injuries, traumatic injury, and asphyxiation. Many thousands of other U.S. firefighters receive injuries in the line of duty each year.[2]

In 1974 experts estimated the number of deaths related to fire as approximately twelve thousand per year, the same year the USFA was established. At that time, a goal for reducing the death rate by fire by 50 percent within a generation was set, and this goal was eventually met in 2002. In that year civilian deaths were 3,380, and fire deaths continue the downward trend. The ten-year trend for U.S. fire losses (as of 2004) shows that fires and fire injuries as calculated per million people are on a steady decline. Property loss, when adjusted for inflation, also continues to trend downward. The death rate of

13.6 per million is half of what it was in the late 1970s. In spite of that positive report, the United States has a fire death rate two to two- and-a-half times that of several European nations and at least 20 percent higher than many other countries. The World Fire Statistics Centre looked at fire loss records in twenty-five industrial nations and found the United States ranked fourth highest, a rate unchanged for the past twenty-five years.[3]

Most Americans who die from fires do so in their own homes. The principal causes of fires in homes are cooking equipment, heating equipment, arson, electrical, appliances, smoking, open flames, and children playing with matches. Although electrical causes rank about fourth overall, in terms of strict property damage, electricity ranks second. This is likely because many electrical fires occur in concealed spaces (such as behind the walls) and often go undetected until too late. A 2004 NFPA telephone survey reported that 96 percent of all U.S. homes have at least one smoke alarm, and three-quarters of them have at least one working smoke alarm. Using data derived from the National Fire Incident Reporting System (NFIRS, 2000–2004), the NFPA identified the following statistics about smoke alarms:[4]

- Smoke alarms sounded in roughly half of the home fires reported in the United States.
- Sixty-five percent of reported home fire deaths in those years resulted from fires in homes with no smoke alarms or no working smoke alarms.
- No smoke alarms were present in 43 percent of the home fire deaths, and in 22 percent of the home fire deaths, smoke alarms were present but did not sound.

The collected data appear to indicate that smoke detection devices, when properly installed and in operating condition, will cut the risk of dying by fire in half. Automatic sprinklers also play a role in reducing property damage and saving lives. We see sprinklers installed in commercial, industrial, and institutional occupancies. Installation in residential settings, primarily dormitories, apartments, and group homes, is increasing. Residential sprinklers for single-family dwellings have been accepted slowly owing to factors such as cost and technology limitations. That, however, is changing.

As a society, Americans need to ask themselves who should be responsible for fire protection. Responsibility for safety begins with the individual. Candles are the source of ignition for many fires in apartments, dormitories, and single-family homes. Many people treat candles with little regard for their potential to ignite nearby combustibles. Americans appear to exhibit minimal concern for the threat of catastrophic fire. Typically, we deny the possibility of a fire and, should it happen, believe insurance will cover our property losses. Of course, only other people die in fires. This belief may be the product of the inherent optimism of the U.S. psyche. In other industrialized nations, the citizens show a greater public awareness of and individual responsibility for being careful. These countries place emphasis on training and educating citizens in safe behavior, accident prevention, and risk reduction. In the United States, we treasure our individual freedoms and tend to see any attempt to regulate behavior as a threat to personal liberty. We pay a great price for that in terms of both money and lives.

The U.S. fire service has started to take steps in the direction of public education and risk management. In general, though, the public has not wholeheartedly embraced these small efforts to help people help themselves. Even within the fire service ranks, line firefighters often have little interest in public education. National organizations, such as the International Association of Fire Chiefs (IAFC), the Change Your Clock, Change Your Battery campaign, and the NFPA's Risk Watch Program, have launched some good efforts. Homeowners would do well to install smoke detectors and heat detectors, practice fire prevention, minimize risks, and develop and practice a home escape plan. Anyone who owns a building (including residential buildings) can have their own private firefighter on guard twenty-four hours a day, seven days a week, 365 days a year, by installing an automatic fire sprinkler system.

CHAPTER 6

Fire and Human Behavior

A person's age plays a significant part in their overall physiological and mental ability to escape a burning structure. Children aged five and under and adults sixty-five and older are at the greatest risk. In 2002 children four years old and younger had a fire death rate 1.5 times that of the general population, normalized to 1.2 per 100,000. (Federal requirements for child-resistant lighters played a major role in reducing the overall rate of fire death among children.) Adults face increased risk as their ages increase. Again using 2002 data, adults sixty-five years and older had a fire death rate of 2.5 times that of the general population, normalized to 2.4 per 100,000. Age seventy-five and older had a fire death rate of 3.1 per 100,000, or three times the national average. The causes include decreased mobility, hearing loss, and resistance to the use of new technologies. Education, poverty, and race also play a role in risk for fire-related death. African Americans, Native Americans, and Alaskan Natives have higher fire death rates than white Americans, who have higher fire death rates than Asian Americans.[1]

As their name indicates, automatic sprinklers require no interaction with humans. For those who cannot react or are unable to react to a threat properly, sprinklers are essential. To save lives in residential settings, sprinkler systems must activate quickly while heat and smoke conditions are still survivable. To gain widespread usage, they must also be economically feasible. Advances in sprinkler design and materials have made the technology more affordable. We will someday see automatic detection and suppression systems in all occupied

57

buildings. Responsibility for personal safety begins with the individual; hardware alone cannot solve the problem.[2]

Statistics from NFPA studies reveal that in 84 percent of fatalities, the fire developed in intensity for at least ten minutes prior to any action, and in 38 percent of all fatal fires, the fire burned for forty minutes or more before the fire department arrived.[3] Under ideal conditions, without intervention or interruption, enclosed room and compartment fires will produce a flashover. Flashover is a phase point in fire growth development at which all combustibles in a room have absorbed sufficient heat to ignite simultaneously, producing rapid and violent combustion.[4] Fires typically begin small and subsequently grow in size through the interplay of radiation, convection, and conduction and around the various open surface areas of the space. As the surfaces of individual items and building components heat up, they approach the temperature at which they will ignite in quick and violent succession. As each item ignites, it releases more heat energy, thus perpetuating and quickening the point of simultaneous ignition (flashover). Anyone caught in a flashover will not likely survive. To understand the flashover phenomenon fully is to appreciate the futility of expecting rescue of exposed victims by firefighters. After flashover, it becomes a victim recovery effort rather than a rescue effort.

A firefighter wearing personal protective equipment (PPE) and breathing supplied air with SCBA may survive a flashover but will likely suffer some degree of injury. A firefighter's ability to survive a flashover is short lived, and must exit the compartment quickly or die. Flashover may occur within eight to ten minutes (or less) of fire ignition in a confined space or room. With prompt detection of a fire and a quick response by firefighters, the fire department often arrives at about the same time that the flashover occurs or a short time before or after. Firefighters must quickly recognize pre-flashover conditions. Anyone trapped within the compartment where flashover has occurred are generally severely burned and very likely dead.

After a flashover, firefighters usually recover bodies rather than make rescues. At this point fire crews will likely attempt to knock down, or extinguish, the fire and then enter the space to recover the body or bodies. The best way to prevent flashover is to prevent fire ignition, control fire growth, or fully suppress the fire before its transition to the incipient phase of growth. An automatic sprinkler system is the most effective way to suppress fire and prevent flashover. Nothing—not even building more fire stations, buying more fire apparatus, increasing crew size, converting from volunteer to paid firefighters, or lowering your city's fire insurance rating—can make the impact on fires that automatic sprinklers can. A quick response time is imperative for controlling any fire. Automatic sprinklers can respond to the threat of unfriendly open flame faster than the local fire department, no matter how good they are, how fast they are, or how well trained they are. In terms of reaction time, automatic sprinklers trump the firefighter hands down. Essentially, suppression of a fire before it becomes destructive and life threatening comes down to quick detection, prompt automatic reaction, and effective application of water. Firefighters can handle one of these essentials. A detection system can handle two. Automatic sprinklers, however, can do all three.

U.S. fire researchers showed little interest in understanding human behavior in fire situations until the 1970s. By then the United States had suffered many large-life-loss fires, which captured the public interest only for a short time after each event. However, these fires did prompt changes in fire service equipment, training, and tactics. Studies centered on the then-popular concept of panic behavior and emphasized the nature of panic. How people behave when confronted by unfriendly fire in a building depends on several variables. How the fire appears to a person and how they interpret the threat may greatly affect whether or not they survive. Are they smelling smoke but seeing no fire or dark, menacing smoke? Does the building have any built-in fire detection alarms or suppression equipment? Have occupants received training to react properly to the situation? For the most part, those individuals having the most intimate contact with the fire are at greatest risk, and their action or lack thereof will affect whether or not other occupants will survive. The most critical action to take in event of fire is to activate an alarm for other occupants and notify the fire department by dialing 911. Do both at the same time if possible. Fighting the fire yourself is the least practical option unless you have taken the other actions, you have the training, and you have extinguishing equipment at hand.

Collective experience with fire seems to indicate that most individuals when confronted by fire will act altruistically, exhibiting deliberate, positive, life-saving actions. The evidence also negates most claims of panic-type behavior (nonadaptive flight). However, when humans gather in large numbers, such as in theaters or stores or restaurants, an individual may disbelieve what they are seeing because of the general inaction of others. People who witness a large fire in an enclosed space may be dumbstruck. Studies have shown that males are more likely to attempt to investigate and extinguish the fire whereas females are more likely to report the fire and help others evacuate. Also, those who have safely exited tend to reenter the burning structure for any number of reasons. Studies have shown Americans reenter to save personal effects, rescue pets, notify others, and assist the fire department. They have also shown that British citizens reenter to fight the fire, observe the fire, shut doors, and wait for the fire department. Studies of occupant behavior reveal other differences between the U.S. and British population. Americans are more likely to notify others, get dressed, gather the family, leave, and then reenter the building. The British tend to fight the fire, visit the fire area, close the door to the fire area, pull the alarm, and turn off appliances.[5]

There is a connection between the frequency and severity of fires and socioeconomic conditions and climate. A number of fire research studies conducted in the 1970s and 1980s considered the role of climate and the conditions of poverty in urban and rural settings. The findings consider data collected by the USFA, which used fire incident data supplied by U.S. fire departments. The data clearly show that northern states with very cold climates and southern states with very poor populations had higher fire death rates than did the other states overall. Heating-degree days (a quantitative indicator of cold weather) correlated significantly with death rates in the northern states. Rural death rates also correlate significantly with poverty levels and exhibit themselves in the poorer populations of the southern states. In both the North and the South, trying to stay warm and improper use of heating equipment affect fire death rates. In the South, there is widespread use of small fixed or portable electric room heaters. In the North, improperly maintained central-heating systems often malfunction. With fuel-burning heating units, there is also the matter of carbon monoxide escaping from improperly installed or maintained chimneys. This especially includes woodstoves and masonry fireplaces where chimney fires compound the problem.[6] A long-standing problem in Maine has been woodstoves and oil-burning appliances connected to and thus sharing a single flue in many chimneys; education and improved methods of installation are reducing this potential hazard.

Poverty and the type of construction also influence fire death rates. Very old housing, substandard housing, poor building construction methods, substandard construction materials, lack of building codes, and lack of enforcement of building codes increase fire death rates. Where housing units suffer from such effects there is the added danger of the fire spreading from building to building. (The buildings next to or near the fire building are called exposures.) In densely built-up and populated cities, the spread of fire to nearby exposures is a severe problem that frequently confronts firefighters. It is one reason that urban fires are typically worse for firefighters.

A 1998 study for the USFA sought to identify relationships between certain city characteristics such as climate and housing stock and the rate of residential fires. The intent was to identify and explain the relationship between human behaviors, living conditions, and the relative risk of fire. Documenting such relationships and establishing a correlation can benefit the design of intervention and education programs aimed at minimizing risk. The type of construction used for housing units plays a role in fire incidence and severity of fire. So do use and maintenance of the units. Almost without exception, every scientific study of socioeconomic characteristics has shown a relationship between level of income and the risk level of fire.[7]

The principal variables in explaining variations in fire incidence rates have negative correlation with parental presence, good education, adequate income, and home ownership. There may be other factors inherent to higher fire rates, as earlier studies only identified variables that might predict higher fire rates. For example, poverty does not necessarily in and of itself cause fires.[8]

A 1998 study of data collected by the NFIRS further examined the results of the earlier studies, producing data that identified (at least for large cities) climate and the condition of housing stock as indicators of higher fire-incident rates in inner cities. Because the NFIRS data included twenty-seven large cities, researchers were better able to examine and explore previous theories and findings and compare them with this larger data set. The NFIRS data reporting form allows for identifying specific agents of the cause. Identifying fire causes such as arson, children playing, careless smoking, cooking, heating, electrical distribution, appliances, and open flames permitted comparisons of socioeconomic factors with physical conditions and climate using multiple regression. Three factors that explained 64 percent of the variation between residential fire rates in the twenty-seven cities of the NFIRS study were annual precipitation (climate), age of the housing stock (socioeconomic conditions), and percentage of the population under age five (demographics). In simpler terms, a cold climate keeps people indoors and using heating devices to cook and keep warm. There is a correlation between the age of the north-eastern cities studied and the regional climate. The age of a city's buildings generally also applies to its burning stock. Although the study showed that high proportions of very young children result in higher fire-incidence rates, it was not proved that poverty was a factor in the children's behavior. Children simply are inclined to like to play with fire and explore its effects. The researchers found that the rate of children playing with fire was lower in those cities where population growth was strong and higher in cities with popula-tion decline.[9] A 2009 analysis questioned the direct role of climate in urban residential fires, however such a study must take into account that people often misuse heating appliances when it is cold.[10] Even urban dwellers may require the use of auxiliary heating appliances.

CHAPTER 7

Fire in Rural Areas
and Wildlands

Understanding the impact of fire in the United States also requires examining the incidence and types of fire in rural wildlife areas. The U.S. Department of Agriculture Rural-Urban Continuum uses a system referred to as the Beale Codes to determine whether an area is rural. The Beale Codes use a scale of zero through nine, with zero indicating a county in a metropolitan area of one million residents or more and nine indicating a rural areaa with fewer than 2,500 residents that is not adjacent to a metropolitan area. A 1998 USFA study of the rural U.S. fire problem uses statistics gathered from rural communities with Beale Codes 7, 8, and 9 and is cited in this book.[1] The range 7–9 includes any nonmetropolitan community of 19,999 or less. Accordingly, 95.7 percent of all U.S. counties are rural under this definition (according to 1995 data).

Except when the public hears news of a fire with a large loss of life or a western wildfire spreading over thousands of acres and destroying hundreds of homes, we tend to view fire as a small, local problem. Fires in the United States take thousands of lives, injure tens of thousands, and cause billions of dollars in property loss. Taken as separate incidents, the fire problem in each community is relatively unique. Amazingly, though, the distribution of fire by property type is roughly proportional when one compares rural areas with the United States as a whole. Data from the mid-1990s show structure (i.e., building) fires in rural areas at 35 percent and at 31 percent in the United States as a whole. The data also show outdoors fires at 45 percent in rural areas and 43 percent for the United States as a whole. The distribution of deaths and injuries from fire between the United States as a whole and rural areas is similar. Open flame, arson, and natural causes are the three top contributors to outside fire in rural areas, while arson is the leading cause in nonrural areas.[2]

The NFIRS study further broke down the analysis to separate North and South as well as East and West to examine regional differences. Significant differences were noted between the North and the South, while the East-West comparison revealed some differences in relative frequency and causes of outside fire. Although open flame accounts for 40 percent of all outside fires in both the East and the West, arson as a cause is a greater problem in the East. In the western United States, outside fires account for 55 percent of all rural fires, but they make up only 36 percent in the East. The four causes of rural residential structure fires in the North are heating, electrical, cooking, and arson. In the South the four leading causes are heating, cooking, arson, and electrical.[3]

Firefighters refer to the place where a fire starts as the area of origin. The prevalent area of origin for rural fires in the North is the chimney (three times higher than in the South). The leading area of origin in the South is the kitchen or cooking area. Imagine what firefighters face when responding to a creosote-plugged chimney connected to a woodstove with a fire roaring inside. Creosote is a mixture of burned and unburned resins and tar that are the by-products of the combustion of wood. Mortality data from 1983–88 reveal that fire death rates in rural areas were higher than the rates in nonrural areas, with the majority of victims being white. However, on a strict per capita basis African Americans and Native Americans were more likely to die by fire.[4] Rural structure fires are more likely to extend beyond the area of origin to involve the entire structure. One reason for this is the longer distances between neighbors so that a fire in an occupied house may go unnoticed.

A discussion of rural fires is incomplete without a mention of the phenomenon of wildfire, both naturally and culturally. Natural wildfires originate from lightening strikes. Stephen J. Pyne, author of *Fire in America: A Cultural History of Wildland and Rural Fire*, writes that approximately eighteen hundred thunderstorms erupt around the world every hour, each having the potential to ignite a fire. Estimates are that lightening strikes may account for 10 percent of the total fires in the United States each year. His study on wildfire in the rural United States focused on the cultural relationship humans have with fire. Perhaps his statement that fire and life itself share a common chemistry of carbon and oxidation best explains the relationship between man and fire. Fire may have been man's first tool. Stone Age hunters lived together in small groups, and fire helped ensure their survival. In nature, without human interference, a natural wildfire will eventually burn itself out when it runs out of fuel or is extinguished by natural means. Cultural use of wildfire enabled the human race to evolve from hunter-gatherers to farmers. As humans learned to master fire, or rather the combustion process, uses for fire turned from cultural to industrial, permitting rapid growth and development of society. Pyne writes that human history and fire are intertwined and have an inherent relationship. Many technological and agricultural developments resulted from our use of fire, with fire itself frequently taking on certain characteristics based on the cultural environment in which it occurs.[5]

Indeed, it is a challenge to comprehend life without fire. The history of human development depended on controlling fire. Our fascination with fire stems from its capacity to overwhelm us, and we are preoccupied with trying to control and master this unpredictable force of nature. Humans in all areas of the world used fire to facilitate hunting animals, clearing forests, clearing land for pastures, clearing brush to expose land for mining, and promoting the growth of certain types of crops. Governments of colonial America imposed controls on fire, restricting its use to certain seasons for land clearing. Colonial governments outlawed the use of fire to aid hunting.

By the seventeenth century, losses caused by uncontrolled fire or escaped fires spurred governments into action to protect property from fire. Most efforts were reactive in nature. The few preventive measures put into practice concerned chimneys and use of noncombustible materials for building construction. The need for the control of fires was and is both legal and practical. Seeking protection and security, we as a society recognize the power of fire and expect governments to assume responsibility for its control and regulation. Essentially, the government has a general duty to protect the public at large. The economic standpoint provided good reason for fire protection. Because one person alone cannot extinguish an out-of-control fire, some provision must be made for the members of a community to assist one another in order to prevent a fire from destroying everyone's property, thus resulting in a loss of their valuables and livelihoods.

In terms of survival, losing a center of economic importance to fire or any other threat is unacceptable. The risk of destruction by fire was so high that it demanded action by the entire community. Americans were generous in helping their neighbors, even those who were hundreds of miles away, in times of need. Sending donations to areas ravaged by conflagrations was common practice. Eventually, however, the concept of insuring one's losses against destruction by fire began to take hold in the form of fire insurance companies, where the insured paid the insurer a fee (a premium) in return for an assurance of a payment of money in the event of a loss by fire. Americans liked this idea. As long as the insurance company is fully capitalized (i.e., maintains sufficient funds in reserve to cover the total replacement costs for the policies written), this system works.

That the concept of fire insurance worked so well is interesting. Purchasing fire insurance requires the assumption that a fire could occur on your property. Yet, Americans act as if fire is something experienced by others. Perhaps we accept a small risk of fire, but believe it will happen only if another building catches fire and the flames spread to our property. Thinking of insurance coverage in that way is essentially hedging your bet on your own perceived risk. This rationalization allowed one to believe in their own good fortune and still have someone bail them out should they have a fire. The problem is that this promotes irresponsibility. People have failed to take ownership of the problem and instead look to society (i.e., government or other people) to handle it. This irresponsibility manifested itself in the prevalent use of wood to build buildings in the early United States. Buildings constructed of wood caught fire, could not be extinguished by the neighborhood bucket brigade, and spread to other wooden buildings, often with disastrous results. Towns or portions of towns burned and were subsequently rebuilt using wood construction, only to be lost again to fire. This scenario played out in U.S. towns throughout the eighteenth and nineteenth centuries. The response to this cycle of destruction was to form volunteer fire companies, install water supplies, and buy more fire insurance coverage against the inevitable.

The United States lacks a strong cultural incentive for preventing fires. We see fire as inevitable, an unfortunate accident that happens to other people, whom we think of as victims. Moreover, we rely on insurance to cover our property losses. There are cultures in the world that view fire as a preventable and even a shameful occurrence. These countries use a mixture of strategies that involves educating people about fire and their responsibility for fire prevention, as well as regulating the built environment in which they live and work. U.S. fire departments have typically put little effort or few resources into fire prevention efforts. In the United States, fire prevention is a local responsibility. A fire department that places an emphasis on building code enforcement, regulating the types of structures covered by building codes, providing specialized training for firefighters, requiring higher education levels for supervisors and managers, and providing a public fire safety education program will help change the U.S. culture of fire.

3
THE FIRE SERVICE
UNDER FIRE

CHAPTER 8

Transformative Forces to Make Firefighting Safer

The legacy of the United States' nineteenth-century volunteer fire departments is evident in the history, tradition, and culture of the twenty-first-century fire service. For the purposes of this book, the term "fire service" refers generally to those agencies, both career and volunteer, providing a range of fire, rescue, and EMS response. Each department is unique in what it provides, but the typical services are structural fire suppression, EMS, wildland fire suppression, hazardous materials spill response, and special or technical rescue. Fire departments providing EMS today find that emergency medical calls outnumber fire calls.

When firefighters claim the service represents "250 years of tradition unimpeded by progress," they are unknowingly referring to their collective tendency to retain cultural artifacts, or traditions and practices from the past. Some of the traditions and practices are not rational, as they have no basis or need in the present. The leather fire helmet falls into this category. The saying hits the mark because the U.S. fire service is tradition bound, for better or worse. The tradition is part of the culture, and the unique culture is part of the tradition, the glue that binds to form a common bond of sacrifice and duty, something to believe in and depend on in good times and in times of crisis. Our fire service esprit de corps prompts the boast that we (Americans) possess the best fire services in the world. In certain terms, such as effectiveness, it may be true. In strictly rational terms, such as efficiency, it may not be as true.

The cracks that exist in this foundation of culture and tradition are becoming more evident year by year. We are losing active volunteers, and nobody can quite figure out how to stop the migration. The trendy phrase among those concerned with volunteers is "recruitment and retention." How do we find new volunteers to fill the ranks and keep those we have now?

There is a static tension between career and volunteer firefighters, yet many career firefighters from large urban departments also volunteer for the suburban fire departments in the communities where they reside. The largest firefighter's union, the International Association of Fire Fighters (IAFF), refers to these individuals as "two-hatters," presumably because they wear different fire helmets for the agencies they serve.[1] The union takes issue with this practice and has threatened action but not followed through with discipline or censure. Although the union leadership can take action against members who wear two hats, directly censuring volunteers carries consequences. The tension between two groups becomes clearer with an understanding of the types of fire positions and fire departments in the United States. A career firefighter is a full-time position within any fire department. A volunteer firefighter agrees to work without expectation of receiving payments. Paid-on-call or call firefighters are a hybrid form of volunteer, paid on a per-call basis, usually by the hour. In the statistical data, the call firefighter is almost always grouped with the pure volunteers, and so useful generalizations about numbers are impossible. This is unfortunate because we cannot determine, using data, whether paying volunteers a small amount of money would serve to motivate more people to join or continue their service.

The NFPA defines two categories of fire departments. However, the de facto result of the definition leaves a third type not covered by their standards. According to NFPA classification, a career department is at least 80 percent paid, while a volunteer department is at least 80 percent volunteer. A department with less than 80 percent either paid or volunteer is a combination department. In applying NFPA standards to a combination department, one must determine whether it functions more like a career department or more like a volunteer department. This system makes data collection more difficult.

As a labor union, the IAFF has a valid duty and responsibility to pursue more paid firefighter positions and improve working conditions for their members. Some of its actions may affect the volunteer service, but overall, when carried through, the result is often long-term improvements in occupational safety and health. The IAFF has no publicly stated agenda to push for the outright dissolution of the volunteers; the union leadership appears to maintain professional neutrality toward the volunteer fire service in the United States. A primary focus of the IAFF is improvement of the occupational health and safety of all firefighters. Their interest in safety ranges from staffing of apparatus and fireground staffing to medical evaluations and long-term health. It is difficult to argue with those goals.

The IAFF is doing only what we all do naturally; we maximize our situation by increasing advantages and diminishing disadvantages. The IAFF has used its influence in the federal OSHA rule-making process to advocate safety rules to protect firefighters, such as respiratory protection and the two-in/two-out rule for interior structural fire attack.[2] The IAFF also influences the NFPA standards-making process by supporting such NFPA standards as 1500, 1710, and 1720.[3] The union's efforts have forced many career and volunteer departments to improve firefighter working conditions and operational procedures. States following OSHA rules for public sector agencies (as well as a few non-OSHA regulated states) implemented the OSHA Respiratory Protection Standard as a requirement for career and volunteer departments. There have been no formal studies to prove or disprove the benefits of the respiratory protection standard. However, common sense holds that protecting your lungs from the products of combustion (heat and toxic smoke) is a positive step.

Certainly many fire departments have embraced the rules and are providing much-needed medical screenings for members who must wear SCBA. They maintain SCBA more diligently and ensure a backup rescue crew when firefighters enter a burning building. Some departments resisted implementation of the respiratory protection standards, specifically the two-in/two-out rule, claiming they impeded their ability to fight fires in an aggressive manner. The doomsayers are always lurking; they are the same ones who criticized plans to pay firemen, steam-powered fire engines, the use of horses, motorized fire apparatus, SCBA, full-body turnout gear, fire-based EMS, NFPA 1500, NFPA 1710, NFPA 1720, and so on.

A major change, implemented across the country in all but a very few departments, is requiring that firefighters wear a full-body set (coat, trousers, hood, boots, gloves, and helmet) of Nomex PPE. In the late 1980s and early 1990s, when it was first suggested that Nomex PPE and fiberglass-reinforced helmets with impact liners would greatly enhance protection over canvas duck turnout coats, three-quarter-length rubber boots, and leather fire helmets, many firefighters (volunteer and career) scoffed at such nonsense. Firefighters wondered how they would know a room was too hot if they were wearing a hood that covered their ears. Indeed, the Nomex hood does mask the heat, giving credence to that argument. However, the solution was not to throw out the Nomex hood but rather to train firefighters to recognize signs of deadly fire behavior. Post-incident analysis of fires usually reveals that firefighters caught in a flashover were perceptually lost (disoriented from knowing their surroundings and location), were not reading the fire behavior conditions properly, or did not have a protective hose line at hand. There are situations where it is accepted procedure in some fire departments for firefighters to be inside, near, or above the fire room without a hose line for protection, but such cases typically involve active searching for or rescuing an occupant trapped inside the building.

Firefighters must consider how far will they go to save a life. The answer depends on whether the victim is savable. The fire service is internalizing the concept that property itself (buildings and contents) is not worth personal sacrifice. The fire service needs its lifesaving tradition, but it also needs educated, combat-experienced leaders who can make difficult decisions. Firefighters must not sacrifice themselves for uninhabited, dilapidated buildings or attempts to rescue a hopelessly trapped or already dead victim.

Traditionally it has been possible, theoretically at least, for any rookie firefighter to imagine that he or she could become chief of department someday. Promotion to rank in the U.S. fire service runs the gamut from annual election of officers in some volunteer organizations to civil service examinations based on test scores, experience, and actual ability (merit). Preparing for, qualifying for, and ultimately receiving a merit-based promotion is an exhilarating experience that reaffirms one's hard work. Sometimes the merit system fails to promote the qualified for political and legal reasons. Legal challenges are sometimes raised against these failures of the legitimized system.[4]

Strange as it may seem, no overreaching or governing authority ensures that a local fire department is an efficient and effective organization. Unlike the local police department, which interacts and associates with larger law enforcement agencies (e.g., county sheriff, state police, FBI, federal border patrol, Department of Justice), a local fire department generally has no active partners other than its neighboring departments. Local departments typically work with area departments, the state fire marshal, and sometimes law enforcement. We have a federal resource agency, the USFA, for training and education, but it has no regulatory powers. Departments may work with the state fire marshal or other state police agency in cases of suspected arson and sometimes for code enforcement issues. Fire departments also work with the state forestry department, and here is a trend to working with or within the emergency management framework. But, except for submitting to rating by the ISO for fire insurance purposes, local departments are mostly unregulated.

There are valid reasons to regulate or standardize fire services. Think of a large-scale disaster on which many fire agencies would work together. If the members of those agencies received similar training, configured apparatus similarly, and used similar operational procedures, their ability to come together and function as a unified entity would improve the effectiveness of the response. Constrained municipal budgets are the rule and not usually the exception. Scrutiny of department budget requests is increasing, and fire departments frequently experience denial of their requests for additional funds. There is more talk of regionalization and consolidation of both local fire departments and governments.

The distribution or deployment of fire stations or trucks need not overlap. In other words, each station and its apparatus can effectively cover a given geographic area, with stations and apparatus sited strategically, irrespective of political boundaries. The question is this: why build more stations and buy more apparatus than is needed? Stretching tax dollars by sharing resources makes good sense. However, there is too often resistance to such efforts from firefighter unions, volunteer stations, and career fire chiefs, who are afraid of losing control or, even worse, their jobs. Techniques and methodologies such as systems analysis and operations research can provide for accurate, predictable, and effective deployment of resources. One tool in this arsenal is geographic information systems (GIS).

Although more and more firefighters have undergraduate degrees, few senior fire officers have graduate degrees. There is a lack of appreciation of any similarities between fire service operations and service-related business models or the military. At one time, it was common for firefighters with college degrees to want to hide their education from their coworkers. Anyone speaking out or questioning the authority of ranking officers quickly learned that career survival required them to dummy up. This is changing, fortunately.

Decision makers at the municipal level can look to standards for fire service deployment published by the NFPA. The one player on the national level that can and does provide guidance on municipal fire protection matters is the ISO, which is an insurance industry trade organization supported by member insurance companies. The ISO, usually on a ten-year interval, evaluates municipal resources that have a bearing on local-level fire protection. The local resources reviewed by the ISO include the public water system, the emergency-911 dispatch system, and, of course, the fire department.

Using their Fire Suppression Rating Schedule, the ISO evaluates resources, assigns a credit, and then issues a Public Protection Classification (PPC) rating. The PPC ratings run from one through ten. A Class 10 indicates no recognized local fire protection. A Class 1 is relatively rare among fire departments. Communities with a recognized fire department but without a public hydrant system are at some disadvantage under the rating system and rarely receive anything better than Class 9. Insurance underwriters use the ISO PPC for guidance in setting or determining what premium to charge a property owner for his or her fire insurance coverage.

Today, more often than not, the PPC mostly affects specific commercial properties because homeowners insurance is now packaged for dealing with multiple perils, fire being only one of them. Nonetheless, fire chiefs will frequently use the ISO rating schedule as leverage for justifying the building of additional fire stations, buying more equipment, or hiring more firefighters. The ISO cannot mandate anything, and their rating schedule strictly focuses on reducing property losses, not on saving the lives of civilians or firefighters. That is about the worst one can say about the ISO. Yet they admit this fact and always make every effort to work cooperatively with public officials to improve public fire protection. How the ISO (and its predecessor, the NBFU) came into existence provides an interesting background for understanding how the autonomy of local fire services affects us all today.

Fire insurance maps were one of the first tools developed by the underwriters. Usually updated every ten years, the maps provided a visual representation in the form of highly detailed plots with all buildings, usually drawn at a scale of one inch for every fifty feet. A fire protection expert cannot look at an urban downtown scene without recognizing the influence of the NBFU and the nineteenth-century fire insurance underwriters. Moreover, an expert cannot look at today's fire service and not see the influence of the NBFU and NFPA. To understand the technological and cultural development of the fire service in the United States, we need to study the late nineteenth through the mid-twentieth century. Understanding the influence of technology and its role in shaping the fire service culture will give us an insight into the values and traditions that today exacerbate the societal, demographic, and economic forces at play in the fire service—both career and volunteer.

CHAPTER 9

Cultural Change Needed to Improve Firefighter Safety

In March 2004 the National Fallen Firefighters Foundation and the USFA sponsored the Firefighter Life Safety Summit in Tampa, Florida. The purpose of the meeting of over two hundred emergency service leaders representing over a hundred organizations was more than spring break in the Florida sunshine. The gathering was to gain support for an effort to reduce firefighter fatalities by 25 percent within five years, and 50 percent within 10 years. This is a noble goal, as we have been holding steady for over ten years at an average of a hundred deaths per year. Before this, the average death rate was typically over two hundred per year.[1]

This reduction apparently comes through a multifaceted effort that included increased training, new equipment, new procedures, and a new philosophy toward fireground command. Beyond immediate improvements in the record, the summit participants must have realized that their lofty goals would require radical transformations in how the fire service does business. The sixteen initiatives formulated by the summit participants could well change the U.S. fire service.[2]

The 16 Firefighter Life Safety Initiatives:
- Define and advocate the need for a cultural change within the fire service relating to safety, incorporating leadership, management, supervision, accountability, and personal responsibility
- Enhance the personal and organizational accountability for health and safety throughout the fire service

- Focus greater attention on the integration of risk management with incident management at all levels, including strategic, tactical, and planning responsibilities
- Empower all firefighters to stop unsafe practices
- Develop and implement national standards for training, qualifications, and certification (including regular recertification) that is equally applicable to all firefighters, based on the duties they are expected to perform
- Develop and implement national medical and physical fitness standards that are equally applicable to all firefighters, based on the duties they are expected to perform
- Create a national research agenda and data collection system that relates to the initiatives
- Utilize available technology wherever it can produce higher levels of health and safety
- Thoroughly investigate all firefighter fatalities, injuries, and near misses
- Grant programs should support the implementation of safe practices and/or mandate safe practices as an eligibility requirement
- National standards for emergency response policies and procedures should be developed and championed
- National protocols for response to violent incidents should be developed and championed
- Firefighters and their families access to counseling and psychological support
- Public education must receive more resources and be championed as a critical fire and life safety program
- Advocacy must be strengthened for the enforcement of codes and the installation of home fire sprinklers
- Safety must be a primary consideration in the design of apparatus and equipment

No one argues against preventing needless firefighter deaths and injuries, but there are strong feelings regarding how to approach the issue of the firefighter's occupational culture.[3] In 2004 the backers of the summit initiatives had no plan, mechanism, or funding for their implementation, but that has changed.[4] The initiatives amount to reengineering the fire service and changing firefighter occupational health and safety through nonregulatory means. If everyone who attended the summit took on this challenge as a lifetime crusade and devoted the remainder of their careers to the cause, they would likely retire without ever seeing full acceptance within the ranks. What they suggest is radical change, which has never come easy for the U.S. fire service. The campaign will move forward one firefighter, one fire chief, and one fire department at a time. Consider that the nine Charleston firefighters died in the Super Sofa Store fire in June 2007, just three years after the 2004 Life Safety Initiatives were born. Worse, they died on the Monday that kicked off National Firefighter Safety Stand Down Week.

Chiefs who embrace the life-safety effort for the well-being of their personnel may find themselves pitted against cash-strapped towns and cities. Other chiefs will find themselves battling the status quo, culture, and tradition within their own departments. In the face of such entrenched resistance, how many chiefs yield to the futility of their efforts? When one has a family to support and a mortgage to pay, sacrificing a position for a crusade is difficult to rationalize. To achieve these initiatives requires substantive change. In effect, the initiatives attempt to professionalize the behavior of firefighters. Such change may be easier to accomplish in paid departments than in volunteer departments. There is less control over volunteers in most states, and the volunteers exercise a larger degree of autonomy over their own actions. Successful cultural change demands a careful and steady approach. People have to be reeducated. This is somewhat easier with full-time employees, as management has some advantage, but how do you convince volunteers to do something they may not have any interest in doing?

Fire chiefs belonging to the IAFC will likely find support for the summit initiatives from that organization. Paid firefighters represented by their own labor organization, the IAFF, will definitely find support for the initiatives. But, what about the volunteers? The NFPA, OSHA, and the various state employee safety agencies will surely support the initiatives. OSHA regulations might apply only to volunteers in some states. Other states might have control over volunteers. The NFPA can set standards, but it cannot enforce rules. The unfortunate reality is that these initiatives may eventually wither in the wake of difficult economic times, entrenched culture, another terrorist attack, or simple complacency. Paid firefighters protect roughly 80 percent of the U.S. population, while the volunteers protect a roughly equal geographical percentage. Many volunteer fire departments are isolated and thus are difficult to reach, literally and figuratively. The crusaders will have to reach out to all U.S. fire-fighters to make change happen. How do they reach out to thousands of volunteers in the rural and suburban United States who lack a unifying national organization?

Hundreds of these small rural departments survive on miniscule operating budgets. Many have to raise their own funds just to purchase the basic equipment needed to protect their community from fires. A number of the initiatives will require purchasing equipment and training programs. Asking for more taxpayer money is generally not well received. Volunteering for fire service is significantly different from volunteering as an elected or appointed public official. Taxpayers may also have to choose between heating school buildings in the winter and buying new turnout gear for the fire department. What choice will they make?

Culture is the powerful force in this equation, as demonstrated by the still widely popular leather fire helmet. In 1977, when the helmet was almost ready to be replaced by modern materials, one would have paid approximately $55 for the leather New Yorker–style helmet. Today at nearly $500, the helmet is still in vogue among firefighters seeking the traditional look. In fact, it is not simply about tradition. It is a statement against the restrictiveness of the current safety culture. Those who wear the modern leather helmet swear it is made of the best material, superior to anything else, comfortable, and iconic. Looking good is important to the fireman's ego. In reality, the modern leather helmet is no match for the similar helmet of thirty or more years ago. The older version certainly fit and wore better, as it was sized correctly and eventually molded to the shape of the wearer's head. Today's leather helmet is heavier in weight, unbalanced, and awkward to wear in tight spaces. Fit and cost are the primary reasons many are opting for a look-alike leather-style helmet made of plastic. Regardless, wearing the leather (or the look-alike) says something about the wearer and tradition.

In some of the largest cities (Boston, New York, Baltimore, Chicago, Houston, and San Francisco) as well as hundreds of smaller departments, fire-fighters wear these helmets proudly. At the same time, some of the best departments (Phoenix, Los Angeles, and Seattle) and thousands of smaller ones wear the modern-style helmet with no infringement on the manhood, or woman-hood, of the firefighter. The modern helmet is lightweight, is smaller, fits well, is balanced, and costs less. Still, many U.S. firefighters and fire departments swear by their traditional leather helmet and do not mind that taxpayers pay more money for the firefighter's special look. (Note: Some firefighters do pay for their own helmet of choice, and those who cannot afford leather purchase the lower-cost look-alike in plastic.) Only in the United States do firefighters make fashion statements. In the end it does not improve performance or make one smarter or safer; it merely costs more.

Tradition, resistance to change, and plain ignorance may lie beneath some firefighter deaths and injuries. Chance also plays a role. Between 1981 and 2007, there was only minor variation in the percentage of injuries across a range of situations. The NFPA, along with other fire service organizations, suggests that the fire service adopt and follow the NFPA's consensus-driven, American National Standards Institute (ANSI)–approved, published standards and guidelines. Neither the NFPA nor any other organization or entity provide evidence that following the standards and guidelines will result in a reduction in fires, injuries, and fatalities. The National Institute for Occupational Safety and Health (NIOSH) investigates firefighter fatalities and injuries and publishes reports of the significant cases. A review of NIOSH investigative reports (available online through their website) shows some common factors present in firefighter deaths.

There is frequently a link between the causative factor(s) and the direct behavior or actions of firefighters killed and injured in the line of duty. Even when equipment or clothing is involved, the failure is frequently attributable to the human element.[5] NFPA standards and guidelines cover aspects of firefighting clothing, equipment, apparatus, organization, management, and behavior. Safe behavior evolves from a state of mind. One can make safety rules, but one cannot force people to be safe unless they internalize and believe in these rules. In addition, firefighting activities can never be absolutely, guaranteed, 100 percent safe. The root cause of the safety problem in the U.S. fire service is generally not with poor equipment or a lack of national standards; it is a matter of training, attitude, habit, and workplace practice.

Certification of training has not made us safer, nor will licensing, since licensing does not prevent malpractice among physicians. NFPA 1500, the Standard on Fire Department Occupational Safety and Health Program, provides guidelines for a fire department safety program. What we really need is proof or evidence that this program works. A long-term, comparative study of firefighter fatalities and injuries in departments that follow the recommended

NFPA standards compared with those that do not might prove very interesting. Unfortunately, conducting such a study would be difficult because of local variations.

The U.S. Firefighter Fatality Database (compiled from NFIRS data) shows a very disturbing trend in fire training–related deaths. While the average number of firefighter deaths holds steady at about a hundred per year on average, the number of training-related deaths is on the rise. In 2003 fire training–related deaths accounted for 10 percent of the total. Moreover, it is not just new recruit firefighters who die in training; it includes all department ranks. No surprise again that the leading cause of death during training is cardiac stress and overexertion. The USFA technical report *Trends and Hazards in Firefighter Training* states that between 1987 and 2001 there was a 31 percent decrease in structure fires in the United States. With fewer actual fires to fight, firefighters cannot gain the essential body of experience that will make them safe and effective on the job.[6]

Fire officers make decisions under conditions of extreme stress. In these situations, individuals make crucial decisions, even life and death decisions, based on previously known or similar situations. Inexperienced firefighters will make poor decisions in real-life situations. To compensate, firefighter training has evolved over the years from being done on the job by one's peers to being conducted in a semicontrolled environment by professional trainers. With fewer fires to fight, firefighters have had to train more, and train harder, under realistic but simulated conditions designed to impart that vital reservoir of knowledge.[7]

Society expects, even demands, a certain level of service and proficiency of firefighters. Meeting that expectation requires training and maintenance of a certain level of competence in a wide range of skills. Such skills would include interior fire attack, wildland fire attack, hazmat incident control, emergency medicine, vehicle extrication, high-angle rescue, collapse rescue, cold-water rescue, driver/operator, and operating pumps. To maintain basic proficiency in such a range of skills requires extensive training, on-the-job experience, and continual retraining. These activities alone are enough to keep a full-time firefighter busy when not responding to calls and maintaining stations and apparatus. When does the volunteer firefighter find time? If that is not enough, all government employees must receive recurrent training in workplace safety, blood-borne pathogens, airborne pathogens, lifestyle diversity, sexual harassment, and department policy and procedures. In addition, firefighters have

routine duties such as reviewing streets, roads, and hydrant locations, and sur-
veying buildings to develop incident action plans. Is it any wonder the number of volunteer firefighters is declining and the number of paid positions is
increasing?

The need for live-fire training is becoming increasingly important to
maintain basic proficiency and help develop a repertoire of knowledge that
permits rapid decision making in high-stress situations. Live fire offers a contextual training experience and is as close to the real world as is safely possible.
There are two ways to provide live-fire training in building fires. The typical
is the constructed or prefabricated "burn building" located at a training site
with other firefighting props. Also used for live-fire attack training are
acquired structures. These are everyday buildings, usually older homes, set for
demolition and used by the fire department for a one-time training opportunity.
Generally, only the states, urban counties, or metropolitan-size departments
have dedicated, fully equipped training sites that accommodate the range of
required training evolutions.

Sadly enough, some states (mostly large, poor, and rural) lack a dedicated,
full-service academy. The recent increase in training-related deaths requires monitoring, and an active investigation of each incident should identify the causative
factors and then make them public. Realistic, contextual training should be
mandatory for any training program. These programs should also be compe-
tency-based, with practical skills taught to a standard and then tested, thus
ensuring a demonstration of measured, evaluated proficiency by the candidate.
On-the-job training (OJT) is a poor substitute for developing critical skills in a
candidate. This route places the rookie in situations of stress and danger in the
company of veterans, who may or may not be qualified to train someone. OJT is
acceptable once individuals have completed basic or advanced training and are
assimilating into their roles as members of an operational company. Military
training and law enforcement training also lend themselves to structured, com-
petency-based programs employing varying degrees of training-in-context.

Modern urban firefighting and wildland firefighting are similar in certain
ways to military action. As such, working as a member of a team becomes a
critical element in achieving efficiency, effectiveness, and safety. The goal is
for everyone to go home alive. Given the number of injuries and fatalities that
occur while responding, a more appropriate slogan is "Arrive alive, go home
alive." Working as a team stands in stark contrast to what firefighters refer to

as "freelancing," or working alone or without direction. From a standpoint of safety, teamwork is essential. Firefighting is labor-intensive work, and effective operations are based and even dependent upon crew members working in teams. Aside from perhaps operating a fire pump, serious task-level evolutions usually involve teams of at least two people; most require three or four, with some tasks requiring even more people. Some studies of task-level firefighting activities indicate that effectiveness and efficiency increase, up to a certain point, with additional staffing. Field experience proves that apparatus crews for engines (pumpers) should include a driver/operator, an officer, and two to four firefighters. Aerial (ladder and platform) apparatus should have an additional member. From advancing hose lines to raising ladders and ventilating roofs, working as a team is safer than working alone. Unbelievably, there are departments in which one or two firefighters may attempt, usually unsuccessfully, to complete the tactical operation.

Anyone who has worked in one of these departments quickly recognizes the added risk and physical stress of working alone. Not only is the risk of firefighter injury or death higher, but the quality of the work suffers. This translates into higher levels of property damage, civilian injuries, and civilian deaths. There are methods and rules of thumb to determine adequate staffing needed to perform a given task. The NFPA provides guidelines for conducting an initial attack based on training evolutions for the same activity. Since the 1970s the staffing levels of most U.S. fire departments have declined. Career departments lose staff through attrition and layoff. Most volunteer departments in the United States are also losing members. Because of the variability in actual availability of volunteers at any given point in time, such departments must have large memberships. The rule of thumb is that you need three to six active volunteers to equal one full-time position. Thus, to field sixteen firefighters for a safe attack, a volunteer department must have approximately forty-eight to ninety-six members on the roster to ensure coverage. Maintaining a roster of trained volunteers is no easy task, and managing such a department is challenging.

CHAPTER 10

Transitional Forces Create New Fire Service Model

Fire departments in the United States come in a variety of organizational schemes and staffing arrangements. Some receive funding from a government entity while others, such as volunteer departments, operating independently of government, may receive nothing. Some departments are part of local or county government while others form into special fire districts with the power to assess protection fees or seek subscriptions for service. Some volunteers receive no reimbursement for personal time while others receive a small stipend or hourly wage. Until the last few decades, most volunteer departments raised all or part of the funds necessary for the department to function.

This was good for small villages and towns while it lasted, but fund-raising requires effort and time. It is costly to operate and maintain a modern fire service. Today, municipalities generally provide some support toward operation of volunteer departments. This lifts a large burden from the members; otherwise, their limited time for volunteering would include fund-raising in addition to firefighting. Fund-raising efforts include bingo games, raffles, fairs, miscellaneous games of chance, facility rental, or charging a fee for service. So, volunteering to be a firefighter is not simply volunteering to fight fires; it also means volunteering to raise money (serious money) to keep the department functioning.

Functioning means different things to different departments. For some it means keeping enough gas or diesel fuel in an outdated, second- or thirdhand fire truck and keeping a dilapidated fire station heated so the fire pumps do not freeze. For others it means purchasing a new $500,000 pumper or $750,000 ladder truck every few years so as not to be one-upped by the department in the next town. Also consider the need for PPE for each member. There is the cost of training courses, educational programs, and medical exams for the members. Take all that into consideration and think about the levels of management skill, leadership ability, and technical expertise required to operate any fire department, whether volunteer or career.

It is becoming increasingly difficult to recruit new volunteers and retain the experienced ones. There are many reasons for this, including the demands and influences of our modern society, cultural trends, and the economy. As a result, more and more volunteer positions evolve into paid positions every year. Another trend has many volunteer departments entering into formal agreements with other nearby departments to respond automatically (i.e., simultaneously). Such policies create what is essentially an automatic system for mutual aid. Such arrangements were once required only for major fires; now they are activated on a daily basis for otherwise routine building fires.

Departments that convert to paid positions so that they become part paid with some volunteers are called combination fire departments, and these departments make up third category, along with career departments and volunteer departments. The combination department offers an alternative arrangement used more frequently every year as departments transition from volunteer to career. Combination departments are not without their problems, though. Imagine that your workplace included people willing to work without pay. How would you, as a paid employee, feel about people who volunteered to do the same work as you? On the other hand, what if they were your bosses and had less training and experience than you had? Existence of a formal labor contract creates more potential for problems. Put both groups together in a high-stress, life-or-death situation, and emotions sometimes run high. Being the chief of a combination department certainly has its unique challenges and demands a person with special leadership skills, excellent management skills, and a tolerance for job stress.

Working in a combination department can be as difficult for the members as it is for the chief. The common thought is that the same training and job performance standards should apply to both volunteers and career personnel in a combination department. There are pros and cons to this argument. Combination departments come in various configurations. As of 2008, an NFPA survey of

U.S. fire departments reported 30,185 fire departments with 8 percent full-time career, 6 percent mostly career, 17 percent mostly volunteer, and 70 percent all volunteer.[1]

The hybrid staffing of a combination department presents many opportunities and challenges. This arrangement is both effective and efficient. It requires an understanding of two principal types of firefighter: volunteer and career. In their book *Leading Career and Volunteer Firefighters*, researchers John Benoit and Kenneth Perkins offer a four-level typology for classifying combination departments. Their purpose is to improve understanding of the combination arrangement because, as hybrids, these departments come in many forms and exist for many reasons. At the first level is the simple-previously-volunteer combination department. These departments are found in rural areas (forty to seventy miles from a central city), have a relatively prosperous local economy, and can afford to hire a small number of career personnel. The career staff may or may not be unionized, and they typically cover the day shift on weekdays when most of the volunteers are off working in the central city. At the second level is the simple previously career combination department. These organizations are in towns or cities facing a bleak or uncertain economic future. As career members retire, the vacant positions fill not with a new career member but with additional volunteers. These departments often take on additional duties, usually EMS response, to help justify and fund their existence. Third in the typology is the complex previously volunteer combination department. This type is typical in the exurban fringe, approximately forty miles from a central city. Growth and development in this suburban environment has fueled the local economy, permitting the hiring of career firefighters to supplement the volunteer force. Some of the volunteers perceive the adding of career personnel as a threat. The fourth type is the complex previously career combination department, usually found where several suburban departments merge with a larger central city department. Sometimes the central city is economically disadvantaged. The move may also be part of a regional governmental consolidation effort. The key difference between this type and the complex previously volunteer type is that one involves an economically thriving suburban fringe area and the other an economically declining urban core area. Consolidations or mergers generally have a relatively lower proportion of volunteers.[2]

Benoit and Perkins base their concept in part on the previous history of the department and the degree of complexity of the fire service delivery system.

The authors contend that history is important because tradition is both the inertia preventing organizational change and a potential reservoir of strength during times of threat. In addition, whether the department was fully career or fully volunteer will affect the choice of management strategy. Benoit and Perkins also hold that the degree of complexity of the fire service delivery system is a significant factor affecting the trust relationship between the individuals and the component parts of the delivery system network. In the end, it all comes down to trust and performance. Do the members of the new department trust each other? Do the members trust the department management and vice versa? Do the local governing body and the fire department trust each other? Is there a level of trust among the various departments involved in the merger or consolidation? Do the citizens (as potential customers) trust the department? Performance is an important element of the trust equation. Does the department perform at a high level, satisfactorily meeting its duties and obligations to the public? Does the department's performance meet or exceed the level of performance of nearby departments? The total capability of a department affects its performance. Capability involves staffing level, training, education, experience, and available resources. These factors intermix, forming an interorganizational dynamic subsequently reflected in the public's perception of the department.[3]

The true essence of any fire department is how it functions and performs at a fire or emergency. It is not about resources (equipment, paid or volunteer personnel, thriving community, or declining community); it is about how well the organization handles the emergencies it faces with the resources it has available. In addition, it is about everyone going home as healthy as they came. Authorities may set benchmarks as measures of cost-effectiveness, implement new policies to minimize legal liability, implement safety programs to minimize risk, reduce staff, and close stations to save money, but it is what happens on the fireground that matters most to property owners and the insurance companies. In addition, most of the time taxpayers' demands drive political decision making.

City and town officials often feel frustrated by or resent the perceived inefficiency of on-duty firefighters. Actually responding to emergency calls may account for as little as 2 to 3 percent of the time spent on duty for many career firefighters. This fact gives firefighters leeway to spend at least some of their on-duty time in creative ways and playing out firehouse rituals, like cooking. Not seen by outsiders are the on-duty hours spent maintaining equipment, cleaning the station house, and training. Many critics focus only on rituals of firehouse life such as cooking, watching television, and sleeping. It would seem that the majority of taxpayers do not have a problem with the culture, as they frequently rate their level of satisfaction with community fire services as very high. People who experience a fire do not care what the firefighters were doing before the alarm or even what they will do afterward—they are only concerned with who is going to save their property.

There is a nationwide trend for both large and small fire departments to merge EMS into their operations or offer EMS as a new service. What EMS will do in terms of improving, enhancing, or even harming the traditional fire department is relatively unknown. Future histories of the U.S. fire service will likely tell a story of revolutionary change in the U.S. firehouse and the operation of the service attributable to the influence of EMS. Fire department–based emergency medical response as practiced in the modern era began in the early 1970s but has really only begun to revolutionize the fire department in the past ten to fifteen years. As more individuals with a primarily EMS background receive promotions to the higher ranks of the fire service, they will begin to effect subtle change. So will the elevation of female firefighter/EMTs to the officer and chief officer ranks. The process is a slow one; by 2008 only 150 women in the career fire service had reached the rank of battalion chief or deputy chief, and thirty-one were chiefs of department.[4] While this fact alone has been seismic to the formerly all-male foundation in urban U.S. firefighting, consider that in 2008 there were approximately 365,000 career fire service positions in the United States, of which 55,200 were supervisors and managers, according to the U.S. Bureau of Labor Statistics.[5]

EMS is as different from firefighting as firefighting is from law enforcement. Firefighting and EMS as occupations both combine art and science. The principal difference is that the science of EMS is biology-based while firefighting involves applied physics and chemistry coupled whereas practical mechanics. Law enforcement primarily combines sociology, psychology, and forensics. People who believe that the three fields are closely similar and that one can combine the skills of all three into a super public safety officer are fooling themselves. The phrase "jack of all trades, master of none" is as true in this case as it is in any other. Any public officials attempting to sell such an idea should prove their case by providing an example of successful, long-term implementation in a U.S. community.

Those vexed by what firefighters do while on duty are afflicted with a form of thinking that holds onto perception as reality. What do firefighters do, or what should they do, while on duty? For volunteers, the answer has two parts. For the limited time they are actually on duty, they are either training, maintaining equipment, or responding to calls. (If they are lucky, the fund-raising chores are minimal.) The rest of the volunteers' time is their own, taken up by family, work, and recreation. Today, volunteers carry a tone-alert radio pager. If they choose to wear the pager all day and keep it near their beds at night, they are on call around the clock. The choice to respond or not respond to a particular call or alert is their own to make. Their motivation to volunteer their own time with minimal compensation is truly personal. Serving as an active volunteer for any extended length of time requires commitment, dedication, and sacrifice.

Serving for any extended length of time will help firefighters develop a reaction that allows them to respond to notification promptly and efficiently. This is true of both volunteer and career firefighters. However, being on call during one's work shift and being on call around the clock are very different. Paid firefighters are usually subject to emergency callbacks, but for the most part when paid firefighters are off duty, they are off duty. Volunteer firefighters, however, are usually on duty and rarely make themselves unavailable for calls. Volunteer departments may encourage their members to back their vehicles into the driveway to ensure a speedier exit when called out. Most volunteers will develop habits such as arranging their clothing near the bedside and always leaving their keys in a certain place to make leaving quickly easier. Once the alarm sounds, the race is on. Too often, the race to the fire results in a personal tragedy as relatively minor as a wrecked vehicle or, in the extreme, a traffic death, either civilian or firefighter. Firefighter job injuries and deaths caused by vehicle accidents when responding to and returning from emergencies are statistically significant and represent a serious problem. We can make the response fast, but it need not be at the expense of safety. The trouble is that U.S. firefighters (career and volunteer) are having wrecks with personal vehicles, fire trucks, and ambulances.

There is a difference in the basic motivation between volunteers and full-time career firefighters. For most of the United States' paid firefighters, the motivation is a secure position with good benefits. Public opinion polls repeatedly rate firefighters in high regard. Individuals with family members in the fire service often seek full-time positions. Until recently, individuals coming from military service and the construction trades sought fire department positions. Beyond benefits and prestige are the excitement and challenge of the job. This is true for both volunteers and paid firefighters. The retention rate among paid firefighters is high, and recruitment is not an issue. For the volunteer service, recruitment is an ongoing challenge, and retention is a strategic issue. It is strategic because the future of the volunteer service is in question. Nationwide, there is a developing shortage of volunteers to serve local fire departments.

There are no definitive scientific studies on the motivation to be a volunteer firefighter. Also lacking is solid guidance or a body of knowledge for maintaining a volunteer force. Without such information, any attempt at recruitment and retention is nothing more than hoping for the best. A common sense approach involves seeking recommendations from trustworthy individuals known for making good decisions, careful screening for suitability, and an employment interview. Good potential choices may be family members of serving firefighters, people who work with members or are associated with other members, and people with a family tradition of firefighting. Without understanding the motivation to serve as a volunteer firefighter, we will continue on the treadmill; we will take any reasonably capable, breathing, warm bodies and invest resources to train them for fire and EMS work, only to see them leave the service after two or three years.

The cost in personal time and public money to train an individual to minimum competency is large. Full training at the entry level, including both fire and EMS, amounts to approximately four hundred hours (depending on the state requirements). The cost is in the neighborhood of $3,000 to $4,000. To buy safety equipment for them amounts to another $1,000 to $2,000. Certainly you can prepare someone at a minimal level of competency and provide them with used gear for minimal cost. In most cases, though, we get what we pay for, and minimal training is a potential liability we cannot afford. Providing someone with barebones training and secondhand equipment and then requesting that they show up at all hours of the day and night for what could be hazardous work is asking a lot. Few chiefs have the leadership capital to make such a request. The history of the U.S. fire service is rooted in the volunteer system, but the culture of today's fire service has its origin in the spirit of duty to the public.

The concept of fire insurance as we recognize it today has its origins in the Great London Fire of 1666.[6] English fire insurance companies had charters to operate in colonial America as early 1720. Around 1730 Benjamin Franklin furthered the concept of fire protection. His plan involved volunteer fire organizations and was loosely based on the concept employed in Boston, which used designated firemen, portable hand pumps, and a citizen bucket brigade as early as 1711.[7] Franklin's plan also included fire insurance offered through locally owned companies with owners who were also the insured so there was a mutual benefit derived from the protection. This was the start of so-called mutual fire insurance, as opposed to the form offered by stock fire insurance companies. The latter type is a profit model with benefits derived by those who hold stock. The mutual-fund insurance companies played a major role in fire protection in the early days of the United States. It is likely that Franklin's public notoriety and general fame, here and abroad, played a role in the myth that he created the U.S. fire service. U.S. fire history virtually ignores the facts that firefighting, organized fire services, fire insurance, and the development of basic fire protection equipment all originated in Europe. Franklin's volunteer fire company is notable only in that it was an idea sold to men who held and shared a spirit of commitment to their community. Within the ongoing discussion of democratic governance in the colonies was a strong belief in civic duty as a virtue. It is in the context of virtue that the U.S. volunteer fire department was born.[8]

History contains many stories of the colonial and early industrial age volunteers. Equipment sabotage and street brawls between rival fire companies over access to water or who was the first to get water on the fire make for colorful tales but suggest out-of-place aggressive or competitive behavior. These tales of excess fail to stand up to the reality and outcomes of the socioeconomic revolution that was the industrial age. Nor do they hold water when we consider that volunteer departments today still provide first-rate public fire protection for Americans. If the volunteers could barely extinguish fires, why do they remain with us today? A competing theory states that the demise of the volunteers was caused by the need for a stable workforce to operate industrial machines.[9] In colonial and early America, residents' principal concerns were farming, transportation-related tasks, and the professions. As the United States transitioned from an agrarian society to an industrial one, factories and mills began to open and required human labor. Factory production tasks and schedules demanded readily available and dependable workers. The factory owners likely had little tolerance for workers dashing off to answer the fire bell, if they could even hear the bell in the noisy factory. This is also the time when workers began commuting to their places of work. Suburban communities sprang up outside cities along new rail lines. Factory hours were long, as was the workweek. Time off was minimal, and the precious few hours workers had free were spent with family. After twelve hours of work in the factory, the idea of spending free time at the firehouse might have lost some of its charm.

This is the point made by Amy S. Greenberg in her book *Cause for Alarm*, which puts forth the theory of volunteer transition. The theory proposes that the makeup and character of the membership of volunteer companies (primarily urban fire companies) began to change during the industrial age. Up to that point, volunteer firemen had been held in high esteem by the community. Women and children especially honored marching volunteers by throwing flower petals in their path during parades. In this era, being a volunteer was a matter of civic virtue. Some volunteers may have pushed the issue by expecting tribute, believing it was a debt owed them by the public. This expectation ultimately caused them to lose public esteem. Incidents of street brawls and equipment sabotage and other competitive behavior likely prompted community leaders to consider making a change. Concurrently with the industrialization of the United States arose a new economic idea of community. The idea of growth as good and threats to growth as something to fear formed in the collective public mind. Tradespeople lost their livelihoods as cheap factory-made goods became readily available. Along with those desiring to escape farm life, they headed for factory jobs in the rapidly expanding cities.[10]

The United States' agrarian social and economic norms were in transition. An industrial society sprang up, and the number of volunteer firefighters declined. The consequence was a decline in the turnout response to fire alarms. Where volunteer membership once included only men of excellent character who lent the company credibility and respectability, now men of lesser character were taking up residence in the firehouses. Even as the standard of living improved (implying more time available to volunteer), volunteers in the professions and other higher-ranking occupations began to spend less time at the firehouse. Fighting and the level of violence among volunteer companies began to increase. Racial and social tensions within the communities of immigrants in the cities potentially contributed to the fighting among rival fire companies. Having the best citizens among the membership had been the key element of the volunteer units' success. The best citizens were highly motivated individuals with a sincere interest in community service to improve and uphold local standards, a key to local economic success.[11]

As cities grew and populations increased, fires became a more potent threat, and the higher potential risk raised the stakes. There was much to lose, and fire insurance could not rebuild or replace everything. Urban fires in densely built-up areas with sidewalks and buildings of wooden construction and with poor to no water supply were disasters in the making. In the densely built cities, there was the potential for many fires every single night because people cooked over open flames and used candles for lighting. An urban fire burning out of control required a determined and coordinated effort to suppress it. Then as now, the task of knocking down a building fire required labor and equipment. Quelling a conflagration multiplies the basic requirements.

To bring order and coordination to the efforts of many companies requires strong leadership in the form of a fire chief (referred to early on as a foreman). Under normal conditions, you would expect the chief of the area where the fire is located to be in command. As circumstances dictate, the chief assumes responsibility for overall command and control of the fire incident, with the goal being prompt suppression with minimal damage. Each being a separate and independent entity, the various volunteer organizations held their territory as sacred, their autonomy as a privilege, and their chief as king of their domain. Yet, as the number of urban fires and consequent threat of total destruction grew, order and control among the independent volunteer units proved difficult.

An independent company ceding control of a fire scene required high-level intervention by influential community leaders and politicians. Attempts by municipal governments to organize the volunteer companies into municipal departments met resistance. This same pattern of resistance replayed later on, with suggestions that the volunteers use horses to pull their beloved hand pumpers, hose wagons, and the hook-and-ladders apparatus. Successful public demonstrations of steam-powered fire pumps hardly diminished the ardor of the volunteers. The push behind the move to steam came from businessmen who wanted to see their financial investment adequately protected and the local economy preserved. The eventual placement of steam-powered fire apparatus opened the door to the institution of a paid municipal fire service because operating a steam fire engine required highly specialized knowledge, skill, and ability.

Americans and especially our fire service have paid scant attention to the means and methods of fire protection in other countries. A comparison study of the development of fire protection in England and the United States reveals similarity in types of fires and variance in numbers. This lack of appreciation reveals itself in the parochialism among U.S. fire departments because public fire protection is a local affair. In Britain the fire service is regionalized and under the oversight of the Home Office, which promulgates policy and procedure. In the United States, however, there is no formal, nationwide overseer to overcome the well-entrenched and localized parochialism. Eyre Massey Shaw, commanding officer of London's Metropolitan Fire Brigade from 1866 to 1891, summed up his opinion of the U.S. fire services after his visit to the United States in 1872:

> A fireman to be successful, must enter buildings . . . he must get in below, above, on every side, from opposite houses, over back walls, over side walls, through panels of doors, through windows, through loopholes cut by himself in the gates, the walls, the roof; he must know how to reach the attic from the basement, by ladders placed on half-burned stairs, and the basement from the attic by rope made fast on a chimney; his whole success depends on his getting in and remaining there, and he must always carry his appliances with him, as without them he is of no use.
>
> When I was last in America it struck me very forcibly that although most of the chiefs were intelligent and zealous in their work, not one that I met even made a pretense to the kind of professional knowledge that I consider so essential. Indeed, one went so far as to say that the only way to learn the business of a fireman was to go to fires. A statement about as monstrous and contrary to reason as if he said that the only way to become a surgeon would be to commence cutting off limbs without any knowledge of the human body or of the implements required. There is no shortcut to proficiency in any profession and the day will come when your fellow countrymen will be obliged to open their eyes to the fact, that, as a man learns the business of a firemen only by attending fires he must of necessity learn it badly. Even that which he does pick up and may seem to know, he will know imperfectly and be incapable of imparting to others. I consider the business of a fireman a regular profession requiring previous study and training as other professions do. I am convinced that where training and study are omitted and men pitch forked into the practical work without preparation, the fire department will never be found capable of dealing satisfactorily with great emergencies.

It is rather amazing that Chief Shaw said this in the late nineteenth century, and today, in the early twenty-first century, we still have volunteer and paid-call departments electing their officers based on popularity, not selecting them based on merit. That alone speaks volumes about our outdated traditions and their influence on the United States' significant fire problems.

Lloyd Layman, a fire chief from Parkersburg, West Virginia, quoted Chief Shaw in his 1953 text on firefighting tactics. Chief Layman, a visionary thinker and experimenter, authored two notable fire service texts. He advocated for advanced training for fire officers as early as the 1950s, something only now given widespread attention, which is truly a sad and shameful commentary on the collective fire service.[12] It took only about 150 years for that concept to advance. When taken solely in the context of the United States' fire services, it may, if you wish to be kind, be considered that our progress in eighty years was the ability to confine fires to a single block of buildings rather than multiple city blocks or even whole cities. Sadly enough, in terms of leadership and any inherent concept of professionalism, it was not so much the collective fire service that pushed change as it was a few notable fire chiefs and the NBFU.

Chief Layman introduced several new and important firefighting concepts and innovations, though today some have fallen away as a result of new research or been modified to meet new conditions. Unfortunately, the newest generation of firefighters has ignored or forgotten Chief Layman altogether. In place of a history of progress, we instead stand on myth, legend, and romance. "Iron men, stout horses, wooden ladders." "Leather [helmets] forever." "First in, last out." To be fair, there are many progressive and even evolutionary elements in the fire service; however, the process of change is often slow. In the past, it sometimes took thirty or forty years or more for a new idea to be established. Today, the lag time may be somewhat shorter in length. Our slowness to change or evolve is rooted in the fact that we are local entities without much outside influence. Enforceable regulation, if it exists at all, comes mostly from state government. This is in contrast to Great Britain, where the British Fire Service organizes regionally with general organizational policy and procedure coming from the Home Office. The service was nationalized at the outbreak of World War II, when it was expected that English cities in range of Nazi bombers (and later rockets) would be hit, significantly increasing the chance of fire and conflagration.

Fires are mostly local and rarely become a regional or state problem. In colonial times, citizens banded together to fight fires and thus performed a vital and necessary civic function. In time, an organized response developed based on local resources. The newly organized fire department took its form according to local need, thus meeting a vital function. Form followed function with the creation of thousands of independent local fire companies throughout the United States, and thus a culture of independence was born. Today we see attempts to integrate and implement national standards and guidelines running into resistance. Organization and control from the top down is pushing desired outcomes on companies with a history of independence. This push from above conflicts with the mode of thinking in the fire service.

The fire service of the nineteenth century solved its own problems or borrowed ideas from other departments. The first attempts to regulate or standardize local fire protection came from the fire insurance industry. The NBFU attempted to exert influence on both the fire insurance industry and local fire departments. The NFPA, born of needs that arose from the work of the NBFU, is today the single greatest influence on both private and public fire protection. Most U.S. firefighters have no idea how the service became what it is today, and few of them realize or acknowledge our origins in Rome, Amsterdam, Edinburgh, and London or the influence of the U.S. fire insurance industry.

4
LEARNING TO FIGHT GREAT URBAN FIRES

CHAPTER 11

London and the Development of a Fire Service

Two things are essential for any fire department to function successfully: trained firefighters and competent leadership. Those two elements are so critical that they trump inadequate or incompetent department management. Traditionally chief officers rose through the ranks. The fire chief, or a deputy chief or assistant chief, typically takes command of serious fires and holds responsibility for setting the overall strategy to control the emergency. While chief officers focus on the strategic goals for incident management, the lieutenants and captains act as first-line supervisors who carry out tactical objectives by leading their crews in task-oriented evolutions.

There is a simple but effective method for division of labor on the fireground. Since the mid-nineteenth century, larger departments have divided firefighting tasks between the engine and truck companies. Engine crews ride the pumper and handle the hose lines, water supply, and overhaul of the fire. Truck crews ride the aerial apparatus (ladder, platform, or tower) and handle forcible entry, search and rescue, ventilation, and salvage. Both engine and truck work involves the tactical evolutions needed to execute the chief officer's strategy. Tactical evolutions include hooking up large-diameter supply lines (hose) to hydrants, advancing hose lines to fight the fire, and cutting a hole in a roof to let out heat and smoke, permitting an advance on the fire inside the structure. These tasks are the elements of firefighting in buildings or enclosed spaces throughout the world. These tasks are nasty, dirty, and dangerous. Assigning people the task of fighting fires is said to have started in ancient Rome with the vigils (men assigned to patrol the streets after dark to snuff out and prevent fires). The duty was given to the soldiers of the Roman legions and implemented throughout the empire. The task may have later fallen on civilian workers under independent control. After Rome's decline, the practice fell out of use as the world entered a dark age. William the Conqueror mandated the covering of open fires at night to prevent the spreading of flames while people slept. However, not until after the Great Fire of London in 1666 did the regular practice of the nighttime fire warden patrol resume.

The Great Fire of 1666 consumed 373 acres inside the old city wall, 63 acres outside the wall, 400 streets, 86 churches, and 13,200 houses, leaving nearly 80,000 homeless.[1] Many English parishes (towns and villages) had manually operated portable fire pumps, each with an attached nozzle fixed atop the tank of water. Acquired throughout the early 1600s, the devices could throw a stream of water under pressure. Several factors made this idea very impractical. No one in particular was responsible for maintaining and operating the pump, and moving the heavy pump to the fire was often difficult. Furthermore, water supplies were poor and alarms were often delayed, allowing fires to grow very large very quickly, thus outpacing the capacity of the pump. Under those circumstances, most parishes found the citizen bucket brigade more effective, so they had leather buckets, along with ladders, and a very large, long-handled, hook-like tool for pulling down buildings. Taking apart a small building by literally dropping it by the walls or otherwise and collapsing it, made the structure less likely to spread the fire. Beds were valuable and something people wanted to save, so the frame was built to collapse quickly for prompt removal in the face of a fire. In 1666 the tool of choice in London was a handheld extinguishing device, similar to a medical syringe that could pump about one gallon of water per squirt. These squirts were useful for small spot fires, for which the larger portable hand pumps were nearly useless.[2]

The great fire convinced business owners and government officials that something needed to be done, or London would suffer more great fires. Rules requiring buildings be built of brick were enacted, fire insurance became common as a means of protecting one's investment, manually pumped fire engines were strategically placed near valuable buildings, and men were hired to operate the new fire apparatus. The fire insurance companies formed engine brigades and hired part-time operators. The purpose of the fire brigade was to protect the property covered by the individual insurance company, which maintained the particular brigade. Fire protection was thus a private business venture rather than an aspect of government.

Property owners holding an insurance policy attached a distinctive emblem, known as a fire mark, to the front of their building to signify it as insured. Each insurance company had its own distinctive fire mark, thus the mark indicated a particular building as insured by a particular insurance company. When a fire was discovered and the alarm sounded, the fire brigades responded, and if the fire building had the mark of their respective company, they would extinguish the fire. If the building did not have a mark, they were not obligated to fight the fire, but they might protect any nearby exposed buildings that did have their company's mark. The insurance underwriters soon realized that this practice was not conducive to their collective economic vitality. They must have realized that fires in general were not good for a city or its economic vitality and future prospects. Over time they recognized that allowing fire to threaten their investments was unacceptable. This led the insurance companies to create agreements to have their fire brigades simply extinguish all fires. They called these agreements pacts of mutual aid.

In 1833 a new broad-based mutual aid pact created the London Fire Engine Establishment under the command of former Edinburgh Fire Brigade chief James Braidwood. The new fire service employed eighty men dispersed among nineteen fire stations and working twenty-four-hour shifts, seven days a week, with minimal opportunity for time off. Braidwood believed effective fire attack involved getting firemen with hose and nozzle inside, close up to what he called the seat of the fire, to apply water directly on the flames. Getting to the seat of the fire remains a basic tenet of fire attack. Steam-powered fire engines were available to Braidwood, but he favored the manual pumps.

In 1834 a housekeeper in the House of Lords noticed a strange odor coming from the central heating system (something new in that era). The ensuing fire destroyed the entire Houses of Parliament. In 1861 London experienced a conflagration in a group of warehouses on Tooley Street; it nearly became the city's second great fire. Braidwood died on Tooley Street in the line of duty from a collapsing wall. A description of this fire has tallow, rubber, fibers, spices, tea, jute, and oil stored in a series of connected buildings of fireproof construction. This form of construction turned each building into a standalone furnace, allowing the fire inside to burn from basement to roof. As the interior structural framework and combustible contents were consumed in the inferno, the walls collapsed into the street and into adjoining buildings, thus spreading the fire. When the second warehouse collapsed, it spewed oil, resin, tar, and tallow, creating the conditions for an explosion which expelled blazing globs of tallow and burning oil in all directions. The burning oil flowed over the street surface and into other buildings, furthering the spread of fire, and into the Thames River, causing wharfs, boats, and barges to catch fire. The torrent of melted tallow flowing over Tooley Street carried with it sizzling hams and burning stock, such as rubber, tea, cotton, jute, and spices, much of which flowed into cellar openings and street sewers, where it solidified after cooling, in some cases to a depth of three feet. Brought under control on the second day, the debris piles and building rubble smoldered for six months while insurance companies dealt with the financial loss (two million pounds). This particular fire was extremely devastating and, like many others, tested the financial foundations of insurance companies. It also softened the resolve of the insurance industry's initiative to operate the fire engine establishment. Following the fire, insurance companies petitioned the government to assume responsibility for extinguishing fires. This request was fulfilled a few years later, when London was in the process of forming a larger metropolitan government. In 1897 a serious fire struck London's industrial area, Cripplegate, fully gutting fifty-six buildings and damaging fifty-six others, amounting to a loss of two million pounds. This area of densely built structures was long a concern of London's fire officers. Ignoring these concerns, the district was rebuilt in a similar manner following that fire, only to burn again during the Blitz in 1940.[3]

In 1866 London officially formed the Metropolitan Fire Brigade and placed it under the command of Captain Eyre Massey Shaw. Although Shaw was well connected in London's highest society and even mentioned in a Gilbert and Sullivan opera, he knew the rough end of the firefighting business from his time in Belfast, where he headed the police and fire brigade. An advocate for innovation he introduced steam-powered fire engines, initiated the construction of a municipal fire alarm telegraph system, and placed a new emphasis on saving lives rather than property alone. He considered lifesaving a fire service function and took over the role from the Royal Society for the Protection of Life from Fire. Established in 1836, the society had placed fire ladders in London streets in the interests of safety. Insurance company fire brigades acted to protect only property and buildings from fire, and the protection of people was secondary, if considered at all. That the society distributed fire ladders is significant in and of itself, as is the London firefighters' decision to take on the responsibility.[4] The insurance fire brigades were not yet concerned with lifesaving, just as today the ISO Fire Suppression Rating Schedule does not reward efforts at saving lives over property. The business of fire insurance underwriting makes saving lives secondary to saving property. Around 1889 London and surrounding towns formed a county government with a new ruling council. Shaw was at odds with the council almost immediately over brigade funding and his authority to make decisions. He resigned in 1891 and was soon knighted. The first years of the new century saw motorcars used in the fire brigade and the name of the service changed to the London Fire Brigade. Motorized apparatus replaced the last horses in 1921.[5]

Although fire services in the United States and Great Britain evolved along a similar path, there is one significant difference between the two countries. German air raids in World War II tested London and its firefighters to the limit. The German bombing blitz over London set many buildings ablaze and at its worst created group fires (many burning buildings within a single block). Group fires could jump natural and man-made barriers (e.g., rivers and streets) to adjacent blocks and thus extend the fire. Depending on the combustibility of the buildings involved, multiple group fires might coalesce and extend across a wider area of the city, increasing the size of the fire through radiation and convection of super-heated air currents.[6] With fire extension over a large area, a conflagration would ensue, requiring the response of hundreds of fire apparatus and thousands of firefighters from the surrounding counties. The need to allocate and coordinate this large firefighting force required extraordinary effort. The government decided to nationalize the fire forces into one agency to bring cohesiveness and a level of uniformity. The new National Fire Service standardized training, drills, rank, uniforms, equipment (hose couplings, for example), and terminology. Despite positive aspects of this arrangement, the service disbanded in 1948; however, the national standards remained. This action reinstituted the separate London Fire Brigade.

The consequences of air raids in two world wars taught the British the inherent benefit of organized, coordinated, and equipped civil defense, fire, and rescue services founded on a national model. Germany learned the same lessons from the Allied forces' saturation bombing of their industrial centers. The United States has not had to learn the same severe lessons of total war by aggressors,

9/11 notwithstanding. However, many of the western U.S. wildfires rank as serious conflagrations and serve to reinforce the idea that fire remains a threat. In the United States, the standards we have for fire service come from the NFPA and OSHA, yet these guidelines and regulations are not universally accepted. The only possible exception is the Fire Suppression Rating Schedule, which provides minimum guidance for equipment and training essential to municipal fire protection.

The ISO rating schedule evaluates three key elements of local fire protection systems: fire dispatch/communications, fire department services, and water supply. Through a system of credits, a score is assigned to each element, and the three scores combined result in classification on a scale of 1–10, with Class 1 representing the best. An individual rating or grade on this classification scale is a PPC. Only a handful of the thirty-thousand-plus fire departments in the United States have a PPC of Class 1 from the ISO. Being an ISO Class 1 fire department is a badge of distinction. The ISO rating schedule itself is a relatively simple mathematical formula; however, the organization's field representatives do apply considerable judgment in assigning credit points or determining equivalencies.

The rating schedule used today is a descendent of a municipal fire department grading schedule developed at the turn of the century by the NBFU. The ISO is a descendent of the NBFU, which formed in the late nineteenth century in response to the losses suffered by insurance companies as a result of the large number of urban fires and conflagrations. The financial interest of the insurance industry lies in making a profit covering risks, not paying out claims for losses. A primary interest of the NBFU was to advocate for improved municipal fire defenses. This translated into hiring more firefighters, building more stations, purchasing fire engines and better fire alarm systems, and improving water supplies. The bottom line for the NBFU was the bottom line of the member stock insurance companies. Any light directed toward saving lives in the United States would have to wait for Boston fire chief John Damrell, the National Association of Fire Engineers (NAFE, now the International Association of Fire Chiefs), and the NFPA.

The influence of the NBFU, and now the ISO, on the U.S. fire service is without question. How it fights fires, deploys resources, and equips its apparatus are all part of the insurance rating schedule. The insurance industry created and funded the London Fire Engine Establishment. The concept of local fire protection and fire insurance brought to the American colonies by Benjamin Franklin thus had English roots. Yet there were two significant differences in how public fire protection evolved in the United States. London eventually banned construction of buildings with exterior walls of wood, and many U.S. cities would come to regret not doing the same. The United States also ignored what England had learned from reliance on unorganized and unregulated volunteer firefighting in its villages. The volunteer forces in the early United States would become the stuff of legend, but they were no match for new industrial technology and the economics of growth and expansion.

Disastrous urban fires were frequent in the United States during the nineteenth century. However, the term "great fire," as used to describe many such events, is misleading because it lacks a definition. Fire experts use the terms "group fire," "conflagration," and "city fire" (the last term used only in Japan) to describe serious fires sometimes extending over wide areas, but they lack standardized definitions within the profession. The NFPA considers a conflagration a "major building-to-building flame spread over some distance," while a group fire is "significant building-to-building fire spread within a complex, or among adjacent buildings." Whether an urban fire extends over a wide area is important in determining the degree of severity for comparison with other fires.[7] Important U.S. cities of the era experienced great fires and conflagrations that burned wide swaths through the cities, consuming individual wealth, corporate capital, business property, personal belongings, and sometimes lives. These fires are notable for their size, intensity, value of property destroyed, and occasional influence on improvements in fire protection.

Giving these fires dimension in order to compare them is difficult because the accuracy of the damages sustained is often in question. In general, this problem is caused in part by the lack of unbiased eyewitness accounts, lack of objective journalistic reporting, lack or destruction of property and financial records, lack of fire insurance survey maps, lack of photographic evidence, and lack of fire department records. Any attempt to make a comparison depends on limited information from more than a century ago. In most cases, the eyewitnesses were more concerned with their immediate survival and preservation of property than with making accurate notes on what they observed. Estimations of the land area burned over in miles or blocks do not always match claims of acreage burned. Estimates of the number of buildings burned appear to vary considerably, likely because the types of structures counted as buildings varied. For example, does the tally include small woodsheds and outhouses or only significant residential, commercial, and institutional buildings? The number of blocks is not a good comparison, as they may be irregular in shape and the sizes may vary between cities. Thus developed acreage burned is the best measure for comparison of area burned. (There are 640 acres in a square mile.) Finally, it is not always possible to convert the dollar loss figures of that era to the value of current dollars. Except for the location and year of the fire, the following list offers only a rough estimate of damages as derived from various sources.[8]

- New York in 1835: 0.08 square miles (50 acres), 48 hours, $20,000,000 loss
- Pittsburgh in 1845: 0.09 square miles (56 acres), 6 hours, $12,000,000 loss
- Portland in 1866: 0.20 square miles (130 acres), 15 hours, $15,000,000 loss
- Chicago in 1871: 3.5 square miles (2,240 acres), 27 hours, $200,000,000 loss
- Boston in 1872: 0.09 square miles (60 acres), 17 hours, $75,000,000 loss
- Baltimore in 1904: 0.22 square miles (140 acres), 25 hours, $150,000,000 loss

The fire in Baltimore is recognized by fire protection experts as the last great urban conflagration of the era. The 1906 fire in San Francisco was significant, but it was the direct result of an earthquake in a city with considerable combustible construction and a public water system susceptible to damage from tremors. The fire in Baltimore solidified the influence of the NBFU and other fire prevention organizations and provided a wake-up call to the fire service. Within a few decades, building codes and operational guidelines for fire departments began to have an effect; where once a fire consumed the entire downtown of a city, fire departments now contained fires to the block of origin. In a few more decades, controlling a fire to the building of origin was commonplace. Today fires are mostly contained to the room or floor of origin. Without the direction of the NBFU, IAFC, and NFPA, this would have likely taken a much longer time to achieve.

Today the battle is for automatic sprinklers in all inhabited buildings. However far we have progressed, it was a costly battle for building owners and

"A Comparison of Old and New Firefighting Methods" by Jan van der Heyden (from his *Brandspuitenboek,* or *Fire Engine Book*). The illustration depicts the old model fire engine and the new model fire engine (left and right, respectively). (Rijksmuseum, Amsterdam)

"A Fire Raging between the Elandsstraat and the Elandsgracht" by Jan van der Heyden (from his *Brandspuitenboek,* or *Fire Engine Book*). The fire occurred on July 27, 1679, and was one of Amsterdam's largest fires to date. It marked a transition of firefighting methods and equipment. The new fire engines and fire hose employed after this fire were designed and built by van der Heyden, a skilled artist and the city's general fire master. (Rijksmuseum, Amsterdam)

Shortly after the 1866 fire, Portland, Maine, installed a municipal fire alarm system. This is a view of the City Fire Alarm Office; note the city street map on the back wall and the suspended electric lighting. (Portland Veteran Firemen's Association)

This is a later photograph of the Portland Fire Alarm Office. Note the larger fire telegraph console, as well as the telephone on the operator's desk, which was probably used for talking directly with city fire stations. (Portland Veteran Firemen's Association)

Ruins of the 1866 Great Fire of Portland, Maine. Near the corner of Congress and Franklin Streets, looking south. (Portland Veteran Firemen's Association)

Ruins of the 1866 Great Fire of Portland, Maine. From the top of the Custom House, looking north. (Portland Veteran Firemen's Association)

Ruins of the 1866 Great Fire of Portland, Maine. From the corner of Congress and Lime Streets, looking north. (Portland Veteran Firemen's Association)

Ruins of the 1866 Great Fire of Portland, Maine. City Hall from Congress Street front side. (Portland Veteran Firemen's Association)

Ruins of the 1866 Great Fire of Portland, Maine. From the top of the Custom House, looking up Free Street. (Portland Veteran Firemen's Association)

Ruins of the 1866 Great Fire of Portland, Maine. From the top of the Custom House, looking west. (Portland Veteran Firemen's Association)

The appliance room (what Americans call the apparatus floor) at the Kennington Fire Station of the London Fire Brigade in 1905. (LFBphotos.com)

Firemen of the London Fire Brigade drill with a Wheeled Escape Unit (what Americans call an aerial ladder) at Southwark HQ, circa 1900. (LFBphotos.com)

Chief John Kenlon of the Fire Department of New York observing a test of the water turrets on the fireboat *New Yorker* in 1909. (Collection of New-York Historical Society)

Two men stand before the frozen aftermath of the disastrous January 1912 fire in the Equitable Building in New York City. (Collection of New-York Historical Society)

New York City firemen attack a developing fire in the Equitable Building, corner of Pine and Nassau Streets, January 1912. (Collection of New-York Historical Society)

LEFT: Firemen climbing ladders and entering the windows of the Winsor Hotel during a fire on March 17, 1899, in New York City. (Collection of New-York Historical Society)

BELOW: New York City fireboats in action off the Battery in 1913. (Collection of New-York Historical Society)

New York firemen on monitor nozzles during a test of the city's high-pressure hydrant system in 1908 at West and Bank Streets. (Collection of New-York Historical Society)

FDNY Engine No. 93, a tractor-drawn steam fire engine, on Washington Bridge. (Collection of New-York Historical Society)

High-pressure water system pumps in the firehouse at Gansevoort Street, New York City. (Collection of New-York Historical Society)

FDNY Manhattan Engine 40, circa 1915. (Photo by Albert Dreyfous/Connecticut Firemen's Historical Society)

Crew of FDNY
Engine 18 drilling at
the Fire College in
Manhattan; Fireman
Shay is the "jumper."
Circa 1915.
(Photo by Albert
Dreyfous/Connecticut
Firemen's
Historical Society)

Delivery photo of an early motorized high-pressure engine in New York City.
(Photo by Albert Dreyfous/Connecticut Firemen's Historical Society)

Motorized water tower operating in New York City, circa 1921. (Photo by Albert Dreyfous/Connecticut Firemen's Historical Society)

ABOVE: High-pressure engines operating in New York City, circa 1917. (Photo by Albert Dreyfous/Connecticut Firemen's Historical Society)

RIGHT: Warehouse fire in New York City, circa 1923. (Photo by Albert Dreyfous/Connecticut Firemen's Historical Society)

FDNY searchlight units illuminate nighttime fire, circa 1922. (Photo by Albert Dreyfous/Connecticut Firemen's Historical Society)

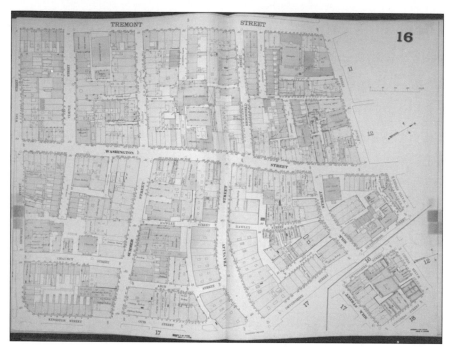

Page from Sanborn Fire Insurance Map Book for Boston in the year 1867. (Library of Congress)

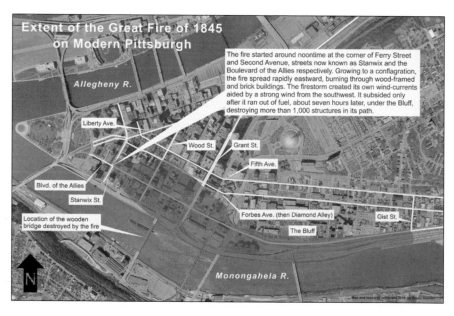

Map depicting extent of the 1845 Great Fire on Modern Pittsburgh. (Map and research by Bruce Hensler)

firefighters. For nearly 125 years, roughly from 1835 to 1960, great fires threatened U.S. cities and towns. The fires destroyed thousands of buildings but claimed a relatively small number of lives. The fires also reshaped the future of cities and changed their course in history. Records of fire losses are important for building on the knowledge of fire protection and creating fire prevention efforts. The fire insurance industry began the practice of keeping records of fire losses. There appears to be a collective tolerance for sustained fire losses in the U.S. psyche. Where one would expect action, there is instead fascination and an underlying sense that fires are inevitable. The greatest advances in fire protection and building technology come invariably after a disaster. Now, wildland-urban interface fires replace the great city fires in our attention. We do not see fires in the forest as a natural environmental process; we see them as something to battle. Every year forest firefighters wage a campaign-style firefight in U.S. forests. Wooden homes susceptible to wildfires in the urban-wildland interface have replaced the wooden buildings in the city as the biggest fire hazard we have.

The frequency and scale of the nineteenth-century fires prompted changes that resulted in improved firefighting techniques, fire equipment, fire codes, and building codes. Solutions to the multifaceted problem posed by development in the wildland interface carry environmental and property rights implications. The interface fire problem falls generally within the issue of suburban development sprawl. Both now and then, society, property owners, and governments are slow to respond to the threat because fire insurance covers the loss. We all pay for the mistakes of the few. As for the urban fire problem in the nineteenth century, the main impetus for change was the fire insurance companies' failure to maintain sufficient capital reserves to cover the actual fire losses sustained in the great urban fires. When the fire insurance companies finally moved to act constructively, they set off a sequence of events that laid the foundation for the modern fire service and the field of fire protection. It was a monetary decision with moral implications that ultimately improved life and security for Americans.

CHAPTER 12

Portland and the Board
of Fire Underwriters

The collective recognition of the U.S. fire problem came in 1866, when a large fire nearly destroyed Portland, Maine. Just months before that fire, insurance industry executives had met in New York to discuss threats to their financial condition. The men of the insurance trade called themselves underwriters. The term "underwriting" (the act of ensuring a financial investment) originated in London at Lloyd's Coffee House in the early eighteenth century. Lloyd's was a known gathering spot for shipowners and merchants involved in trade. The custom was to record the values of cargoes (at sea on ships) on the coffeehouse blackboard. Men seeking to make money speculated on the relative safety of the ships and cargo and for a monetary consideration would guarantee the merchants' investments from potential disasters at sea. These investment capitalists thus wrote their own names on the board below or underneath the records of the cargoes that they insured, and thus underwriting became synonymous with insuring.[1]

Those attending the fire insurance underwriters' meeting in 1866 feared a potential overreliance on fire insurance as well as the rapid post–Civil War industrial expansion. Fire losses in commercial and industrial occupancies were growing, and insurance companies were paying out more for the losses, with the result that the capital reserves of their respective companies were diminishing. These insurance company executives viewed the fire problem as a threat to their viable existence. Remaining solvent and making a profit for shareholders required that the executives maintain an equitable spread between the premiums paid by customers for coverage of losses and the commissions paid to the agents who sold the policies. The spread had to be sufficient to cover potential fire losses, direct operating expenses of the business, and yield a fair profit.

Although the underwriters met primarily to discuss the issue of maintaining an equitable spread and the growing losses, they perceived another problem. They feared the federal government's and many state legislature's growing interest in the business practices of the stock insurance companies. Governments had begun to realize that citizens deserved protection from unfair business practices. The insurance business practices in question were the undercapitalization of reserves and unethical behavior by the agents of the insurance companies. The business of selling insurance was mostly unregulated at that time, with each company acting in its own best interest. Some of the companies recognized the problems. They tried, without much success, to cap the commissions paid to the agents and set a minimum rate for fire insurance. The problem was with the independent agents, who could play one company against another, seeking a lower rate for a potential customer. A company seeking to insure what was deemed a "good risk" might, and frequently did, lower its rates to get the customer who wanted insurance. This undercuts the competition, and the downside is that eventually the undercutting undermines the business foundation. Moreover, having shareholders required that companies turn a profit. To maintain a profit margin in this environment required that the company cut expenses; once there is nothing left to cut, one must cut back on the capital reserve fund. For an insurer, an adequate capital reserve is essential to cover potential losses suffered by the policyholders. If an insurer's reserve is too low and a disaster strikes, large numbers of policyholders file claims. The insurer then runs the risk of bankruptcy. If one company goes bankrupt, it is a small problem; if many go under, it raises concern. Concerned about fraudulent insurance agents and poorly managed companies, state legislatures at this time were starting to take an interest in the insurance business. Failure to maintain an adequate capital reserve to cover potential claims reflects poor, if not dishonest, management. At the mid-century point, there was minimal state and no federal regulation of insurance companies.[2]

In the age of sail, Portland, Maine, was a significant East Coast port. Late in the afternoon of July 4, 1866, a fire started (possibly from fireworks) in a boatbuilding shop on Commercial Street. Flames carried by a stiff southern wind burned uphill away from the harbor. The fire jumped from building to building and into the city's business district. The wind-driven fire torched hundreds of wood-frame, brick, and stone buildings, destroying many businesses and leaving approximately ten thousand people without a place to sleep. The fire carved a swath through the city, approximately one and a half miles by a quarter mile in size. Insured losses amounted to approximately $5 million because only about half of the structures carried insurance.[3]

A serious rumor that some local insurance companies were not in a financial position to cover the insured losses ignited and spread almost as quickly as the fire. Fearing a public relations debacle or, worse, a financial scandal, principals of the insurance industry from New England and New York met on July 7, 1866. They reached a significant agreement. Acting as a unified group, they would meet all claims from the Portland fire. This action set the foundation for the U.S. insurance industry. The men who struck the agreement in July 1866 very likely did not realize the full implication of their proposal, but their action set into motion an industry effort that not only initiated a professional ethic for the fire service but created fire protection organizations that still exist. Mostly through the new U.S. fire service, these organizations gave shape and direction to fire protection in the United States. Their small but significant action ultimately initiated the creation of the NBFU and left a lasting impact on the insurance, building, and fire protection industries, as well as on the fire services of the United States. Initially the insurance executives called for a universal increase in premium rates for fire insurance and for Portland to form a board of underwriters. The Portland underwriters were then directed to adopt a tariff of rates that would in turn be approved by a committee of the larger group, which insisted that an up-front advance of at least 50 percent be charged on all insured risks.[4] Two weeks following their July 7 meeting, they met again on July 18 to form the NBFU and drafted the following goals.[5]

1. Establish and maintain a system of uniform rates of premium.
2. Establish and maintain a uniform rate of compensation to agents and brokers.
3. Repress incendiarism or arson by the apprehension, conviction, and punishment of criminals so engaged.
4. Devise and effect measures for the protection of our common interests and the promotion of general prosperity.

The third goal was important, as it formally recognized the role of arson-for-profit as a devious method of transforming one's economic misfortune by using fire to collect insurance money. Within two years, hundreds of U.S. cities formed local boards of fire underwriters. By 1869 special committees of the national board were formulating standards to classify levels of risk. To classify risks with any degree of statistical accuracy requires data about the building construction, building value, value of contents, cause of the fire, damages attributable to the fire, damages attributable to fighting the fire, and resulting business losses. With a system of data collection, statistical loss record, and uniform standards, the underwriters felt they would be in a position to manage their covered risks and make a profit. The ability to set rates based on accurate loss information would make writing insurance a scientific process. Unfortunately, the freewheeling, competitive nature of U.S. business sandbagged the underwriter's efforts at applying scientific method to managing a business.

On main street America, however, competition remained cutthroat, and the agents easily fell back into the behaviors that helped create the problem. Those insurance executives who best understood the problem realized that government must step in to regulate business. To ensure uniform application and enforcement of regulations between states, they believed that the federal government should take responsibility. In 1869 the U.S. Supreme Court (in *Paul vs. Virginia*) ruled that regulation of the insurance trade was a matter for state, not federal, government. After this legal setback, NBFU influence waned, and their funding decreased. Not even the Chicago fire of 1871, which was almost twenty times more costly than the Portland fire, could turn the problem around.[6]

The next big urban fire struck in Boston in November 1872, and the resulting insurance losses, felt deeply by the various providers, caused rates to increase across the United States. The Boston fire had a long-term effect. Industrialization in the United States began in New England with numerous large factories and mills. New England factory and mill owners sidestepped traditional insurance and instead insured their properties through a collective arrangement, in effect creating their own factory mutual insurance system. They could assume the financial risk of self-insuring because of their confidence in fire protection features, such as hydrant systems, fire sprinklers, and automatic alarms, installed on their properties. Thus in the Boston area, a level of expertise in both fire protection and insurance brought together in one region the best minds in both businesses. This would come to have a significant effect on the future of fire protection in the United States. The mutual fire insurance companies in New England vigorously promoted the prevention of fires in the factories and mills they insured, in stark contrast to the attitude of disinterest in fire prevention measures among the insurance companies owned by stockholders. That disinterest faded after the Boston fire, when preventing fires without government intervention began to seem both possible and beneficial. Investigating the cause of fires to facilitate prosecution of arson, data collection for statistic-based rate setting, and fire prevention were initiatives that the stock insurance industry used to improve their bottom line.[7]

The data and statistics that enabled underwriters to make risk-benefit calculations, which in turn improved accuracy in rate setting, required efficient collection methods, as well as information not just about one building, but about all buildings possible. Think about it: underwriters are trying to predict not only the potential for a fire in the building to be insured but also the potential for other buildings that may cause a client's building to catch fire. Once the underwriter calculates the risk potential in one building, he or she has to look for any other buildings that may reasonably contribute to causing the insured building to burn. In 1873 the NBFU, through the executive leadership of Henry Oakley, called for a focus on fire prevention. The first target in Oakley's sights was the wooden Mansard-style roof atop multistory brick buildings, which was a very popular adornment in that era. His second targets were unprotected, unenclosed vertical shafts, especially elevator shafts. To persuade building owners to correct these deficiencies or developers not to include them in new construction, the companies offered financial incentives. They also offered incentives to towns and cities to construct or improve public water systems with fire hydrants and to upgrade local fire departments. However, rate-cutting practices caused by the competition among local insurance agents negated these minimal improvements.[8]

In the mid-1870s, funding to the NBFU again decreased to a level making effective operation difficult and thus preventing the board from offering incentives and disseminating fire prevention information. Despite these efforts, U.S. cities continued to grow and to burn. In 1889 New York, Seattle, Spokane, Lynn, MA, and again Boston suffered fires, with damages together totaling $123 million. Around this time, the NBFU hired Chief John W. Smith of the Brooklyn (New York) Fire Department to act as its inspector of fire departments. In 1892 under the leadership of DeWitt Skilton, the NBFU assumed the initiative and called for improvements in construction and installation of automatic fire sprinkler systems, as well as an increase in fire prevention efforts. In that same year the NBFU began lobbying federal and state officials to implement formal investigation of fire causes, proper building construction, and regulation of special hazards. The NBFU convened a technical conference and invited architects, builders, and engineers to attend.[9]

A significant result of the conference was the effort to draft a model building code for New York. Although the state legislature defeated a proposal to adopt the code as law, the draft went on to become the National Board Model Building Code. However, it was not strictly the methods and materials of construction that contributed to the fire hazard. Electric lighting was a new invention and rapidly found application in the urban environment. This new form of indoor lighting permitted people to use more hours of the day to work and play. It also lit the streets at night and powered trolley and streetcar systems. Although the use of electricity in buildings was generally safer than gas lighting, it was causing an alarming number of fires because proper methods of installing electrical devices and wiring buildings had yet to be developed. In time, the causes of electrical fires were identified, and with that information, measures were taken to make installations and applications safer. Eventually, the practices were codified in the National Board Electric Code. A spin-off of the testing and research led to the formation of the Underwriters Laboratory of Chicago (now the UL). With the rapid advance in fire protection, a group of engineers, insurance experts, and fire service officials founded the NFPA in 1896.

One of the first efforts of the NFPA was to set up studies of the performance of automatic fire sprinkler systems, portable fire extinguishers, and fireproof doors. In 1896 the organization published the *Handbook of the Underwriters' Bureau of New England*. The book provided rules for insurance inspectors and contained chapters on construction, fire doors, fire shutters, exposure protection, and automatic sprinklers, as well as the principles of safe electrical installations. The construction chapters contained details for building exterior walls for protection and firewalls for separation. Eventually the NFPA assumed full responsibility for publishing the manual and, most importantly, keeping the content up to date. The manual is still in existence as the *NFPA Fire Protection Handbook*. Thus, the underwriters' handbook provided the foundation from which future building, electrical, and fire prevention codes would evolve. The requirements specified in codes are the direct result of field experience, research, and collected data.[10]

The collective experience gained from the urban fires of the nineteenth century formed the basis for the underwriters' handbook and the codes we use today. The NFPA developed and published inspection reporting forms in 1898, inspection guidelines in 1902, and the field practice manual in 1914. The manual lives on, published today as the *NFPA Fire Inspection Manual*. The NBFU eventually merged with the American Insurance Association (AIA). The AIA eventually spun off the ISO. These two organizations have shaped fire departments and the general practice of fire protection in the United States for well over a hundred years.

The fire underwriter's job required knowledge of the risk they were considering. They needed to know about the building's construction, combustibility of the construction materials, contents stored, any hazardous processes conducted, types of nearby buildings (exposures), and the location of the nearest fire hydrant and fire station. This information is vital to profiling a potential risk in order to set a rate to charge for the premium. Obtaining this information, storing it, and keeping it up to date was a monumental task in an age without computers. Where a need exists, an enterprising individual sees an opportunity. In this case it was Daniel Sanborn, a surveyor from Somerville, Massachusetts (near Boston). In 1866 Sanborn received a commission from the Aetna Insurance Company to create a series of fire insurance maps for Boston and parts of Tennessee. Eventually, Sanborn's company mapped as many as twelve thousand U.S. cities and towns into the twentieth century.

Sanborn's surveyors collected information critical to fire insurance underwriters and mapped areas at large scale to provide rich details. They noted construction methods, type of building materials used, processes undertaken inside buildings, and storage. Because Sanborn's crews returned approximately every ten years, the maps represent a long-term record of land usage. Today this information is useful to developers who want to know about hidden risks, to land-use planners seeking the history and previous uses of a location, and to environmental historians.

CHAPTER 13

Boston and the Standardization of Fire Protection

In July 1873, nearly a year after the great fire in Boston, a treatise titled "Fires and Fire Departments" appeared in the *North American Review*, a subscription journal. The author was James M. Bugbee, a Boston insurance executive and father of a future president of the NFPA, Percy Bugbee. In "Fires and Fire Departments," Bugbee (senior) made a careful study of Boston's 1872 fire and the actions taken to quell it.[1]

Bugbee's article praised the application of new technologies in fighting fires, but pointed out that the principal problem was the methods and materials used in the construction of buildings. He noted that Americans have not learned the lessons of the past sixty or seventy years and continue as they have always done. Worse, he noted, was the general lack of personal responsibility for fire prevention. He was critical of what he saw as an entrenched overreliance on fire insurance and a new reliance on paid firemen and steam fire engines to protect U.S. cities. To him this reliance was an abdication of personal responsibility. To an extent, his message still applies in the twenty-first century as towns, cities, and even states struggle to adopt basic building and fire codes against the will of powerful lobbies. The message should resonate with today's firefighters, who are still paying the price of the United States' general lack of responsibility when it comes to fire. Throughout U.S. history, from the time volunteers manned the brakes of hand pumpers through the transition to paid firemen operating steam fire engines and now motorized apparatus, Americans have failed miserably to separate politics and self-interest from the fire problem.

117

Bugbee found a kindred spirit in Eyre Massey Shaw. As London's chief fire
officer, Shaw spared no professional sentiment for his U.S. counterparts.[2]
Bugbee quotes from an article, originally appearing in the *London Herald* on
September 28, 1869, about Shaw's recent trip to the United States to inspect
the fire departments:[3]

> The chief officers, or as they are called chief engineers, of most American
> fire departments, and the principal assistant engineers, are elected, not
> promoted, and that political influence is commonly paramount in the
> elections. In some towns, the chief and his assistants were appointed by
> the mayor, and this was probably the better of the two; but in whichever
> way they obtained their places, the appointments were generally only
> temporary, and varied in duration from one to about three years, accord-
> ing to local arrangements. It was hardly to be believed that in the midst
> of a practical nation like the Americans, the chief of an important depart-
> ment, requiring a considerable amount of skill and special training,
> should be obliged every year to enter into competition with his subordi-
> nates and others, and either to stand continued fresh elections or to lose
> his place. Such was, however, the case, and the effect of the system is, of
> course, fatal to the advancement of the professional work of the depart-
> ment. . . . The Americans had now powerful and weighty machinery and
> appliances, drawn about by large numbers of horses, and worked by enor-
> mous bodies of men; it could hardly be supposed that the cities would
> long continue to supply funds for the payment of heavy expenses ren-
> dered necessary chiefly by the want of skill and practice on the part of
> those concerned. It was a very singular and unaccountable fact, that the
> Americans in their admiration for steam fire engines had forgotten or
> ignored the use of hand-worked engines, and abolished them altogether,
> thus absolutely depriving themselves of the means of instantly extin-
> guishing fires at their own doors, leaving themselves in the particular
> point far behind the most backward nations of Europe. He had asked in
> every city why this had been done, but he had not received as much as one
> reply giving the slightest reason; on the contrary, the answer generally
> was, that hand-engines were of no use, a statement quite without mean-
> ing in the face of the fact that some of the principal cities in the world
> are still entirely protected by them.

U.S. fire chiefs believed that the good fire record of European cities was a
result of widespread use of fireproof construction and rigid enforcement of the

building codes. One wonders what the former volunteer firemen, replaced in the name of progress by steam fire engines, and paid firemen thought about Shaw's observation. It would seem that the retirement of the volunteer system in the name of technological advancement and modernization was misguided. That the transformation to steam and paid staff was forced by well-meaning businessmen and politicians in the name of economic development makes it all the more incredible when today the same groups criticize fire service spending.

Bugbee studied the Boston fire service in the aftermath of the city's 1872 fire and presented a disheartening view of U.S. nineteenth-century firefighting efforts. Americans, in his opinion, prided themselves on their esprit de corps, even going so far as to claim that enthusiasm and dash could trump training and discipline when it came to volunteer fire crews. Those subscribing to this theory went so far as to claim that the more people know about their business, the less interest they take in it.[4] If these were the viewpoints of professional U.S. fire officers, it is clear they were not quite up to the task of organizing their operations to combat the growing urban fire problem, a fact not lost on many who looked at the matter. Officials in many cities created boards of commissioners to oversee fire department management and operations in an effort to force professionalism from the top down. Political influence, so much a part of the old volunteer system in the early nineteenth century, had carried over into the new paid fire service. This time around, however, the politicians exerted influence over management of fire department operations; the firefighters did not exert influence on politicians.

Bugbee laid out the convoluted relationship of the governing entities of Boston at the time of the great fire. There was the Board of Aldermen, the Common Council, and the mayor. Together, the Common Council and aldermen constituted the Boston City Council. The City Council annually elected the chief engineer (fire chief) of the Boston Fire Department, as well as the fourteen assistant chief engineers. The mayor of Boston appointed regular members of the fire department with approval from the aldermen. However, the City Council approved funding, meaning they had absolute control over the actual number of firemen appointed, their pay, their qualifications, terms of service, and job duties. They also purchased the fire apparatus (steam engines, hook and ladders, hose wagons, etc.) and made decisions as to where it should be deployed. Politically oriented deployment of Boston's firefighting resources, stations, and apparatus played a large role in how the 1872 fire was fought. Successive city councils had failed to build new fire stations to meet demand in the growing commercial district, all but leaving the high-value commercial properties (where the fire started) without a fire station. Various city councils had also failed to fund improvements to the public water system and hydrants, as requested repeatedly by the fire department.[5]

The chief engineer and his assistants had control of the fires, but it seems they controlled little else in the Boston Fire Department. Each company of the department had a foreman and assistant foreman, who were elected annually by the company's members. Each engine company (with a steam engine) had a paid driver, paid fireman, and paid engineer, all of which were permanent positions. Each engine company also had eight hosemen (including the foreman), who were all only paid-on-call members. The hose companies (with a hose wagon) each had a permanent paid driver and eight paid-on-call men. The ladder companies (with a hook and ladder) had a paid driver and a complement of either fourteen or twenty-one paid-on-call members. This latter core of members was assigned as follows: one foreman, one assistant foreman, four axmen, four rakemen, and either six or thirteen laddermen. The entire Boston Fire Department had 459 positions. Except for the elected engineers, all other members had tenure based on good behavior. At the time of the fire, the department had twenty-one steam engines capable of pumping 300 to 550 gallons per minute a horizontal distance of 320 feet and a vertical distance of 220 feet with each carrying 450 feet of fire hose. They had ten hose wagons or carriages, with each averaging nine hundred feet of fire hose. The ladder carriages each carried fifteen to twenty ladders of varying lengths. Nine men were assigned to salvage and property preservation work, positions paid for by insurance companies.[6]

For fires below the third floor of a building, firemen connected hoses directly to the nearest fire hydrant without a steamer to boost pressure. The Boston water system at the time had sufficient pressure to allow for friction loss in the hose, nozzle pressure and elevation losses. For fires on the third floor and above, a steam engine was required to boost the pressure lost to friction and elevation. The engine would connect to the hydrant and pump the line to the fire building. The hosemen of the engine and hose wagon companies handled the hose lines while laddermen opened up the building to ventilate smoke and expose hidden fire. Boston also had a fireboat and a Babcock chemical fire engine. This chemical rig was useful for small and incipient-stage fires. It weighed just over three thousand pounds and was pulled by one or two horses. With two chambers to maintain constant pressure and using a one-inch nozzle, it could pump extinguishing agent a vertical distance of seventy-five feet. Bugbee believed that these chemical rigs could take the place of the hand pumps that Shaw thought so highly of and were in use in Europe.[7]

Boston also benefited from a municipal fire alarm system run by the city and under control of the superintendent of fire alarm, not the fire chief. Boston had fire alarm pull boxes located on street corners throughout the city and wired to the city's fire alarm office. Alarm bells were located in the fire stations, public buildings, churches, and the homes of the department's engineers.

Boston's great fire came on November 9, 1872, starting around seven in the evening. It originated in the basement of a warehouse that measured fifty feet wide by a hundred feet long by seventy-two feet high and had a mansard roof. The front exterior wall was granite, and the other exterior walls were brick. The warehouse was at an intersection of two streets, forty and forty-five feet in width. Surrounding buildings were of similar construction and also had mansard roofs. Because it was early Saturday evening, no one noticed the fire until it was at an advanced stage.

By the next morning the entire complement of men and apparatus of the Boston Fire Department, as well as those of surrounding cities and towns, were engaged fighting the fire. Boston at the time of the fire had an area of 15.5 square miles and 260,000 residents. The fire department had 459 assigned personnel and 21 steam fire engines. Contrast this with London, which had a population of 3.34 million and an area of 122 square miles, but whose fire brigade had just 28 steam engines and 396 assigned personnel. On the night of the fire, with a recall of the entire department, Boston could field more firefighters than London. In testimony to a study commission after the fire, Harvard University president Charles William Eliot claimed that he saw a large number of what he termed "superb resources" at the fire, yet the operation was run poorly and lacked overall coordination and control. He was not the only person to make this observation.

In his testimony, President Eliot stated, "In short, the fire department seemed to lack the methods of an army altogether, about receiving intelligence and conveying orders." Others testified to the commission that fire streams were ineffectively applied; some even went so far as to say that the department entered the fray without a plan and fell quickly behind. Some thought that the

Boston firemen, being so accustomed to routinely entering burning buildings to extinguish fires, may have been shocked by the intensity and severity of the situation. Eyewitnesses to the actions of the assistant engineers testified that arriving officers would stop and remain at the first steam engine they came across. Referring to Chief Officer Shaw's observations on the lack of training in U.S. fire departments, Bugbee seemed to agree that a general plan of action did not manifest itself that night. Rather than placing themselves and the apparatus in strategic locations, the firemen simply entered the fight wherever they could. Bugbee writes that Shaw would have been able to offer a dissertation strategy. Shaw demonstrates in his book *Fire Surveys: Or, a Summary of the Principles to Be Observed in Estimating the Risk of Buildings* a thorough understanding of building construction and fire behavior.[10]

> The distance apart of buildings fronting each other should be in proportion to their height; in fact, as a simple rule, it might be laid down that they should be separated by a distance equal to half their combined height. Thus, for instance, a building of sixty feet and a building of thirty feet might occupy sides of a street forty-five feet wide. With a well-organized and properly equipped fire brigade it is found that sixty feet is the greatest height at which a building can be quickly protected, and that the cube of 60, or 216,000 cubic feet, is the largest cubical capacity which can be protected with reasonable hope of success after a fire has once come to a head.

Bugbee used Shaw's formula to determine that the fire department never had a chance to save the building of fire origin in Boston because of its size and the width of the street. The other contributing factors included the delayed alarm, the fire horses' illnesses, and the inadequate water supply. The fire horses suffered from epizootic fever, a virulent form of horse distemper. Fire horses in many other eastern U.S. fire departments had the same disease in November 1872. Because the fire horses were down, the fire chief hired five hundred men, on an on-call basis, to help pull the city's fire apparatus in event of an alarm. Even so, the additional help was only a stopgap measure, as heavy fire apparatus were very slow in arriving on scene, compounding the problem of a delayed alarm on the night of the great fire.

Noting these factors, a fire commander should have set a strategy of fire control focused on defensive posture, first protecting the exposed buildings rather than directly extinguishing the main fire. At some point, if the main body of fire had been controlled, with no threats to exposures and no problem with brands carried on air currents, the operation might have become offensive in posture, if necessary. Given the size of the building, the size of the fire, and the additional problems, protection of exposures was the best tactic. This would have been practical only if well-supplied engines and water towers massed their flow of water on the closest exposures. All of the nearby buildings had mansard roofs, so once the fire jumped from building to building, the battle was lost. Saving buildings that night required a defensive strategy that focused on protecting exposures and controlling spot fires from flying brands. Given that fire crews had to pull their apparatus to the fire because of the sick fire horses, the delay in response time would likely have negated the possibility of a massed attack in the early stages. In addition, Chief John Damrell would have had to coordinate the various arriving steamers, assigning them a hydrant and a location to set up. Eyewitnesses recount apparently minimal strategic coordination. The fire eventually burned some 65 acres of built-up area and destroyed 776 buildings in the heart of the city's commercial sector, with losses of $75 million in 1872 dollars, or about $1.350 billion in today's dollars.

U.S. cities would continue to pay the price for failing to learn what European cities had learned about the mansard wood roof. European cities had banned such construction and suffered fewer such conflagrations. In addition, while U.S. fire insurance companies knew about the problem, they were unwilling to act. As Bugbee pointed out, Americans knew well the danger of wood construction for cities. Consider this partial list of disastrous fires and the number of buildings lost: 1835 in New York, 640 warehouses; 1838 in Charleston, 1,158 buildings; 1845 in Pittsburgh, 1,000 buildings; 1845 in New York, 302 stores and houses; 1848 in Albany, 300 buildings; 1849 in St. Louis, 350 buildings; 1850 in Philadelphia, 400 buildings; and 1852 in San Francisco, 3,000 buildings lost to two fires. In addition, Bugbee reports that Troy, Savannah, New Orleans, Mobile, Portland, and Brooklyn burned. During roughly the same forty-year time span in Europe, there were only two significant urban fires: Hamburg in 1842 and Constantinople in 1870.

Bugbee could not seem to reach a conclusion: was it the attention that Europeans paid to the process of maintaining superior building construction or their trained professional fire departments that contributed to their excellent record of fire protection? Perhaps multiple, interrelated factors were at work in the form of an open-ended technological system. A technological system, or

network in this case, with various contributing factors, many diverse participants, and no entity in control is defined as open ended. The participants in
this technological system included the government, the public, the fire service, engineers, builders, and fire insurance companies. The elements or factors
in the system include duncontrolled fire, water supply, combustibles, high-
density urban development, and firefighting apparatus.[9] Seeking the easy
answer like Shaw, Bugbee agrees that the relative success of European fire
departments is their reliance on the small, portable hand pumps distributed
strategically throughout their cities. Using portable pumps remained a viable
method of deployment for many more years in some of Europe's largest urban
centers. By stark contrast, U.S. departments of that era invested heavily in
powerful steam fire engines drawn by horses.

Bugbee's model of a well-run department was the FDNY, which he
described as being organized like a military unit, with nine battalion districts
and fifty company districts. At the time, the force was fully paid, consisting
of a chief engineer, twelve assistant chief engineers, fifty-two foremen, and
fifty-two assistant foremen. Each steamer was assigned two engineers, and each
company had eight firemen. They drilled and trained regularly and also
patrolled their respective response areas. The department was organized into
three bureaus: one for firefighting and fire prevention under the chief engineer, one to regulate sale and storage of combustibles under the inspector of
combustibles, and one to investigate the cause of fires under the fire marshal.
The mayor of New York appoints a board of commissioners to manage the
FDNY. At times, the posts of fire commissioner and chief of department (chief
engineer) were held by one individual. The annual report of the FDNY in
1879 reported 1,551 fires, and of these, 1,456 were confined to the building
of origin, 25 buildings were destroyed, and 69 buildings were greatly damaged. Buckets of water and portable extinguishers were used to control 1,061
of the fires. Total estimated losses for the buildings were $900,280 and
$4,771,300 for stock. Estimated insurance coverage on the buildings totaled
$7,276,446 and $14,525,264 for stock. In 1,066 cases of fire, the loss was less
than $100. A quarter of the fires were caused by carelessness, and a hundred
were caused by children playing with matches. Four firemen died in the line
of duty, along with twelve citizens. Injuries were sustained by 139 firemen
and 54 citizens. There were 729 uniformed members of the department with
a payroll of $1,030,822, and $1,254,970 was appropriated for expenses. The

FDNY of 1879 had 233 horses, 1 marine steam fire engine, 58 steam fire engines (fiver were self-propelled), 10 chemical engines, 24 hook and ladder trucks, 108 chemical fire extinguishers, and 4 aerial ladders. In 1879 the record time for hitching a team of horses and an apparatus was 9 minutes and 54 seconds, down from 13 minutes and 3 seconds in 1877.

Bugbee also provided a capsulated summary of the details from thirty-three years of firefighting in London (1833 to 1866), a period of time when firefighting was in the direct control of the fire insurance industry. The effort to maintain statistics on fires in U.S. cities lagged well behind that in London. In the thirty-three years covered, London experienced 29,069 fires, with breakdown by reported cause as follows: candles, 3,218; curtains, 2,822; fouled flues, 1,946; defective flues, 301; gas, 1,682; sparks, 1,255; spontaneous ignition, 274; children playing with fire, 471; children playing with lucifers (matches), 95; smokers, 406; intoxication, 155; naphtha lamps, 70; lime slacking, 93; lightning, 12; hunting bugs, 15; reading in bed, 34; smoking in bed, 2; sewing in bed, 3; crinoline, 3; cats, 34; dogs, 9; a monkey, 1; and a jackdaw, 1. There were 9,557 fires of unknown cause, with spontaneous combustion the rational suspect. As for the type of occupancy, the majority of fires occured in private homes and lodging houses. By trade and occupation, for the thirty-three-year period from 1833 to 1866, there were 1,164 fires in carpenter shops; 533 in baker shops; 422 in book and paper shops; 223 in print shops; and 208 in warehouses. By season of the year, most fires occurred in the winter and the fewest in autumn. By time of day, most fires occurred in the evening between 8:00 and 11:00. It is interesting that New York recorded a hundred fires caused by children playing with matches in a single year, while London reported 471 cases of children playing with fire and 95 of children playing with matches over a thirty-three -year period.

In closing his treatise on U.S. fire departments, Bugbee called for the NBFU to organize a committee of engineers to test fire apparatus and report the findings; to establish general rules for managing fire departments; to prepare and maintain fire incident statistics; and to establish standard sizes for fire hoses and standard thread sizes for hose couplings and hydrant nozzles. In 1889 the NBFU hired a fire chief to survey fire departments, but the practice did not gain momentum until after the 1904 fire in Baltimore. Although many East Coast fire departments quickly responded to Baltimore's cry for help, most steamers could not hook up to Baltimore's hydrants, and many hose couplings had incompatible threads preventing their use. Initially, after the 1904 fire, the

NBFU had three survey teams in the field. The number of teams increased to eight in the 1960s. Fire departments in the 1960s finally saw the achievement of most of the goals and the near end of urban conflagrations. The one significant failure that remains is the overall lack of standardization in fire apparatus, hose, couplings, and hydrants, even though the ISO evaluates almost every fire department in the United States.

Today the ISO Fire Suppression Rating Schedule has replaced the NBFU grading schedule. The goal is mostly the same; the major difference is that the focus has shifted from fighting conflagrations and block fires to controlling building fires. The influence of the NBFU and ISO on municipal fire departments is undeniable. The NBFU engineers used a systematic approach in their work, not unlike today's methods. Depending on the size of the city, the survey team spent from a week to several months gathering city data for its report. Cites were surveyed every five to ten years or more frequently if requested by the city government. The NBFU claimed no political agenda, instead adhering to a strict process governed by rules, using specific criteria to quantify findings. Measurable criteria made objective comparisons with fire departments of other cities possible. More importantly, correlating local survey information with the fire loss records of a city and then comparing against other cities allowed for objective analysis. The findings from a survey provided underwriters with information that aided them in determining the potential fire risk in a given city. Specifically, it helped them gauge fire defense as a system that included the water supply to hydrants, fire alarm box coverage, fire station locations, number of pumps, pumping capacity, feet of fire hose, staffing levels, and training of firemen. A city that was prepared to defend itself against a catastrophic fire earned the underwriter's confidence and contributed to equitable rates for insurance coverage. A city that ignored its overall fire defenses might suffer a disaster, and property owners paid higher rates for their fire insurance coverage. The purpose of grading or rating municipal fire defenses is to measure the capacity to prevent the spread of fire. It is unlikely that any fire chief or fire underwriter seriously believed they could prevent fires; their interest was in preventing fires from spreading from building to building or block to block.

The members of the NBFU survey teams were knowledgeable in firefighting techniques, fire chemistry, water supply planning, and waterworks operations. Some of them also had engineering degrees. Their primary qualification was always their overall knowledge of the diverse elements of fire protection. They asked questions, but they also looked for proof or evidence. They would ask the chief if the fire department pressure tested its hose, but they would also examine the fire hose test records. Words were fine, but documentation was necessary.

The grading schedule, known officially as the Standard Schedule for Grading Cities and Towns of the United States with Reference to Their Fire Defense and Physical Conditions, was a hundred pages long. The survey team divided its responsibilities to inspect, examine, count, and measure a city's efforts, equipment, and human capacity. Firemen were as important as fire apparatus because "fire engines don't fight fires, firefighters fight fires." The training and experience of a department's officers was especially important, as a fire department needs competent officers to succeed. They checked the fire apparatus, counted lengths of hose, and determined the total number of feet of ground ladders. They ensured that fire departments conducted annual service tests of pumps and pressure tests of fire hose and that accurate records of the results were made. The age of fire apparatus did not matter, but proper maintenance was critical, as was service testing of pumps. They looked at apparatus staffing to determine whether sufficient numbers of firefighters responded on calls. They examined the department's training records to determine subjects covered and recommended a minimum number of hours of training.

NBFU survey teams looked at the methods for notifying a fire department about fires and the means of transmittal to the various fire stations. They looked at the process of notification as a stepwise operation: alarm receipt, processing, handling, assignment, and dispatch of fire companies. For a fire company or station to respond to a call, they are first notified by the city fire alarm office. In smaller cities, this is relatively straightforward, but in a large city, districts divide the territory into specific response areas for specific companies. A given company's area of responsibility is its first due area. The assignment depends on proximity to the scene of the fire call, and the closest station responds. Additional companies follow according to which is the next closest or has special equipment needed for fighting the fire. This process is much like the military's order of battle when preparing for engagement. Index cards kept on file in the fire alarm office record the order of assignment by street location and fire alarm master boxes. Computer systems handle this function today.

The survey team identified the city's principal business district. They were very concerned with fire risks and fire protection capability within the district, especially the predominant form of construction within each block of buildings. They assigned a level of risk to each block and determined the amount of water needed to fight a large fire. The needed fire flow (NFF) is an estimation of the amount of water required to extinguish that building should it be involved in a serious fire. The NFF for a given building depends on the size, construction, occupancy, and exposure to other buildings. Remember, for an underwriter it is not just about the building being insured—exposure from nearby buildings is just as important, perhaps even more so. Today, the highest required NFF for buildings in the principal business district or built-up area determines the basic fire flow (BFF) for the city. In the early days of the grading schedule, the required BFF also depended on the city's population, which further served to determine the number of firefighters needed.

There is a direct relationship among staffing, the NFF of a building, and the BFF of the city. Hoses carry water, and firefighters carry hoses. More water equals more hoses equals more firefighters. A fire hose of a given size will allow a given volume of water to meet the NFF. Firefighters use the lines to apply the water through nozzles onto the fire. To deploy and advance a hose line requires physical effort by firefighters to maneuver the line. Thus, in the end, the NFF dictates the number of hose lines, which in turn dictates the number of firefighters needed to move the lines and perform other tasks. The design of modern public water systems requires allowance for not only domestic and industrial water supply needs, but also fire flow requirements. In rural areas without public water systems, fire departments rely on various alternative means for water supply.

In fire protection, notification is a deliberate attempt to communicate that an uncontrolled and potentially hostile fire exists. The intent of the message is to prompt acknowledgement and thereby action on the part of the recipient. Before the age of automatic fire alarm systems and telephones, notification of fire presented a huge challenge. The evolution of notification probably started with people shouting, then maybe beating on a hollow log, and at some point, someone likely used an animal's horn. Cannons, church bells, and factory steam whistles also saw use as warning devices. The invention of telegraphy opened up new possibilities in fire protection as a means of notification. Boston employed the first fire alarm telegraph system in 1852. The telephone now affords the means to provide notification of fire.

The rapid growth of U.S. cities in the nineteenth century spurred by economic expansion and industrialization created an urban fire problem. This evolution shaped the development of U.S. cities for a hundred years. It also forced the transition from volunteer fire forces, highly dependent on manual labor, to paid firemen, dependent on machines and manual labor. Transition to paid forces brought changes, among them the necessity for rules to govern employee behavior and essential work. Many of the departments, even in large cities, had a combination of personnel including full-time and part-time paid-on-call, an arrangement that exists today in smaller cities and towns. The introduction of steam fire engines necessitated hiring trained and responsible individuals to operate the machines. Responsibility necessitated rules.

City governments codified fire department rules in their ordinances, something the NBFU probably favored, as codification could serve to keep politics out of fire department administration. Department rules set lines of authority and chain of command. The NBFU expected the chief of the department to have absolute command and control of firefighting operations, as well as general administrative authority over the department's personnel, apparatus, and facilities. Sometimes there was a layer of control over the fire chief in the form of a fire or public safety committee. The duties of a fire chief included general supervision over all personnel, facilities, and apparatus; assignment of personnel; discipline of personnel; and enforcement of city and department rules. The chief was also responsible for record keeping, which included the number of alarms, number and types of fires, causes of fires, dollar value of property losses caused by fire, insurance coverage paid for fire losses, and the names of members and excuses for their being absent from duty. Fire committees might have oversight over department finances and would have to review requests for purchases and approve invoices for payment. Fire chiefs maintain an inventory of all fire department equipment. They submit a payroll reflecting the number of regular hours and overtime hours worked per person, as well as the number of substitutes filling vacancies or absences. Chiefs usually have authority to administer discipline with more severe infractions referred to a committee. In the absence of the chief, a deputy or the assistant chiefs assume the responsibilities of command and supervision. Deputy and assistant chiefs normally have routine responsibility for a bureau or office within the department. Captains are responsible for a station. Captains are supervisors and ensure that crews are present for duty, perform all required duties, wear their uniform properly, keep the station clean, and generally maintain equipment.

Before motorized apparatus replaced horses, maintaining station cleanliness was important, as crew and horses were under one roof. Apparatus drivers were responsible for looking after the horses; they exercised the horses for one hour daily, except on Sundays or within twenty-four hours of a horse's response to a fire call. The exercise route could not exceed two blocks from the station in case there was a fire call. If there were a fire, the steamer would go into action while the horses were unhitched and removed from the scene of the fire. Cold or wet weather required covering the horses for protection. On return to the station, horses perspiring from a workout or wet from rain or snow received a rubdown and grooming. Returning from a fire, drivers ensured that the horses maintained a slow trot.

Firefighters have assignments to perform specific and specialized roles. The basic division of work is between handling hoses and ladders. Before the term "firefighter" came into usage, firemen were assigned as either hosemen or laddermen. In the late nineteenth and early twentieth centuries, assignment to a firehouse meant that one was expected to be there full-time unless answering an alarm or on preapproved time off. The workday likely began and ended at eight in the morning, with firemen having perhaps only seventy-two hours off per month. A day off could not exceed twenty-four hours and could not interfere with night watches for which the particular member was scheduled that month. The department might have provided a helmet for use in firefighting. When on leave, positions were covered by substitute firemen, and the member's helmet was used by the substitute. Alcohol, gambling, profanity, and wrangling were forbidden in the firehouse. The threat of forfeiture of position was intended to keep firemen from entering any business establishment serving alcoholic beverages. Members were expected to act courteously to one another; officers were to be treated with deference, and communications were to be respectful. The rules also stressed personal restraint while at fires, with extraneous talking kept to a minimum. Missing a fire without excuse or good cause was grounds for discipline. Racing to fires was not permitted. If several companies were responding along a street in the same direction, they were to remain in single file. Civilians were not permitted to ride the apparatus or sleep in the firehouse. After a fire, an inventory of equipment was taken, and missing items were reported.

Members were required to wear their uniform while on duty. Arguing with officers was not tolerated. Officers were to be dignified and firm in their interactions with subordinates and were to be careful to abstain from any violent, abusive, or immoderate language while issuing orders, providing direction, or in general conversation. During firefighting operations, procedures stressed keeping property damage to minimum. Before leaving, the fire officer in charge secured the property from further damage, notifying the police department if necessary of a building left open. Members were on duty at all times and prepared to attend any fire, even if on leave. To visit another firehouse, the firemen were required to have permission from a chief officer or the station captain. Applicants to the fire department had to be U.S. citizens, be a city resident for three years, speak English, write their own name legibly, be at least twenty-one but not more than forty years of age, and exhibit adequate intellect and physical capacity as deemed sufficient by the chief of department.[10]

Although the NBFU had made efforts toward reviewing fire departments starting in the 1890s, the full-scale grading of municipal fire defenses by the NBFU expanded soon after the Baltimore fire of 1904. In the first decades of the twentieth century, the NBFU pushed the fire service forward with the help of the NFPA and NAFE (which later became the IAFC). The impact of these driving forces cannot be understated. Improvements in public water supplies, municipal fire alarm systems, and the fire department itself helped to restrain and sometimes prevent serious fires from becoming conflagrations. By mid-century the fire suppression capability of city fire departments was greatly improved, building codes were enforced, two-way radio communication technology was implemented, fires were investigated, arson crimes punished, and records of fires maintained. At the state level, fire marshals worked across local boundaries, and firefighter training programs developed. The goal of the NBFU had been simple: do everything possible to prevent fires from starting, but once a fire has started, have the resources ready to prevent it from spreading. Fire prevention and fire containment became the focus of progressive fire departments. The strategic goals for firefighters from the mid-twentieth century on have been prevention and containment.

Prevention of fires involves education, enforcement, and engineering. Education is teaching people about the hazards of fires and what steps they can take to minimize the potential for having a fire. Enforcement is ensuring that construction of buildings, hazardous processes, and storage of combustibles adheres to codes and safety regulations. Engineering is designing methods and systems to prevent, contain, detect, and extinguish fires in the built environment. Automatic fire sprinkler systems extinguish or contain incipient fires at or near the point of origin. Smoke and heat detectors detect fires near the point of origin and provide notification via an alarm. The alarm may be internal and notify only occupants in proximity, or it may be hardwired to a system that monitors for alarms and automatically notifies an authority. If firefighters arrive soon enough, they will attempt to contain and extinguish the fire in the room of origin. If the fire has extended beyond the room of origin, firefighters will attempt to control and extinguish the fire in this order: on the floor of origin, in the building of origin, and in the block of origin.

Fires involving several blocks have the potential to become conflagrations, depending on circumstances, such as weather conditions. Keeping a fire contained to the building of origin is possible without intervention of the fire department. If a building is equipped with an automatic fire sprinkler; is built of protected, fire-resistive materials; and is subdivided using fire-rated walls and doors, and a fire occurs but is contained, the credit goes to the building inspectors, architects, and design engineers. If the building cannot withstand a fire because of its construction and the fire spreads beyond the building, then it is up to the fire department (with help from the water department) to keep the fire in check. The model building codes of today assume that no fire department will respond. The model codes also provide reasonable assurance that without intervention, a fire will spread in a predictable manner. This is possible through application of height and area limitations. (Recall Chief Shaw's rule of thumb for maximum size of buildings. The maximum volume of an area involved in a fire that can be attacked with hope of success is approximately 216,000 cubic feet, or roughly sixty feet on a side.) The same practical theory holds for the height and area limits in model building codes. Chief Damrell helped develop this concept, basing his ideas on his experience as both a fire chief and a building inspector in Boston. The first model building code published after the 1904 Baltimore fire included this concept in its recommendations: the potential to contain a fire in a compartment relates directly to the area and height (i.e., volume) of the space. The greater the open area, the greater the potential for a large fire to develop if sufficient fire loading is present. With code requirements, you have trade-offs. By installing an automatic fire sprinkler system, the area and height may be increased accordingly and still meet the code. The type of occupancy is also a factor in allowances by code. Codes also address exposures, and they may cause a restriction on what may be done in a given building. As much as fire departments, building and fire codes deserve credit for the decline of building-group fires, multi-block fires, and conflagrations in the United States.

By 1916, the NBFU grading schedule stressed the need for adopting and enforcing building codes. Today the ISO continues to stress fire control through properly equipped and trained fire departments, but until recently, it placed minimal emphasis on codes. In the late 1990s, the ISO began a new program that evaluates municipal code enforcement programs. How building and fire codes developed relates to our experience with large-scale urban fires. Developments in codes link directly to the most serious fires that the United States faced. After every deadly fire or large-loss fire, changes trickle down through revisions in the code requirements.

5
LEARNING TO CONTROL BUILDING FIRES

CHAPTER 14

Fire Protection in Theory

The intensity of today's fires has increased because plastics and synthetic materials have replaced wood, paper, wool, and cotton as the predominant materials in household and office contents. Products made of plastics and synthetics tend to burn hotter (i.e., at higher temperatures) and their products of combustion (smoke and various gases) produce a more toxic and lethal threat. The polyurethane used in furniture burns intensely, producing smoke, gas, and heat similar to a gasoline-fed fire. This fact played a role in the intensity of the Super Sofa Furniture Store fire in Charleston. One way to measure heat is the British thermal unit (BTU). One BTU represents the amount of heat necessary to raise the temperature of 1 pound of water 1 degree Fahrenheit. One BTU equals 252 calories, 1,054 joules, or 1.054 kilowatts. Compare two homes, one from 1940 and another from 2000. Examine their construction, construction materials, features, furnishings, and contents. There are striking differences between the two homes in every detail.[1]

Today we may see fewer fires overall, but these fires burn with intensity and are very deadly. Consider pieces of wood, cut and stacked in two piles, with one weighing one pound and the other weighing two pounds. Ignite the wood and allow it to burn freely. The subsequent output of heat energy produced, as measured in BTUs, is greater in the pile weighing more, thus more fuel leads to bigger fire, which creates more heat. Next, consider two stacks, one of wood and the other of plastic, in equal weights, arranged for burning. The heat output of the plastic fire as measured in BTUs greatly exceeds that of the wood. Of the two materials, plastic as compared with an equal quantity of wood burns hotter. In addition, the products of combustion from the plastics fire are greater in toxicity. Going back to the two houses, the modern home is larger and filled with more content in the form of plastics and synthetic materials. We see less wood, paper, wool, cotton, and linen in the modern home. Pound for pound, plastics and synthetics pose a greater fire hazard than wood, paper, and natural fibers, and the modern home probably contains a greater load of combustibles than the older home. Thus, its fuel load or capacity to produce big, hot fires is higher. As a result, a developed room and contents fire in the modern home will likely be hotter and produce more smoke than a similar fire in the older home; recognizing that fact is critical to the survival of any occupants and the safety of the firefighters who respond. Fuel load determines the amount of water needed to suppress the fire. Water is highly effective for suppressing fires because it has a high latent heat of evaporation, meaning it has the capacity to absorb considerable heat through its conversion to steam. Absorbing the heat of the fire serves to cool, and thus suppress, the fire.

For a given volume of water, in the process of converting to steam, the rate of expansion is approximately 1,700 to 1. Not only is water highly effective at cooling by absorbing heat, but the resulting steam also acts to smother the flames by excluding the available oxygen. The expansion of the steam also tends to aid ventilation by displacing the toxic smoke and gas from the compartment. However, if there is no outlet to ventilate the heat, smoke, gases, and rapidly expanding steam, the interior atmosphere of the compartment and possibly the entire building will become untenable to humans. The result is that the hot steam will burn any trapped occupants.

It will become very uncomfortable very quickly for any firefighter who happens to be in the room or compartment, despite having protective equipment and an air supply. Firefighters frequently receive severe burns from steam and hot gases. Improper application of water from a fire hose can disrupt the layers of hot air and create volumes of dangerous steam. This is why firefighters receive intensive training in attacking a fire and are required to wear protective equipment. A building equipped with automatic fire sprinklers provides occupants and firefighters with a margin of safety. The activation of sprinklers keeps a fire in check, preventing it from growing in intensity and reaching the point of flashover. This allows occupants to escape safely and firefighters to enter a more controlled and manageable work environment.

If you have ever considered using the sprinkler system as a diversion the next time villains chase you, you had better plan on something else. Hollywood movies have provided audiences with a distorted picture of how sprinkler systems function. How many times have you watched characters try that trick as a diversion? They hold a lighter to a sprinkler head or they strike one of heads on the ceiling and suddenly water gushes from every sprinkler in the building. What sort of magic holds back the water in all those heads so that striking just one causes all to spray at one time? A special type of high-volume sprinkler system, designed for special hazards, will allow water to flow in a deluge from all heads simultaneously—such systems are typically found protecting warehouse loading docks and aircraft hangars.

The sprinkler systems found in stores, offices, schools, apartments, and homes have fusible heads. Each head operates independently of the others and is activated by heat. Only those heads nearest the fire will discharge a spray of water. Typically, fewer than five heads open in a given fire, allowing water to flow. Therefore, if you need a diversion and plan to use the sprinkler system, you will need to strike each single head, which will cost you the element of surprise. Sprinklers have been around for a long time, but most people know very little about how they work and, more importantly, just how effective they are at minimizing property damage and increasing occupant escape time. Occasionally one may hear of a library rejecting the idea of sprinklers because of potential damage to the books. What is the alternative to having just some of the books ruined by water and smoke? Losing the entire collection and maybe the building to total destruction by fire.

Here is another way to look at this problem for libraries. If fewer than five heads typically fuse, and each head releases around twenty gallons per minute, the yield is a hundred gallons per minute or less before the fire department arrives and stops the sprinkler flow—approximately five minutes. The worst scenario with five heads opening is about five hundred gallons of water. Contrast that with a no-sprinkler situation. In the four to five minutes it takes for the fire department to arrive, the fire has grown in intensity and size. Firefighters will enter the building with at least one hose line. That line will be spraying around 175 to 250 gallons per minute. The firefighters will likely have to discharge that line for several minutes to extinguish the large fire in the stacks of books. Remember, in the few minutes it took for the five sprinklers to gain control over the fire, they flowed five hundred gallons of water or less. When the fire department attacks the larger fire with hose lines, the total damage—including fire, smoke, and water—exceeds the smaller fire suppressed with sprinklers. Without sprinklers, the smoke and heat produced by the hotter fire will probably ruin much more of the library's book collection than the damage from the smaller fire suppressed by sprinklers. In addition, the more severe fire will necessitate that firefighters make holes in the walls and ceiling to check for extension of fire. It is even conceivable that the fire might require a ventilation hole in the library roof. The water damage argument used against sprinklers is simple minded, unscientific, and economically foolish. More often than not, the fear is not water damage but the cost of installation. Because fires happen only to other people, we feel we can safely ignore the threat. We take the potential risk of having a fire and place it on the shoulders of the fire department, with the cost spread among the taxpayers and those who carry fire insurance.[2]

If we, as a society, accepted the possibility of a fire as a real threat and assumed moral and economic responsibility, we would have building regulations that mandate sprinklers in all occupied buildings. As a result, our community would suffer fewer serious fires, and the cost of running a fire department would be much lower. There are three approaches to managing risk: avoid it, minimize it, or transfer it. When we prevent a fire from starting by installing a new electrical outlet for the refrigerator instead of using a cheap electrical extension cord, we avoid risk. When we store cans of flammable liquid in a metal cabinet, we minimize the risk. When we dial 911, we transfer the risk to the fire department. What is the most responsible course of action regarding risk? Building and fire codes help to prevent and minimize risk, but meeting the code costs money. Sprinkler systems minimize risk, but they cost money.

What makes us think that dialing 911 does not have a cost associated with it? Is it because the cost of code compliance and sprinklers comes out of the individual's wallet and thus is seen as an unproductive investment or even a penalty because fires happen only to other people? Taxpayers directly support the cost of public fire protection. The protection is in the form of fire stations, fire trucks, and firefighters. When we dial 911 and transfer the risk, all taxpayers share in the cost. It may be difficult to grasp that there is a difference between the two costs. However, if we factor in the cost of fire in terms of business interruption, lost jobs, injuries, and fatalities, the picture begins to look different. Fire insurance justifies and sustains our collective irresponsibility regarding the risk of fire. If society cared about saving lives and reducing the cost of fire, we would adopt a systems approach using prevention, built-in protection, and product safety engineering.

The Europeans who immigrated to the United States were resourceful and clever, using their own skills to fabricate structures from natural elements such as wood and stone, often built close together for protection. Because of factors such as location, some villages grew to be towns, and later some towns grew to be cities. First tradesmen built shops and later businesses, and manufacturing would develop in certain areas. People lived close to their jobs, if not actually in the same building. People learned there was strength in numbers in creating a village; and the same held true for commercial interests, but for different reasons. It might be accessibility to main roads or intersections or water transportation. A person stopping for dry goods might also visit the bakery and so on. With the realization that a fire could easily destroy an entire town, the residents attempted to divide their towns into areas intended for specific uses. Placing industry, business, mercantile, and residential buildings in their own districts became in effect simple zoning. The strategy was to keep a fire from spreading beyond the district in which it erupted. The rationale was that if a fire could be limited to a district, then only about one-fourth of the town would be lost to it. The thinking was that in each so-called fire district, the typical buildings would share similar construction. Thus, the buildings in each district would have a somewhat self-imposed height and area limitation. If developers and builders held to the height and area limitation, fires might be easier to control and kept within the building of origin, or at worst the block of origin. The realization that a very serious fire could take out an entire sector of the community soon rose into awareness. Self-imposed height and area limits were logical in concept, but until uniform materials and standardized methods of construction came along, limiting size was only a half measure. With the development of model building codes came classification of construction methods.[3]

Buildings codes today recognize five classes or methods of construction, each with predominant features or elements related to fire protection. The highest class is Type-I Fire Resistive, which features structural elements of noncombustible materials with added protection for rated fire resistance protection. In Type-I, steel beams and columns may be encased in concrete or have a sprayed-on fire-resistive material providing some resistance to fire. High-rise office buildings and hospitals are examples of typical Type-I buildings. They are designed to withstand a total burnout without collapsing and spreading fire to other buildings. In taller Type-I structures, every two to four floors are constructed to slow the fire from spreading vertically. Fire in a lower section of such buildings should burn itself out before it reaches the section above.

Type-II Noncombustible construction also relies on noncombustible structural elements, but they are typically not protected and do not carry the higher fire-resistive rating of Type-I construction. Approximately twenty minutes of direct exposure to fire is sufficient to cause a structural failure in Type-II buildings.

Type-III Ordinary features masonry exterior walls and steel or wooden floors and roofs. Firefighters sometimes called these buildings Main Street USA because they were typical in the downtown business district of nearly every U.S. city and town. Any wood used in a Type-III will contribute to the fire load and severity of the fire, bringing on the potential for collapse. These buildings have long been the focus of the insurance industry and fire chiefs because of the threat they pose and the fact that they comprise the downtown business and commercial districts of the United States. Many also consider these buildings the heart and soul of downtown America. Whether they have shops below and apartments above or are all offices, they are economic engines. Today, they are at the heart of economic development in small towns and cities, and developers are seeking to renovate these old buildings, in order to keep them going for another hundred years. To keep the cherished architectural features and ornamentation, they require special building code provisions to improve but not remake them. Many of these buildings have an extra-wide masonry wall providing a two-hour fire rating to slow down the spread of fire horizontally from building to building.

Type-IV Heavy Timber or mill construction features structural elements of wood with at least a nominal dimension of six by six inches. The exterior walls may be masonry or wood. This form of construction housed mills and factories in the nineteenth century. There are still many of these buildings in New England, and they are commercial, business, or residential conversions. Heavy timber buildings like those of ordinary construction have void spaces. Void spaces in a fire present a unique hazard because they may fill with smoke, gases, and heat. These spaces may lack sufficient oxygen after a time, and the combustion process will slow down until a firefighter opens the space, introduces air, and sets off a smoke explosion or a backdraft. Type-IV buildings are slow to burn because of the large-dimension timber framing, but they make for spectacular fires once they get going. Older firefighters refer to these fires as lawn chair fires because they make for a good, long show.

Last is the Type-V Frame construction with small dimension wood or steel framing. Americans who live in single-family homes probably live in a Type-V, even if it has a brick veneer.

Fireproof buildings (i.e., those built of noncombustible materials) were just what the fire insurance industry was looking for in its efforts to keep fires as close as possible to the area of origin. A false sense of security was associated with them at first, before several notable fires in these buildings resulted in significant losses of life. Even though nineteenth-century U.S. cities experienced large-scale block fires and even conflagrations, there were very few lives lost in these fires. When large numbers of people began to die by fire and smoke in so-called fireproof buildings, fire chiefs, building inspectors, engineers, and architects took note.

The answer at first seemed to be exit codes, which would set requirements for size and location of building exits for emergencies, but this did not stem the number of fire deaths. With careful examination and study of fire behavior, a connection between combustibility and flammability of materials and fire spread provided the clues to what was killing people in fire-resistive buildings. The answer involved flame spread, the speed of flame travel over the surface of certain materials. With this realization came the move toward comprehensive building, fire-prevention, and life-safety codes. Codes address fuel load, unprotected vertical openings, concealed spaces, interior finish, smoke control, sprinkler system coverage, fire-detection devices, fire alarm systems, and isolation of compartments. All of this factored into the classification of building occupancy—who inhabits the building, for what intent, and what is their capacity to deal with an emergency.

CHAPTER 15

Deadly Fire in a Fireproof Hotel

Advertised as being fireproof, the Winecoff Hotel in Atlanta, Georgia, lacked the fire protection features common in modern hotels—enclosed and protected vertical openings, fire doors, automatic fire sprinklers, and an alarm system. It even lacked fire escapes. The hotel turned into a furnace on December 7, 1946, and 119 people lost their lives. The fire also injured ninety people and remains the most deadly hotel fire in U.S. history. Some victims burned alive, some suffocated from smoke, and others simply leapt from windows rather than burn. NFPA engineer James K. McElroy wrote, "The screams of the Winecoff's occupants and the dull thud of bodies hurtling to Peachtree and Ellis Streets should eliminate for all time the illusion that this and other buildings, classified as fireproof in fire insurance rating schedules and many building codes, are secure against all perils to life safety without adequate safeguards for combustible interior finish and content."[1]

This fire among other fires in fireproof buildings of that era forever changed life-safety codes in the United States. Earlier in 1946, sixty-one people died (one of them a Chicago fireman) and more than two hundred were injured, including thirty city firemen, in another fireproof hotel, the thousand-room, twenty-three-story LaSalle Hotel. Canada also had a deadly hotel fire in 1946. Eleven occupants died and eight people were injured in the fireproof Barry Hotel in Saskatoon, Saskatchewan. In these as well as other fires in fireproof buildings, people died or were injured as a direct result of being trapped by flames or overcome by asphyxiation caused by smoke inhalation.

144

A contributing factor in these fires was rapid flame and smoke development from highly combustible interior surfaces and finishes. The fires grew and spread rapidly, feeding on furniture surfaces and wall finishes, extending horizontally and vertically, unchecked by sprinkler systems, fire doors, or protected vertical enclosures.[2]

In 1946 architect Maurice Webster had served as a member of the Cook County investigating jury that reviewed the deadly LaSalle fire. He also served on a similar jury investigating another deadly hotel fire in which fourteen occupants died. He was not the first person to recognize the inadequacy of fireproof construction, but he wanted to make sure that Americans knew of the problem, so he wrote an article for *The Atlantic*. According to Webster, fireproof construction simply meant a building was designed to eliminate the possibility that a fire would result in anything more than a minimum and predictable loss to the structure. In Webster's view, fireproof construction was a child of the fire insurance industry, a group that exhibited little concern for the safety of building occupants. He quoted a consultant from the Underwriters Laboratory, who stated that such buildings should act like a "good stove," retaining the heat inside and thus preventing fire from spreading to exposures.[3] Those people trapped within the fireproof hotels during a fire must have surely felt they were inside a stove.

Given the right conditions and resources, a capable fire department of the late nineteenth century would have had the capacity to hold a severe fire to the building of origin with some damage to nearby exposed buildings. The problem seemed to be fire-induced structural collapse that in turn released fire and by-products in a violent outpouring, thus causing more fires to ignite nearby. Fire insurance underwriters needed predictability to determine probability of outcome to, in turn, determine insurability. When buildings collapsed, calculation for probability went up in smoke. The fireproof building offered relatively secure odds. A fireproof building could withstand a total burnout without collapsing, raising the odds for the predictability that any claim for insurance would not be for a total loss. As an added benefit, the fireproof building also offered assurance for the underwriters of nearby buildings that the first building would not collapse and spread fire to exposed buildings. The owner and underwriter of a fireproof building knew that the building offered a quick return to use after a fire, requiring only replacement or restoration of interior surface features.

The deadly hotel fires of the mid-twentieth century were obviously of great interest to fire chiefs and were carefully studied by the NFPA and others. All reached the same conclusion because of the similarities in the pattern of the fires' development. There was a commonality in the scenario of these deadly hotel fires. They usually started on the ground floor near the bar, dining room, lobby, or an adjoining store. They grew quickly, igniting nearby combustibles, and produced such rapid flame development that employees failed to control or suppress them using portable extinguishers. The flames and smoke spread outward, and where it found a vertical opening, the mixture rose upward rapidly. Where no vertical channel existed, the heat and smoke mushroomed horizontally and filled confined areas. In all cases, the movement of flames, heated gases, and smoke were aided by any natural air drafts existing in the buildings.

Seeking a vertical outlet (stairwells, elevator shafts, ventilation shafts, and windows are convenient), building fires spread upward on convection currents bolstered by the pressure created from the products of combustion released into a confined space. In simple terms, fire in a confined space produces by-products of combustion that result in an increase in the ambient air pressure. If the air pressure cannot be released, a rupture or explosion is likely at the weakest point, often the windows. If a vertical opening exists, the increased pressure acting in conjunction with the natural convection of heated gases will produce an upward movement of the flame front so powerful that it will create its own draft, sucking in air at the lowest level. (This is why firefighters will cut a hole in the roof of a burning building—to release the built-up heat and smoke, a tactic known as ventilation, which relieves the toxic atmosphere inside.) Rapidly expanding fire gases will always seek release to those areas where the pressure is lower, unless natural air currents within the building are powerful enough to influence it to act differently. The natural animation inherent to the behavior of flames and smoke gives us the notion of fire as a living, breathing thing.

The power of combustion in the confines of a building causes flames, smoke, and hot gases to spew violently from every opening, something witnesses often describe as a building filled with fire. Firefighters call it a fully involved structure fire. For anyone inside, it is hell, but only for a time. Of those trapped in the rapid advance and spread of the fire, the fortunate die quickly of asphyxiation while the unfortunate experience the flame front and die from the heat's intensity. As in a stove, the fire gases rise upward in a fireproof building with unprotected vertical openings. Those trapped inside are indeed inside a furnace. The experts who studied the fireproof-hotel fires focused on the high combustibility and rapid flame-spread characteristics of the interior surfaces of the buildings (walls, floors, and ceilings), the lack of enclosure for horizontal and vertical spaces, the lack of adequate means of exiting, the lack of alarm systems, and the lack of automatic sprinkler systems.[4]

In Webster's opinion, the safety of the occupants in a building is best ensured by taking these steps: prevent fires from starting; extinguish fires in the incipient stage; once started, keep the fire from spreading; and direct the fire gases to the outside to prevent spreading inside. Webster pointed out that although the first three have received attention, the fourth has been overlooked because it isn't well understood. He further claimed that building codes of the day treated ventilation of fire gases in a confusing manner.[5]

Understanding fire behavior in confined spaces and compartments such as those found in buildings is critical to understanding the problems of combating fire either manually or with automatic systems. A fire heats the air, causing it to expand. Combined with the added heat and gases from the building elements and furnishings, the mixture expands rapidly, building in pressure. In a closed compartment, overpressurization causes the windows to blow out, assuming there is sufficient entrapped air to keep the fire burning long enough to reach the critical point. Where the fire compartment is open to other areas, the fire and products of combustion will expand under pressure and extend into other parts of the building, traveling both horizontally and vertically. The fire acts as though it were a living being. Once the fire front finds a vertical path or channel, it travels upward seeking an outlet. If the open channel is a stairway, any open doors to rooms or hallways off the stairs present an invitation for fire extension. This condition existed in the fireproof hotels where so many died.

These were the days before central air conditioning when each guest room had a transom window above the entry door. Transom windows facilitated air movement for cooling or heating. Hotel occupants also opened the windows to the outside for fresh air. Both transom windows and exterior windows played a role in the behavior of the fires studied. In hotel fires, guests frequently died from smoke inhalation while sleeping because of the open transom windows. Webster and other experts suggested installation of a large opening at the very top of stairwells to permit ventilation to the outside in the event of a fire. In other words, put a chimney (stairway vent) on the stove (fireproof building). He based this idea on Bernoulli's principle regarding fluid and gas behavior.[6]

Making a vent hole created an opening in which the air pressure would be lower. The higher-pressure fire gases would travel upward to the area of lower pressure, creating a strong updraft sufficient to keep any hot gases from flowing horizontally into hallways, through open fire doors, and into transom windows on the guest room doors. The national advisory building code and the fire service of the time recognized this fact. Nevertheless, many locally developed building codes required that vertical shafts have a secured enclosure at the top with an automatic closer; some codes even specified using a slab of concrete. The LaSalle Hotel had these enclosures.[7]

Even with existing requirements for vertical venting of theater fly galleries and explosive handling rooms, some codes of the day missed the concept when it came to venting vertical shafts in hotels. Webster thought the prevailing perception that fireproof buildings offered built-in safety provided local code officials with reason to relax requirements for exits and ventilation in such buildings. Webster's thinking on codes in general was that they were perhaps too restrictive and that common sense should prevail in some matters of safety. For example, pay strict attention to hidden spaces (voids) and closets, limit fuel loading in hotel lobbies and connecting areas, install sprinkler systems where possible, provide separation between lobbies and sleeping rooms, and ensure adequate venting of vertical openings that communicate with the hallways of guest floors.[8]

Materials burn differently. For example, on a plaster wall with a painted surface, the plaster resists combustion, but the oil-based paint is flammable. The plaster wall affords protection from fire spreading to separate compartments, but the painted surface is a mechanism for fire spread across the surface. The rate at which flames spread across a surface plays a role in building fires. Consider wood paneling or cloth attached to a wall. Both the wood and the cloth are combustible and offer fuel for combustion. The vertical surface contributes to the rapidity of flame spread because the fire moving upward preheats the material above, raising its temperature and causing it to burn faster. Contrast the same material on a horizontal as opposed to a vertical surface. The development and progress of the flames across the horizontal surface will be slower than they are across a vertical surface. Fire behavior then is dependent on the combustibility or flammability of a material, and how that material presents itself as a potential source of fuel also affects the rate at which flames will spread. Highly flammable materials, paints, and draperies have played significant roles in many deadly fires, especially in hotels and nightclubs.

Automatic sprinkler systems in those fireproof hotels would have provided a large measure of safety if installed. Sprinklers would someday be required in new public buildings where the public assembled and slept. However, retrofitting sprinklers in older buildings has always sparked complaints of excessive cost and unsightliness. If fireproof construction ensured structural integrity under fire conditions, what about the other methods of construction? What are the advantages and disadvantages of other methods? The codes will frequently relax strict provisions as a concession to the voluntary installation of sprinklers. Rather than require sprinklers in the first place, we take a backdoor approach. Even the fire insurance industry is not a big proponent of the widespread installation of sprinkler systems in all occupancy classes.

In building design, sizing structural elements to span open areas is important. Support columns bear the loads carried by the structural elements that span open spaces. The greater the area in size, the more support called for and the more columns needed. However, from a designer's perspective, columns get in the way of things. Recall the relationship of height and area to fire protection. Installing sprinklers may in turn trigger an allowance to permit an increase in the open area. Larger open areas require more support. Wood can be used for columns and its mass does afford endurance under fire conditions but it does not work well for spanning wide areas unless in very large dimensions. Today wood beams for large spans exist, but the technology to make them did not exist in the late nineteenth and early twentieth centuries. Firefighters learned early that iron columns do not offer much protection against fire. Steel is better, but its structural integrity is affected starting at about 800 degrees Fahrenheit. One can protect the steel and buy some added time by increasing its fire rating.

The cost-effective solution to the span problem came with the invention of truss construction. Masonry arches spanning a wide area require a massive bearing wall. The method was costly and dangerous to construct. Timber trusses offered an alternative to the masonry arch. Relatively speaking, they are light in weight, offer a high strength-to-weight ratio, cost less, and are easier to construct. This is also true of today's lightweight wood and steel trusses used in commercial and residential construction. In commercial construction, the open, lightweight bar-joist truss is widely used and often left exposed for an industrial look or otherwise covered by a drop ceiling. Applying fire-coating materials is sometimes difficult to do properly. It is difficult to spray them in place, and subsequent damage by workers may compromise the protection. Wood trusses now find widespread application in home construction and, in contrast to traditional wood-frame construction, are quickly installed.

Wood trusses are factory built under controlled conditions, shipped to the job site, and installed by a small crew using a crane or hoist. A new variation is the solid web truss featuring plywood or oriented-strand board (OSB) glued in place between two solid wood chords. A truss has several component parts, all of which serve to provide high strength with minimum weight. Truss integrity depends on the web, chords, and means of connection. A failure of any one component sets up the potential for a structural failure. Under fire conditions, trusses may fail relatively quickly. They present a significant cause for concern for firefighters, even though manufacturers of wooden trusses claim they are safe. In a given situation, with fire impinging on a truss, the point and moment of failure is not predictable under field conditions. Firefighters making entry to attack a fire may not be able to determine quickly where the fire is located. Should the trusses sustain attack by fire, firefighters may have no way of knowing the danger at hand. If they were to discover that the trusses were burning, their tactical option would be to exit immediately from the building because of the potential for catastrophic failure. The failure of a truss can precipitate collapse of floors or roofs, trapping fire crews. The manufacturers of wood trusses contend that their products receive ratings for use and provide a safe means of construction.

With regular frequency, U.S. firefighters die or receive injuries in the collapse of truss floors and roofs under fire conditions.[9] This scenario happens with such regularity in the United States that some states require that buildings built with structural trusses have a label or placard affixed to the front of the building to warn firefighters of the presence of truss construction. The manufacturers of trusses swear to the safety of their product and obviously argue that their product should not be labeled dangerous. Experts believe the truss flooring in the World Trade Center buildings failed, setting off the successive collapse of floors. Investigators and engineers concluded that burning jet fuel weakened the trusses, the trusses then failed, and the floors began to fall. An unprotected truss in a small commercial or residential building may fail under fire conditions in as little as twenty minutes. Thus, without solid information about the starting time and location of the fire, it becomes almost impossible for firefighters to gauge the period of safety, if any, that they have before a potential collapse.

By the time the fire ignites and develops in intensity and the occupants discover the fire and call 911, several minutes may have elapsed. Allow a minute or so for the 911 center to process the call and notify the fire department, a minute or so for the station to acknowledge the alarm, and another minute for firefighters to turn out and get the trucks on the road. By this time, the fire may have been burning for six to ten minutes. Allowing up to four minutes travel time for the fire trucks and then for crews to set up for the attack means a total of ten to fifteen minutes the ignition of the fire. Fire crews now make entry and attempt to locate the seat of the fire. If trusses are involved, the firefighters are at a critical time threshold; if the fire has grown to severe intensity, a failure of the trusses is very possible. The officer in charge has to decide whether to pursue the attack. Only in a very dire situation in which civilian lives are at risk would a fire commander allow crews to move on with the attack instead of retreating, yet even then the command would be questionable. One must weigh the potential hazard to the firefighters' lives against the unknown of whether trapped occupants are still alive and savable.

CHAPTER 16

Firefighting, Building Codes, and Technology

One nineteenth-century firefighter who grasped the concept of building safer buildings was Boston fire chief John S. Damrell. His background as a builder, his experience as fire chief during the 1872 great fire in Boston, and his later service as chief building inspector provided him with a unique perspective into the fire problem in the United States' combustible cities. His advocacy went beyond the city of Boston to the nation through his influence on architects, builders, fire chiefs, and fire insurance underwriters while serving on a model building code committee. Ultimately, his work and that of others resulted in a National Model Building Code. He died in 1905, the same year the NBFU published the model building code. Damrell focused on height and area limitations in Boston just as Eyre Massey Shaw did in London.

A new issue for firefighters to consider involves the building code's ability to protect firefighters. The issue is related to risk management. Should firefighters change their strategy and tactics to avoid hazards that compound the inherent risks of the job? There are the two schools of thought. One group accepts the full risk of the mission as being part of the job, but others think that members of this group have a death wish. The core belief held by the first group is that they should risk all to save a life. The other group seems to feel that society has collectively chosen to build lightweight, disposable buildings, and in doing so, everyone should shoulder some responsibility for living in them and should not expect firefighters to die trying to save them.

The moral responsibility of society as a whole is to ensure that these buildings afford an acceptable level of safety to occupants as well as firefighters.

A good example of taking responsibility is installing automatic sprinklers in all occupied buildings, including residential dwellings. Beyond poor endurance in fire conditions, lightweight construction poses a problem in areas threatened by earthquakes, hurricanes, and tornadoes. Again, insurance covers some of the risk, and we see insurance-funded rebuilding after hurricanes in coastal areas. Fortunately, the rebuilding is required to follow tougher building requirements so that new structures may better withstand hurricane-force winds. Code developments follow disasters, such as major fires with loss of life and natural disasters. We rarely see code changes, however, after firefighters die. Is that because we assume firefighters are expendable? Given the way society and our economic market respond, that belief may well exist deep in our collective consciousness.

Ensuring the public's health, safety, and welfare is the intent of the model codes. Related areas include cultural and historical preservation as well as environmental protection. The codes in the United States do not provide explicit protection for firefighters engaged in fighting a fire covered by a code. This is not necessarily intentional, as code writers should have given this need some consideration as they drafted the code. Codes supposedly take the safety of both firefighters and building occupants into account.[1] Apparently, one umbrella covers all. The presumption is that firefighters are trained and equipped to meet the task, and the building codes inherently assume there will be no outside intervention by firefighters—it is a very convenient way to cover all bases. Code writers also presume that firefighters have situational awareness and know the potential hazards and level of risk. The presumption is proved false whenever firefighters die in up-to-code buildings. Provisions to mitigate stupid mistakes by occupants are built into our codes, but the same protection is not provided to firefighters. The presumption is then that firefighters do not make mistakes, but we know that to be terribly incorrect.

Bad decisions do not start and end on the fireground; in fact, most result from managerial decisions made at fire department headquarters and budget decisions at city hall. Failing to properly fund fire investigations and building inspections and follow up on code violations are at the root of many firefighter fatalities. Included in that list is the failure of some fire departments to identify and recognize hazardous buildings. If they do not recognize the hazards, they will undoubtedly fail to devise a plan of action to minimize the risk. Developing a plan of action for fire attack should be standard procedure. Some firefighters distort the concept, taking the attitude that because every fire is different, it is impossible to develop, let alone follow, operational guidelines. Having intimate knowledge about buildings is essential to situational awareness. Lacking action plans, operational plans, and standard operating guidelines or procedures is a failure worse than mere incompetence—it is neglect of duty. It is a failure of action that places the firefighter's life as a low priority. Incompetence and neglect of duty are not unique to fire departments. City building inspection and code enforcement offices are notorious for failing to do the right thing. Sometimes there is political pressure to go easy, but these offices sometimes fail to work in conjunction with fire officials. When both departments fail in their duties, civilians and firefighters are at risk.

Details of construction are important to ensuring safety. Structural elements themselves, as well as configurations of structural elements, have fire ratings that describe their ability to resist fire. The rating is time-based, such as a one-hour fire door, a twenty-minute door, or a two-hour firewall. Incompetent builders, cost cutting at the job site, or incompetent workers may compromise fire ratings. The job of inspectors is to ensure the proper installation of building, electrical, and plumbing systems to meet code requirements. Overall, structural integrity under fire conditions is dependent on fire-rated materials and assemblies maintaining their integrity and performing to their design. Occupant and firefighter safety depends on the building's ability to remain intact by defying the power of gravity. When structural components fail, gravity wins and occupants and firefighters lose.

Traditionally codes have been prescriptive in nature; in other words, they tell you what to do and how to do it. A new type of code, called a performance code, is gaining some interest. A performance code is nonprescriptive; instead, it specifies the safety goals and leaves the details up to the architects and engineers. The details include not only designing the building for its specified utility but also including safety in the equation. Designers and engineers are given the latitude to introduce new ideas, provided they include functional and fail-safe protection in the design. Each building design offers something new, and code officials have to learn to analyze the design features to determine compliance with performance goals. New Zealand has implemented performance codes that address firefighter safety as it applies to building fires.

In the United States, a new concept has been introduced in the discussion regarding firefighter safety: while firefighters are trained and equipped under certain conditions, codes should address their personal safety.[2] In this view, the code assumes that firefighters will not abandon a civilian or put another firefighter at risk. The code provisions assume that in certain dire moments, the firefighter's intense focus on search and rescue efforts may prevent him or her from recognizing threats coming from the building's design or construction. In other words, firefighters lose their total situational awareness because they are in a situation involving compound physical and mental stresses. This view also includes the assumption that firefighters will not call off their efforts until situations deteriorate to the point that their own lives are imperiled. This viewpoint acknowledges that fire commanders may pull their forces out of the interior when conditions are unsafe and no lives are at risk. In this mode, they will take a defensive position on the outside and press the attack from a safe vantage. The key for fire commanders and tactical officers is developing a seasoned knowledge of building design and construction, acknowledging of the hazards, and having an action plan.

Should performance-type building codes gain in popularity, the fire service will have to engage at a deeper level in order to adapt their traditional approaches to fighting fires. Buildings that meet both types of codes will require heightened situational awareness, pre-incident planning, data collection, and accessibility to databases from the field. The fire service will need to rewrite their rules of engagement. The matter of knowing the buildings you protect—or rather not knowing them well enough—is dramatically evident in the Worcester, Massachusetts, fire.

Early in the evening of December 3, 1999, the Worcester Fire Department received a call about a possible fire at the Worcester Cold Storage Building in the city's downtown area. The building was a nightmare waiting for a triggering event. It came when two transients (a man and a woman) using the building as a home lit some candles. A fire started, and they left the building. On arrival, there was light smoke coming from the building, and fire crews learned from someone on the scene that homeless people frequented building. The crews divided to enter the warehouse to locate the fire and search the building for occupants. Surviving firefighters do not mention any question about searching this monster of a building for people based on an unsubstantiated report. In fact, some of their apparatus in 1999 had a decal in side window of the crew's jump seats depicting a Tasmanian devil dressed as a firefighter and ready for action, with wording to the effect that "We are ready for action, no questions asked." The sticker itself is simply another example of fire service culture. One has to wonder about the statement "no questions asked" and how that slogan has affected department culture. Did an attitude of "no questions asked" serve to get six firefighters killed? By the accounts of the survivors, the idea of forgoing the search apparently did not cross their minds that evening.

The former cold storage facility was six stories high and windowless, with two different interior levels and a maze of passageways. The different levels posed a problem for the various fire crews inside the structure. They had entered through different doors and counted the floors they climbed, but they did not realize (or know) that the floors between the two sections of the building did not match perfectly. The matter of there being two different levels resulted in confusion in the radio communications among interior crews and the incident commander standing outside. Without a pre-action plan, without floor plans on site, and because neither they nor anyone in their department regularly checked the buildings in their district, the Worcester firefighters lacked essential information about the layout of the building. In addition, they did not fully appreciate the potential for the building's insulation to burn vigorously and produce highly toxic products of combustion. (The building incorporated various petroleum-based insulation materials, including rigid expanded polystyrene boards and blown-on polyurethane foam. These improvements served to prove the temperature performance of the building.)

As a serious fire developed, visibility inside the warehouse rapidly deteriorated, and disorientation set in as the firefighters lost their situational awareness. Lost in a hot, dark, confusing maze, they ran out of air. As other crews tried to help their comrades, the situation worsened, and the incident commander called for everyone to exit the building. There was a problem identifying who got out, and a new search was initiated. Eventually, three two-man teams perished in what grew to be an inferno. Lack of knowledge about the building, absence of a pre-action plan, absence of a policy for a fire in an abandoned building, poor accountability of personnel, and loss of situational awareness were the coincidental factors. It was a perverse scenario of fire service system failures stacked one upon the other, and it took six lives. Is it fair to criticize or second-guess the actions, inactions, and system breakdown that evening? I think it is fair. It could have been different if that fire department operated differently. All U.S. firefighters share a responsibility to remember these events and learn from them, because it should not happen again.[3]

U.S. firefighters can learn something about crew or personnel accountability from their counterparts in England. British interior crews always wear SCBA, and their status is constantly monitored by the incident command team. The command team continuously tracks every individual in SCBA for time on-air, predicted air usage, and approximate position. Knowing and monitoring positions is difficult, but the difference in England is that the interior crews, unlike U.S. firefighters, use guidelines when working under the most severe smoke conditions and in large-area buildings.

The guides have knots tied in series in a pattern to indicate direction, and they are spaced at frequent intervals. The knots indicate to firefighters wearing heavy work gloves, by touch alone, in which direction they are heading, such as inward or outward. Since more than one guide may be in use, each line is tagged with a metallic disc. Each disc has punched holes to represent its ID number. For guidance, U.S. firefighters usually rely on a hose line they have stretched into the building for extinguishing the fire, although some searches may be conducted without advantage of a hose line. Hoses have male and female couplings, and these serve to help indicate direction. A male coupling, unlike the female, has exposed threads. Put another way, the female coupling has protected threads to receive the exposed threads of the male end. The male end (with exposed threads) always points toward the fire or the direction of the water flow.

Thus, if a firefighter, through a gloved hand, discerns that the male coupling is pointing in the direction he is moving, then he knows he is moving toward the nozzle end of the hose line or generally toward the fire. An English firefighter may also tie off to the guide with a leader line if he or she is going to be working in one place. If a U.S. firefighter loses contact with the hose line and cannot recover it, he or she is in trouble. The biggest difference is that a guideline is a lightweight rope, and even multiple guidelines are easily deployed at one time. A hose line filled with water is heavy and not easily moved. The guideline system offers a viable, low-cost, low-tech option. Guidelines are easy to make, maintain, and replace. Branch lines tied off from the main guide allow search teams to deploy in more directions. You cannot easily create branch lines with a hose line. A hose line also extinguishes fire and thus protects the crew. A guideline can be burned through, but then so can a hose line.

Here is another interesting difference between the two services. In the United States, building exit signs are up high on the wall. In thick smoke, firefighters or other building occupants may not be able to see the sign. In England, the exit signs are lower so that someone crawling under the smoke might actually be able to see it. Thermal imaging technology has made major inroads in U.S. fire departments. A thermal imaging camera (TIC) is essentially a night-vision goggle with infrared-sensing ability, useful in low-light conditions such as smoke-filled buildings. The reflected infrared heat energy patterns show up on the screen for the user to see. Because objects have different heat-absorption characteristics, they present their heat signature in shades of color and patterns.

Therefore, in smoky conditions, a firefighter with a TIC can identify victims by their shapes and differences in their color shade from surrounding and nearby objects. With a TIC, fire crews can move quickly through thick smoke, but they must always remember their path of travel unless they have a hose line or use a guide to find their way back out. If they have located and recovered a victim, then getting him or her out quickly to medical care is imperative. The thermal imager also reveals fire extension behind walls, ceilings, and other void spaces by reading the heat reflected from surfaces. The U.S. fire service would do well to monitor time in SCBA, SCBA air management, accountability of personnel, and systematic searching to enhance situational awareness.

Every department has certain ways doing things. When they document their procedures and methods, the result is a set of standard operating procedures (SOP) or standard operating guidelines (SOG). Once again, there are two schools of thought: are they guidelines (only advisory in nature) or are they procedures (must do it this way)? Does it really matter? Do firefighters have better things to do than sit around and debate guidelines and procedures? One could discern a difference in philosophy on this important fire service subject in two types of scenarios. The method a department uses to stack a fire hose on fire trucks may be standardized (done one way throughout the city). We might call that a department SOP for hose loads. Then there are tactical evolutions that a department typically uses, such as when they respond to house fires as a two-piece engine company. Here the first engine to arrive goes straight to the house, and the second engine always reverse-lays a supply line from the first engine back to the nearest hydrant. The second engine connects to the hydrant and pumps the supply line to the attack truck. If the department has four-way hydrant valves, and the first engine has an option to lay in with a supply line, the second engine then simply goes directly to the hydrant and uses the four-way valve to hook into and pressurize. That sounds complex, but it is very simple, and because the crews have options available, we can call the evolution an SOG rather than an SOP.

There must always be latitude for judgment calls or common sense. Using the house fire example once again, let us say that the first truck turns into the street where the house is located. Pulling up to the house, the crew members spot a hydrant located just a hundred feet away on the same side of the street as the house. The company officer orders a four-way valve and supply line hooked up to this hydrant and instructs the second engine to come straight to the scene, go directly to the hydrant, and pump the line. In this scenario, the company officer used judgment and ordered the first crew to connect to the hydrant instead of waiting for the second engine crew to reverse-lay. In some departments, the officer making this call could be subject to a reprimand; in others, nothing would happen; and in others, the officer would have to justify the decision. In the last case, justifying a decision helps the senior officer understand the junior officer's tactical decision-making ability and makes it a learning opportunity instead of a disciplinary opportunity, as in the first case.

The knowledge and skills of a department's company officers are critical to that department's success. This fact is lost on many in the fire service. Also lost is the fact that chief officers require special skills and knowledge. In the United States, there is a long-held notion that every firefighter is a potential fire chief, just as any American can theoretically grow up to be president. There is equal opportunity to rise through the ranks. The same is true in the military; in theory anyone can go from a private to a general, but how often does that happen? It is relatively rare because being a general requires special skills and knowledge. Being a good soldier and being a good general are two different things.

In the nineteenth century, the training that existed for firefighters was limited to drills. No formal programs existed until early in the twentieth century. Certainly there were a few manuals of drills for firemen, but they were limited and strictly practical. The first college curriculum leading to a bachelor's degree with a fire protection focus came into being in the 1930s at Oklahoma State University. Drill schools were set up in the largest city fire departments at the turn of the century, but there were no state-operated fire academies until the 1930s. Around that time, the body of knowledge for fire protection and firefighting started coming together. In the early 1970s, a two-year college-level program known as fire science technology appeared. The intent of the associate's degree in fire science was to transform officer-level leadership in the U.S. fire service.

Before mass-produced buildings, builders used locally available materials. The methods used were also local and reflected materials, tradition, and heritage. In the first half of the nineteenth century, U.S. cities grew rapidly both economically and in physical size. People migrated to cities to take jobs in industry and manufacturing. Americans took to heart the idea of a free market economy. Even as it became evident that the urban poor were living under terrible conditions in substandard apartments with inadequate sanitary conditions, Americans expected the market to take care of the problem. Building design and construction methods were often haphazard. The widespread use of wood for framing and covering buildings inevitably fed urban fires and conflagrations. Serious fires involved blocks of buildings. Civic leaders and business interests decided to replace the hand pumpers and volunteers with steam fire engines and paid firemen. Though the United States' first part-paid fire service was in Boston, Cincinnati took the lead with steamers and full-time paid members. The process of transition, however, was slow and played out for more than half a century. During the same period, U.S. cities and towns experienced their worst fires. Fire insurance companies coped with disaster after disaster and wrestled with challenges to their economic survival. By the late twentieth century, volunteer fire departments operated and functioned in the image of their paid brethren because of the influence of fire insurance underwriters. Both firefighters and fire underwriters depended on trained fire protection engineers for the technical aspects of the complex system of fire protection.

6

FIREFIGHTERS, ENGINEERS, AND UNDERWRITERS

CHAPTER 17

New England Mills and the Factory Mutual System

As cities grew, both density of population and intensity of land use increased. The fire risks increased and placed a greater demand on fire companies. In turn, this placed a greater burden on the volunteers, and thus, more fire companies were organized. These companies began to specialize so that some supplied water with pumps and others provided ladders and hooks. The complexity of combating large urban fires required more firefighters. Losing the commercial district or a factory to fire severely affected local economies. In the United States' free market capitalist system, business owners were key leaders of the community. Investment in businesses, buildings, and stock produced profit; any threat to the ability to make profits caught the business owners' attention. Large-loss fires posed a threat to fire insurance company profits, spurring that industry to action. In general, business and insurance interests were involved in the evolution of fire services through their influence on politicians. The improvement in fire protection and the resulting decline in great fires came in part from improved fire services and public water supplies. However, these two factors alone did not turn the tide in the war on fire. Improved building construction methods and materials played a large, perhaps the most significant, role in controlling urban fires.[1]

The owners of the New England textile factories and their insurers were especially interested in fire protection, and they looked to England for answers. The industrial age in England began roughly fifty years before that in the United States. In the mid-eighteenth century, English mill owners began trying new forms of construction to create fireproof buildings in order to protect their investment. They adapted an old method known as vault construction that used bricks for floors and ceilings, thus making each room like a vault. Using wood frames as a temporary form over which brick was laid, they built barrel, groin, and intersecting vaults. Because vault construction required massive foundations to support the greater weight of bricks, they next experimented with using hollow tiles. The method was introduced in the United States in the early nineteenth century when the U.S. government used it to build munitions stores and customhouses. These structures were cold and dark inside, and although such buildings were fireproof, they proved too costly for most applications.[2]

The English realized these facts and quickly turned to the use of iron with masonry and brick. Iron columns and girders allowed open areas to be spanned in brick buildings. It did not prove to be superior in the construction of mills, so owners in England continued to construct mills out of heavy timbers through the first half of the nineteenth century. Problems with iron and brick fireproof construction surfaced quickly. In 1844 a fireproof mill building collapsed and claimed an estimated twenty lives, and in another mill, an entire section collapsed. One expert on fires questioned the fire safety of supposedly fireproof buildings.[3]

James Braidwood, the superintendent of London's firefighting force, pointed out the fallacy of fireproof construction. Although the building's structure was indeed technically fireproof, the inside was open and lacked compartmentalization, the vertical openings were unprotected, and the contents were combustible. An unchecked fire developing under these conditions could grow quickly. The heat and flames developed by such a fire would begin to attack, break down, and weaken the building's unprotected structural components. Under these conditions, exposed iron was vulnerable and could fail rapidly, with catastrophic and deadly results. Fire causes iron to expand. Expansion of structural elements causes displacement, which in turn causes the connections to fail. Firefighters also learned that cold water applied to hot cast iron could cause the metal to fracture. Braidwood cautioned his firefighters about these concerns.[4]

Unfortunately, the lessons learned in England about fireproof construction did not make the trip across the Atlantic. In the United States, as in England, the concept of a particular material being apparently fireproof continued to be confused with the concept of that same material exhibiting measurable resistance to fire. For example, cast iron may initially appear to be fireproof, but under prolonged exposure to a hot fire, it will fail. Thus, it lacks sufficient resistance to fire. By comparing the inherent degree of fire resistance in cast iron with that of another material, such as steel or masonry, measures of relative fire resistance are possible. By the 1850s Americans were producing iron for structural components. The U.S. government was a notable leader in experimenting with iron and brick construction because of the need to construct many new government buildings to meet the demands of an expanding country. Although the French and British did it much sooner, U.S. iron mills learned how to roll iron just in time for the Treasury Department's new building contracts. In the 1850s mills in New Jersey and Pennsylvania started producing solid, wrought-iron beams.[5]

The construction of iron and brick fireproof buildings took off in the United States just as it had years earlier in London and Paris. However, fireproof construction was a fallacy. The conflagration in the Tooley Street warehouse district of London in 1861 involved iron and brick fireproof buildings. Braidwood's death in the fire was tragic enough, but all too ironic, as the fire chief had denounced the iron and brick form of construction. He knew the dangers and had issued the standing order to his firemen that they were not to enter such buildings when fire heavily involved the structure. His successor, Eyre Massey Shaw, also condemned this form of construction. Shaw promoted fire-resistive construction employing heavy wood timbers. He felt timber construction provided warning to firefighters of impending collapse. In his book *Fire Surveys*, he prescribed limiting height and area, thought of masonry as an acceptable building material (provided no iron was used with it), and condemned stone as a material for building stairs.[6]

The durability of fireproof construction would be tested in Chicago and Boston. Shortly after the 1871 fire, Peter B. Wright, an architect and expert on fireproof construction, inspected the burned district of Chicago. He noted that iron columns had failed, but iron beams (used as cross members) held up better with only their lower flange showing deflection. He was most likely looking at wrought-iron structural components, which have less carbon than cast iron and so have poor compressive strength, but good tensile strength (resistance to bending). Cast-iron columns would likely have held up better and supported their load under the fire's attack. What Wright thought of next would have a lasting effect on structural fire protection. He conceived of applying a protective barrier to structural iron to give it resistance to fire. He suggested using cement, plaster, terra cotta, or artificial stone. This was a great leap forward. Wright had recognized that something being fireproof was not sufficient—it also had to offer resistance to fire and extreme heat. The fires of Chicago and Boston provided other vital lessons: Brick is better than stone in a fire, and iron is noncombustible but not fireproof. Also, high-pressure water from fire hoses causes hot stone to crack and spall, brick showed more durability from hose streams. What came of the experiences of burned-out buildings and cities was a debate over the benefits of fireproof construction versus fire-resistive construction. From the concept of fire resistance came the idea for slow burning or mill construction.[7]

The advocates of slow-burning construction came from the ranks of New England mill owners and the mutual fire insurance companies that insured the mills. Their study of the subject area was so intense that they developed guidelines for what they referred to as standard mill construction. Because they were insured with mutual insurance companies, the mill owners were also part owners of their insurance companies. This offered them a strong incentive to build and operate in a manner to maximize fire safety. Lower rates for premiums and fewer losses served to maximize profit. This profitable arrangement stood in contrast to insuring with a stock- or investor-owned insurance company, which meant rates were higher and profits went only to the stockholders.[8]

Differences in ownership aside, what set apart the New England mutual insurance companies was their focus on informed decision making using collected data about the risks they covered and their determination to minimize risk in the mills. The latter caused them to focus on the slow-burning characteristics of heavy timber construction. Stock insurance companies differentiated their risks by classifying the materials used in construction, as well as the use of the building or the activities that took place inside. Unlike the mutual companies, the stock companies offered their customers no incentive to build fire-safe buildings. By controlling hazards, the mutual companies lowered the potential risk, allowing them to charge lower rates and keep the revenue that they might have otherwise had to pay out to cover losses.

The stock companies had to maximize revenue to maintain sufficient capital on hand to cover losses. The market segment for the mutual companies (extremely high-risk factories) built to the mill standard actively practiced fire safety. The incentive for factory owners to practice safety was that they, as part owners in their mutual insurance company, would have to help cover losses for other mill owners out of their own pocket if the company had insufficient capital. In return for low rates (often 25 percent), the mill owner agreed to follow the safety rules of the mutual method and allow regular inspections by insurance inspectors. The inspectors from the mutual companies (called mill men) went beyond simply inspecting; they offered safety advice. The principal requirements involved keeping the mill clean of dust and combustibles, having watchmen on duty, and having an on-site water supply source.[9]

In 1850 the mill owners around Lowell, Massachusetts, hired James B. Francis to oversee fire protection for their mills. Francis had experience managing water supply systems. The safety record of the Lowell mills was such that the owners did not carry fire insurance. Their mill complex was protected by its own water supply system, including force pumps driven by a water wheel. The force pumps filled the gravity-flow roof tanks that fed the sprinkler system and standpipe fire hoses used for fighting fires inside. The pumps could also feed the standpipes and the yard hydrants. The standpipes had been in the Lowell mills since 1823. The complex of mills had a private water system even before Lowell itself. The sprinkler system was a dry system consisting of open-hole, perforated pipe. In the event of a fire, an employee would open a valve so that water could flow into the open hole piping to extinguish the fire. The Lowell mills had exterior stair towers and ladders on the outside walls. Fire doors separated and thus protected the opening from the stair tower into the mill. The exterior ladders and platforms provided an access from which firefighters could work. In 1828 the mill owners agreed to connect the piping from their respective mills to form a grid system to improve volume and pressure characteristics. They also installed standpipes in the stair towers for fire hoses. These were American ideas, not seen anywhere else at that time. Another strong feature was the plank flooring laid directly on the girders to eliminate the need for joists.[10]

The idea for large-dimension planking laid on top of girders for flooring came from observing the characteristics of heavy timbers in fires. As flames attack wood surfaces, charring occurs to a certain depth. The char forms a protective layer, in turn offering some resistance to the effect of the flames for a short while. This added time results in resistance to fire; this is how the concept of slow burning became associated with large dimension timber. Heavy timber and built-in fire protection features came to be standard mill construction, as defined by the associated factory mutual companies.[11]

In his 1882 book, *The Fire Protection of Mills*, Charles J. H. Woodbury, an inspector for the factory mutual companies, defined standard mill construction as follows: Such construction included exterior brick walls with piers between the windows to support the ends of floor beams; floor beams were large timbers sixteen to twenty-five feet in length on eight- to ten-foot centers; and the floor beams rested on cast-iron caps set atop wooden posts. Subfloors were planks three to four inches in thickness with grooves and splines. Finish floors were one-and-a-quarter-inch boards with grooves and splines. Roofs were near flat and constructed like the flooring using two-and-a-half- to three-inch boards covered with gravel, duck cloth, or tin roofing. Inside, compartmentalization separated vertical and horizontal spaces. No hollows, voids, or concealed spaces were permitted. Fire protection features included water buckets, sprinklers, and standpipes fed through a system of tanks and pumps. There was often a fire brigade. Fire hoses had clear access to all parts of the underside of the roof and floors because there were no joists to break the stream. Sprinklers were also more effective without joists. The standard mill was almost unique to the New England states, particularly Massachusetts.[12]

In 1886 John R. Freeman, an engineer, went to work for Charles Woodbury and the associated factory mutual system. Freeman's work in hydraulics set the foundation and basic formulas for the practice of fire protection engineering and fire service hydraulics. Today, as in the past, firefighters use Freeman's calculations. The tables of friction loss in pipe and discharge from nozzles developed by Freeman stand the test of time, appearing today in fire service textbooks. Like Woodbury, Freeman promoted the fire prevention and protection philosophy of the factory mutual system. He conducted tests of fire equipment to determine its hydraulic characteristics. He developed and published tables of data related to friction loss in piping, hydrants, fire hoses, and nozzles. The tests also included tests of fire streams to determine their reach at various angles of elevation and nozzle pressure. Line illustrations of hose streams arching upward toward buildings appeared in fire service texts and manuals for many years. Freeman and Woodbury were a good team, with Woodbury specializing in building materials and construction and Freeman in fire protection equipment.

The debate over fireproof versus fire-resistive construction, seemed to favor the slow-burning method. The late nineteenth century saw slow-burning buildings erected outside of New England and for buildings other than mills.

The standard mill was relatively safe from fire because of many special features as well as the owner's attitude toward safety—it was more than the method and material used for construction. This key point was overlooked with costly results. Because some slow-burning buildings burned in unexpected ways, the method under investigation. Critics often ignored the fact that the rules for the standard mill construction method were violated. The fire chief of St. Louis denounced slow-burning, as well as fireproof, construction in 1892, claiming that slow burning is more dangerous because the buildings fail to collapse quickly. He apparently believed that exposing adjacent buildings to fire was less of a threat than a collapsing building violently disgorging fire and burning brands into the area. The early twentieth century would see the first real advances in fire-safe construction, and nearly the entire century passed before the two concepts of fire protection and life safety came together.[13]

The leap forward came with technology that combined reinforced concrete and a skeleton frame to achieve both fire resistance and compartmentalization. Add the essential features of built-in fire protection, and U.S. cities could now have very tall buildings covering a small area and still offer a degree of safety to the occupants. The work of the association of factory mutual insurance companies made a lasting impact on fire protection and fire service in the United States. Fire underwriters of the stock insurance companies finally embraced the proven results employed in the factory mutual system and implemented many of its ideas.[14]

Urban fires also affected stock insurance companies. Their underwriters grew to be cautious about the types of buildings they would cover. As it turned out, people in rural areas and isolated small towns found it impossible to buy fire insurance. The idea of forming mutual insurance companies for local coverage took hold, and state legislatures passed laws to legalize local mutual insurance companies. The states were regulating the insurance industry because they generally feared that companies would not pay claims from big fires. The stock insurance industry was also beginning to form compacts, in which companies agreed to set rates. This occurred early in the era when businesses were forming trusts, and there were antitrust sentiments developing among lawmakers. A number of states passed anti-compact laws to prevent stock insurance companies from forming compacts to set rates. These laws threatened the stock companies' existence. The insurance companies were not necessarily to blame for all of the United States' fire problems, although their policies and practices had created much of the problem. Moreover, central to the problem was an attitude in the United States toward fire and insurance. The potential for profit by arson was very real, but only a minor effort to fight the crime was made because arson was so difficult to prove in a court of law. In fact, without a confession or credable eyewitness, the chance of a conviction was, and still is, remote. Undetected arson was probably costing insurance companies of the day a considerable amount of money.

Two things help fight arson: investigation of fires to determine cause and collection of data about the causes of fires. Arson-for-profit is thought of as a victimless crime because no one is physically hurt, and the building owner collects the insurance money. The stock insurance companies offered a plan to state legislatures: the insurance companies would agree to allow the states to levy a tax on them if, in return, the states would pass laws to require investigation of the cause of fires, collect data on the causes of fires, and prosecute more vigorously the crime of arson. The effect of this reform lives on today: the money the fire insurance companies pay the states funds state fire marshal programs and firefighter-training programs and provides revenue to volunteer fire departments. Today the states have fire marshals to collect data and investigate fires.

The stock insurance companies eventually agreed to fund the NBFU, making it a permanent entity. The NBFU in time merged with another group, the AIA, and formed the ISO, which met special needs for insurance industry data. This era saw the introduction of electricity, and electrical fires emerged. The reform effort resulted in the creation of a testing laboratory for electrical uses and products, called the Underwriters Laboratory, which is still in existence. Many new ideas came from those involved with the NBFU and Underwriters Laboratory, as well as from fire chiefs of larger cities. One of the ideas resulted in the formation of a private organization dedicated to the interests of fire protection and fire safety.

From this organization grew the NFPA, founded in Boston in 1896. In the following decades, the focus shifted from large-scale fires involving blocks of buildings to fires in single buildings. Americans began to see their fellow citizens die in large numbers inside presumably safe fireproof buildings. In Chicago the fireproof Iroquois Theatre burned, taking 602 lives in 1903. In New York the fire-resistive Triangle Shirtwaist Factory fire claimed 146 lives in 1911. Both buildings withstood the fire and saw later use. While the NBFU continued to protect fire insurance interests by conducting inspections of fire departments and water systems (grading them according to their capacity), fire protection experts took a closer look at why people were dying in building fires. Their attention quickly focused on egress, or exiting, from buildings.

Fireproof or fire-resistive construction alone was not enough, not even with automatic sprinklers installed. As early as 1905, the NBFU had formally published their recommendations for building construction. These recommendations eventually became the National Model Building Code. In 1913 the NFPA convened a technical committee to study emergency egress. By 1923 it had drafted a building exit code. This code would eventually become the Life Safety Code. The influence of those early pioneers lives today in a wide range of standards published by the NFPA and the Fire Suppression Rating Schedule of the ISO.

CHAPTER 18

Fighting Fires:
From Art to Science

The modern fire service and the profession of engineering owe a debt of gratitude to the work of two men familiar with the 1872 great fire in Boston: engineer John R. Freeman and fire chief John S. Damrell. Freeman provided the basic engineering concepts of fire protection, and Damrell played an instrumental role in leading the development of the country's first National Model Building Code. The work of both men directly contributed to the end of the conflagration threat. Freeman, born in Maine and educated at the Massachusetts Institute of Technology in Boston, first worked for the Essex Company as an assistant to hydraulic engineer Hiram Mills. This apprenticeship laid the foundation for Freeman's future, giving him the conceptual and practical understanding of flowing water in piping systems. He joined the associated factory mutual system of companies in 1886 and, with Charles J. H. Woodbury, helped define the fundamentals of fire protection. Freeman started his studies at MIT in September 1872 and no doubt witnessed firsthand the devastating effects of Boston's great fire in November. If he was not a witness to the fire itself, then he certainly saw the destruction afterward and learned about the water supply and pressure problems that plagued Chief Damrell's firefighters during the battle to save Boston.[1]

At that time, civil engineers who designed public water systems saw the potential to supply domestic, commercial, industrial, and fire protection needs from one water system. However, they needed a method to compute both the amount of water for fire flow needs and the optimum pressure at a hydrant's discharge outlet. They determined that the needed fire flow from the system correlates directly with how many fire hose streams firefighters put into use to control a given fire. Because the size of the fire is a function of building size, a city's needed fire flow depended on the types and sizes of buildings in its most developed or built-up area. Also critical to that calculation was the population, because the greater the population, the larger the city and the larger the congested or built-up area. The civil engineers believed that a high density of people and buildings equaled congestion and therefore an elevated risk of fire. They finally decided to concentrate on a population-based formula. Of the many formulas offered, Freeman's was the experts' choice on the subject. If they had based the risk strictly on the size of grouped buildings, they would have probably underdesigned the new systems. The supply of water for domestic needs drives the design of water systems, as it usually represents the highest demand. Properly engineered systems easily meet the additional needs for commercial, industrial, and fire protection. Because of Freeman's experiments with fire hose streams, he determined that the standard fire stream was one flowing at 250 gallons per minute delivered at a pressure of 40 to 50 pounds per square inch gauge. Freeman correctly determined that a formula based on population would work in most cases, but the system needs had to be carefully determined so that the system met all user needs. To give some idea of what the formula predicted, systems supplying cities of up to 1,000 people would need to supply 2–3 standard fire streams; for populations over 200,000, the system would need to supply 30–50 standard fire streams. No matter the size or population of a city or town, Freeman recommended ten streams, or as large a proportion thereof, for any compact cluster of large, high-value buildings. In 1892 he published his findings in the *Journal of the New England Waterworks Association.*[2]

In that report, titled "The Arrangement of Hydrants and Water Pipes for the Protection of a City against Fire," he pointed out the fundamental difference between the needed flow for domestic use and the needed flow for fire protection. According to Freeman, what he called fire draft required a concentration of water at specific points, whereas domestic draft was itself simply a problem of distribution. For a domestic system to be able to supply large quantities for fire protection at specific locations, distribution systems would require engineered design rather than a predetermined schedule of pipe sizes. Freeman estimated through hydraulic calculation the type of flows anticipated

for fire draft and determined that six-inch-diameter pipe was the absolute minimum size of pipe for residential districts and that eight-inch pipe was only
suitable when part of looped-grid network of pipe. He discouraged random
placement of hydrants, pointing out that additional hydrants should be strategically located in such a manner as to enable the fire department to concentrate
fire hose streams at specific blocks or groups of buildings. He recommended
250-foot spacing for hydrants in commercial and industrial districts and 400–
500 feet in residential areas. His most important recommendation was that
the needed flow for fire protection purposes be in addition to the needed flow
for domestic service. For gravity-fed systems, he suggested a six-hour reserve
held in reservoirs or standpipes to be available to meet both domestic and fire
flows simultaneously. For systems with pumps, he called for a one-hour reserve.
The early work of Freeman and other engineers remains the standard for water
distribution systems.[3]

In the early 1890s, the NBFU started a program to survey the fire and
water departments of the largest cities. This effort grew to include all cities and
towns after the Baltimore fire of 1904. Building on Freeman's work, NBFU
engineers developed a more precise formula for calculating needed fire flow in
high-value commercial districts. This formula also relied on population to
determine fire flow needs. NBFU engineers estimated the needed fire flow for
areas outside the commercial district. In 1948 NBFU engineer A. C. Hutson
recommended a new formula based on a building's construction type and size.
The formula eventually became the standard for determining needed fire flow,
now published in the ISO Guide for Determination of Required Fire Flow.[4]

Almost as soon as solutions came for many long-standing fire protection
problems, a new one captured everyone's attention—the introduction of electricity. In 1881 at the factory mutual system, Woodbury reported the installation of electrical lighting at sixty-five of their insured mills and, in six
months time, twenty-three fires of electrical origin resulted. Thomas Edison, who
advocated for direct current as the standard for electric circuits, recommended
the installation of insulated wiring and fusible elements into wiring circuits to
provide protection from overly high draws of current. Electric lighting was
featured at the 1883 World's Fair in Chicago; however, the installation created hazards, and an expert had to be summoned. William Henry Merrill, an
electrician from Boston, went to Chicago to examine the installation. Merrill
was the first to suggest product safety testing for electrical components under

controlled laboratory conditions. With the backing of insurance underwriters, Merrill opened his testing lab and called it Underwriters Electrical Bureau. It would later become Underwriters Laboratory. The next step was a set of standardized rules for the installation of safe electrical systems. In 1882 the NBFU adopted a set of guidelines developed by the New York Board of Underwriters. However, within the next five years, there were four other sets of rules in the country and no consistency between them.[5]

The same problem existed for sprinkler installations. In 1896 a group of fire and electrical safety experts in Boston decided to form a nonprofit association dedicated to solving fire safety problems. The new organization was the NFPA. The NBFU eventually joined as a member, as did the Underwriters Laboratory. In the mid-twentieth century, they opened membership to the fire service. The mission has evolved over 110-plus years to include advocacy for scientific-based consensus codes and standards, supported by research and education on fire and related safety issues. Today the NFPA headquarters is in Quincy, Massachusetts. The organization thinks of itself as a place of ideas, concepts, and ways to organize in the fight against fire.[6]

The Puritans who settled Boston brought a strong work ethic and built the city into a commercial and shipping center. The settlement featured modest, closely packed, lightly built structures of wood, often with thatched roofs and open-hearth cooking inside. Fires were a problem and, when they grew large, required the help of the entire community to extinguish. Participation in bucket brigades was a moral responsibility and a civic duty. Each householder was required to provide a leather bucket. Long poles with a hooked end, along with chains, were the means to pull down burning structures to expose the fire and stop it from spreading. They acquired hand-tubs equipped with mounted nozzles for pumping a stream of water directly onto fire. The tub's reservoir was filled by the bucket brigade. The wooden tubs, referred to as fire engines, measured roughly three feet by one and a half feet; they had an open-top reservoir and a piston pump. Operated by hand, the piston pump forced water out through the nozzle under pressure, producing a focused stream of water that could be thrown a reasonable distance.

Peter Stuyvesant formed the rattle watch to patrol New Amsterdam. The watch was a group of fire wardens whose purpose was to enforce local fire prevention measures and to sound the alarm when a fire broke out. In 1718 the Boston Fire Society formed for the general but limited purpose of rendering aid only to other members. The concept came from London. It was later the basis for Benjamin Franklin's volunteer fire company in Philadelphia. Those small villages and towns of early America—their survival threatened continually by attack, starvation, and fire—would come to see the volunteers of the local fire brigade as the embodiment of civic life and virtue. Currier and Ives captured this image in a nineteenth-century print series of firemen. Speaking before the Charitable Fire Society in Boston in 1809, Alexander Townsend said, "Volunteers in the service of beneficiaries are the glory of civilized life." At the heart of the volunteer culture was the machine—the engine. For the community, a good deal of civic pride centered on the local fire engine and the men who pulled the machine. A town could boast of the bravery and devotion to duty of its volunteer company. Mottos such as "We come, we conquer" and "Fear not, we come" were typical. The competition among individual firemen and between companies was fierce. The bravest firemen were revered. Companies strove to be the fastest to respond and first to put water on the fire. Boston began using primitive fire engines in 1678; the devices had handles, and men carried them to the scene, where a bucket brigade formed to fill the tank. The next evolutionary shift in fire-engine design was the work of William Hunneman of Boston. His engines were well designed, well constructed, and cherished by the firemen who used them.[7]

In 1823 Hunneman built No. 16 for Boston. Named the Torrent, it drafted water through a suction hose placed into a water source. The design would soon relegate the bucket brigade to history, as these new engines could draft their own water, with the handles pumped by the firemen. The pump discharge outlets of No.16 accepted hoses with nozzles to attack fires directly or as part of a relay of pumps that moved water over a distance to the fire scene. Response time was critical for quelling blazes quickly and for first-water bragging rights. The competition between companies grew fiercer. Some companies plotted and hatched their plans to thwart or slow down the response of rival companies. Adoration of the public, self-image, and pride were at the root of the trouble. Musters or competitions served the purpose of channeling the excess energy constructively. Parades were very popular events with firemen and the public. Some let the adoration of the public get the best of them. Firehouses received exceptional care, with open house events held frequently. Volunteers could wear their prized uniforms at parades, musters, and community events. Their enthusiasm helped them do their job, which was difficult and at times dangerous. Without moral leadership, though, things could and did some-times turn negative. Exuberance and pride sometimes morphed into prejudi-cial behavior toward those seen as lesser or as lacking the qualities to be members of the department. The volunteers affirmed their manhood through their sense of pride in what they did and the consequent heroic status con-ferred by their fellow citizens. Anything that challenged or minimized their manhood may also have challenged their status as firemen. That firefighting was hard, difficult, and dangerous was a part of the allure. Anything perceived as lessening the work and danger thereby lessened their manhood, at least in their eyes. This perhaps is why they so resisted technological innovation.[8]

A nineteenth-century official of New York City said, "I esteem the fire department as one of the most difficult departments into which to introduce any changes or innovations, even though they may be exceedingly important, and command themselves to common-sense judgment of every man." The reluctance carried through every innovation, from bucket brigades to hand tubs, from hand tubs to hand-brake pumpers, from brake pumpers to steam-ers, from hand pulled to horse pulled, and on to modern-day motorized appa-ratus. Boston firefighters disdained anyone who poured water on a fire from a perceived safe distance. Real firefighters wanted to be in close, right in the smoke, next to the flames. Often the display of manhood trumped common sense. The hand tubs and brake pumpers would eventually evolve into the two-piece engine company (pumper and hose wagon) and the hook and ladder.[9]

Trust in fire hose increased with improvements in design and manufacture. Two Philadelphia firemen patented riveted leather hose in 1817. Hose before this was sewn by hand. The new hose met a strict standard of quality, includ-ing the best heavyweight leather, copper wire for rivets, and specifications for number of rivets. A fifty-foot section without couplings weighed in at sixty-four pounds and could withstand a pressure of two hundred pounds per square inch. Some innovations, like the new hose, made sense and were adopted.[10]

During the American Civil War, some volunteer fire companies enlisted as a group to serve in the battlefield ambulance service. The idea of the ambu-lance was taken back home after the war, and some volunteer companies began to run an ambulance from the fire station. Another new idea found acceptance: the fire alarm telegraph system. Most likely this was because it made a quicker response possible, and more calls for help could be turned in and responded to. The fire alarm boxes started a new tradition that lives on in some form today, with bells remaining in some fire stations. The chief of department could also use the system to direct firefighters. Each district had a specific identifying number—the signal from the alarm box traveled by wire to the central fire alarm office. There it was decoded, revealing the approximate location of a possible fire within a fire district. The alarm office staff would then transmit an alarm signal to the respective fire stations. The bells struck the number of the box activated. To strike an alarm meant to send the signal for a fire through the telegraph system. Firefighters today will still say strike an alarm even though the bell system is now gone in most places. Interestingly, only reputable citizens and police officers had keys that allowed them to open a street fire alarm box and turn the crank handle. Regular firemen were not issued fire alarm box keys. Later, a spring-loaded mechanism replaced the crank, allowing an alarm to be sent by pulling down on a handle. A telegraph tap key was then added to the box, allowing a fire chief officer to tap out a message to the alarm office. The officers might report a false alarm, place a request for additional alarms, or report a fire under control. An alarm system wired to an air horn or factory whistle alerted volunteers. This would provide a loud outside signal to all volunteers that there was a fire and they should respond. This was not needed if the department was paid and firemen lived in the fire stations. Telephones, 911 emergency call centers, two-way radios, and private central-station alarm companies eventually relegated the telegraph system to history.[11]

The culture of the U.S. fire service is rooted in the old volunteer system. In place where there is no volunteer history, there is little resistance to change. In these places, fire service is almost like any other job. What did the volunteers stand for? What did they believe in? How did they perceive themselves, their department, and their mission? What influenced the decline in public esteem for volunteers? How did they go from civic-minded heroes to rowdies in just a few decades? What happened to the leadership within the companies and departments?

CHAPTER 19

Volunteers to Paid Firemen

Those who study the history of firefighting in the United States often forget that we still have volunteers. In fact, the majority of U.S. firefighters are volunteer, paid-call, or part-time. Once historians move beyond the transition to paid firemen, they ignore the volunteer service as if it suddenly disappeared, replaced by a paid service professionally administered with bureaucratic structure, created as a result of the influence of the fire insurance underwriters. In reality the deeply rooted concept of civic virtue and the idea of independence held by the founding volunteers carried over to the paid service in the great transition. The Franklin volunteer system started roughly in the 1730s and persisted in urban centers into the mid-1800s, a span of about 125 years, or the first era of the volunteer.

The next few decades, into the late 1800s, saw the volunteer system modernize. Independent volunteer companies began to reorganize through charters or incorporation as volunteer fire departments under limited municipal government control. This system continues to this day as more volunteer departments now require financial support to continue providing essential emergency services to small towns and cities. This period of a hundred-plus years constitutes the second era of the volunteer. Just as the core volunteer traditions carried over to the paid service, the new philosophy and technology of firefighting used by the paid service saw adoption by the reformed volunteers during the twentieth century. The two services organized on similar lines, used similar equipment, fought fires in similar ways, and used the same training programs.

179

It is difficult to discern a difference when watching a fire fought by both paid and volunteer firefighters. Both services manage to exert a great degree of control over their own labor and thus feel that what they do is a calling, something very special and unique, not merely a job.[1]

The events of September 11, 2001, forever changed the fire service. This point marks the end of the second volunteer era and the start of the third era of the volunteer. In the near future various pressures—social and economic—will force the volunteer service to become even more like the paid service. If it fails to adapt, the system as we know it will die. If we separate the early volunteers from the U.S. social system, thus isolating them for examination, the traditional stories and mythology regarding the volunteers seems to make sense. They were manly rowdies who liked to drink and run with the engine. This behavior got them into trouble, and so paid forces replaced them. It makes for a very colorful story that sells well but does not fit neatly with modern history.

Common sense should inform us that more than fighting and drinking was afoot. A deeper look into the social and economic changes taking place reveals something about the demise of the nineteenth century volunteer. We owe it to the contemporary volunteers who serve their communities faithfully to tell an accurate story. Some of the early culture still exists with volunteers, but it also exists in the paid service. The volunteer firefighters of today reflect the paid service more than they reflect the old volunteers. The volunteer culture has evolved with the loss of financial independence; there is usually oversight by local government, but the volunteers receive training and grants, and they interact with paid forces frequently. The volunteers' pride, energy, enthusiasm, and courage live on. Their ranks are thinning, but those remaining may be the best of a long line.

In *Cause for Alarm*, Amy S. Greenberg put forth a theory of the decline of the nineteenth-century urban volunteer based on social change. She supports her case through examination of fire company rosters, meeting minutes, city directories, and other sources. Her story rests on the premise that the demands placed on volunteers in the shift from an agrarian to a commercial-industrial economy compromised the ability of individuals to volunteer.[2] This theory has social and economic undertones and appears valid—so much so that it may also help explain the decline of the late-twentieth-century volunteer. Family survival now often depends on two incomes, which reduces time available for volunteering; coupled with joint childrearing responsibilities, responding to a fire can be next to impossible. Factor in requirements for training, both in firefighting and EMS, increased call volume, and higher physical demands, and it is very easy to begin to understand the reasons behind the second decline.

Greenberg takes us to the antebellum period, the era of Jacksonian democracy, party politics, and economic transition; it was a time of rapid growth of cities and change from an agrarian lifestyle to a commercial one. The United States was entering the industrial age. Greenberg uses two Currier and Ives lithograph print series titled, "Life of a Fireman" and "American Firemen," to show how people of the times viewed their volunteer firemen. The prints reflect a composite image and an ideal. In no way can they reflect the typical volunteer of the time. Many individuals with varying capacities and motivations made up the volunteer company. The prints were more likely intended to honor the collective spirit, courage, and sacrifice of the U.S. fireman. Greenberg writes that the clergy fights one devil and firefighters the other. Police officers never had a Currier and Ives series, perhaps because neither Nathaniel Currier nor James Merritt Ives served as a police officer. Currier, however, did serve as a fireman. The prints epitomize the volunteer as selfless, heroic, respectable, and masculine.[3]

Between 1977 and 2009, an average of 111 U.S. firefighters died while on duty each year. That figure excludes the 9/11-related FDNY fatalities; if we include the 343 New York firefighters, the average becomes 122 per year.[4] Whether it was a collapsed building, flashover, rolled-over tanker, heart attack, or fall from a ladder while changing a light bulb at the station, they died on duty. We do not memorialize every one of these people. We celebrate the heroics, especially when firefighters die in clusters of 6, 9, or 343. Moreover, while society initially celebrates the quality of a sacrificed life, the ceremony is short-lived. Only the families and those who serve really remember the fallen. The profession of firefighting is changing, but it retains elements of the warrior culture. That culture is essential to order and discipline in the face of chaos, and the essence of firefighting is bringing order to chaos. It is what makes possible what we do and why we continue to die in the line of duty. The push for safety can go too far, and overburdening firefighters with national standards will eventually dilute the warrior culture. The factions pushing for change today in the fire service—whether through risk management, stop-loss control, job creation, job preservation, or homeland security—gain their impetus from social and economic motivations. How else can we explain why someone wakes up one morning and decides they have had enough of the volunteer fire service?

In the post-revolutionary era, U.S. heroes were the founders, the minutemen, the soldiers of the Revolutionary War, and the volunteer firemen. Greenberg questions the rationality of this view in light of the circumstance of their ultimate demise. The volunteer firemen were not heroes in the classical mode but were men serving their city. Newspaper accounts of the period portrayed them as heroes, however, and overlooked their frequent inefficiency and ineffectiveness. As Greenberg implies, how trustworthy are the newspaper accounts of firefighting of that era? The situation then was not unlike today; the media spins firefighters and all firefighting as positive, unless they are telling the story of a firehouse sex scandal or a case of firefighter arson. Experience reveals situations in which fire departments screw up, badly, and the media reports the fire in a positive manner even with heroic undertones. What aggravated the post-colonial volunteers, as it does now, was an attitude of contempt toward them that played out through unwanted intrusion from outsiders and attempts to control their actions. The volunteers' demise came when local government, justifiably concerned about fire protection, tried to look into the affairs of the volunteers and met steadfast resistance and hostility. The early volunteers actually believed they were untouchable warriors whose intentions were unquestionable. What they did was very difficult, challenging work, and they felt they did their best. When circumstances overwhelmed their capacity, they felt failure but believed they alone could solve the problems. The politicians and businessmen saw it differently.[5]

The urban volunteers, in some instances, poured their department funds into building and outfitting firehouses worthy of warrior heroes. This apparently irked some politicians, newspapermen, and businessmen. Perhaps the real threat was not extravagant spending but rather the growing political influence of firefighters. The membership of the first volunteer companies included the highest classes of citizens. It stands to reason that in urban areas, as the fires grew worse, the type of person who volunteered changed. If departments are mirror images of the community, what is important is the type of person representing the community. If the new membership was mostly from the mid- and lower levels of society, they represented a new threat to traditional political power. The fire insurance industry was also a factor. Paying out fire loss claims takes profits away from stockholders. Controlling fire losses saves money. The fire insurance industry had a stake in the ability of volunteers to provide fire services. If the volunteer system showed any potential for failing, fire insurance interests would take immediate notice. Recall the situation in

London, where the fire insurance companies provided both coverage and protection. The invention of the steam engine, which led to the appearance of steam-powered, water pumping engines for fighting fires, also played a role. The decline of the volunteers began in the 1830s and 1840s, possibly because the composition of the membership of their organizations included too many new immigrants. Certainly no one questioned their devotion to duty or their bravery, but their attitudes, behaviors, and customs came into question.[6]

Another interesting theory, which deserves to share a place alongside Greenberg's, holds that the real motive for replacing low-cost volunteers was not their problems (relatively manageable ones if there was a desire to do so), but instead the potential for political patronage through appointments to paid city positions in the fire department.[7] Paid fire departments were certainly more costly, an expense difficult to justify if the volunteers were extinguishing fires successfully. Fire insurance cost money, and yet people saw a need to purchase coverage to protect investment in property and business. The fire insurance industry pushed the hardest for conversion of the volunteers to paid forces they presumed they could control and manage, which was in their best financial interests. They deemed a paid force more reliable. They were obviously looking at the situation in London, where insurance companies funded and ran the fire brigade. However, by mid-century the insurance industry turned over firefighting responsibility in London to the metropolitan government; in the United States, government would also take over control of firefighting to help the floundering, mismanaged stock fire insurance companies. Thus, insurance companies pressed their case, with politicians painting the volunteers as a threat to order, the common good, and economic advancement.[8]

The stock fire insurance companies had no interest in preventing fires; they just wanted to control them, making things predictable enough to ensure regular profits. Under attack and with their character, manhood, and motivation in question, the volunteers quickly degenerated sufficiently so that no one questioned whether conversion of the force was in everyone's best interests. The steam fire engine manned by sober, reliable, controllable, paid men was the fire insurance industry's solution to maintaining profits. What the insurers failed to appreciate in their calculation was the propensity for concentrated groups of wooden buildings in urban locations to burn violently. They would soon learn that combustible cities, even with steam fire engines and paid firefighters, still burned down.

The influence of the fire insurance industry and urban reformers had a lasting influence on how the U.S. fire service was organized, deployed, and equipped. The type of buildings in a city and how they burned also dictated how the fire service was equipped and operated. Very frequently, politicians who were influenced by special interests ignored the valid recommendations of the firemen. Our fire service might have developed differently if not for the early influence of the fire insurance industry. The motivation of that industry was purely self-centered and focused on profits. The businessmen ignored experts, made bad decisions that resulted in the loss of millions of dollars, and saw cities nearly destroyed by fire. Architects and builders built some beautiful but flawed buildings, sometimes out of pure ignorance and sometimes in spite of knowledgeable fire advice. In this regard, hundreds of people died in building fires for the sin of ignorance. Through it all was the firefighter's singular devotion, eternal vigilance, and courage under trying conditions. Despite it all, despite the past, Americans still knew it was the firemen and the fire department they could always depend on in a dire emergency.

Whereas volunteers relied heavily on courage, strength, and common sense, paid firemen needed advanced technical skills and knowledge. The paid firemen (engineers) who ran the steamers were expected to have the technical and mechanical skills to understand, operate, and repair the engines. They also needed a basic understanding of hydraulics. This was the new job of the fire service. Hosemen and laddermen, whether volunteer, paid-on-call, or paid full-time, performed the same function, had the same duties at a fire, and did the same jobs. The interest of the fire insurance industry was the deployment of steam engines drawn by horses, assignment of paid firemen to stations, and expectation of a quick response to fire alarms twenty-four hours a day, seven days a week, 365 days of the year. The motorized fire apparatus replaced the horse-drawn steamer, and firemen became firefighters and received better working conditions, but the vested interest of the fire insurance industry continued to dominate and shape the U.S. fire department into the next century. As the paid service evolved from and borrowed characteristics of the volunteers, so has the modern-day volunteer evolved, by accepting training and adopting the methods of the career service.

CHAPTER 20

Legacy of the Combustible City

Learning to combat the great fires of the nineteenth century forged a fire protection industry and revolutionized firefighting in both Europe and the United States. Great fires arose largely owing to the economic expansion and rapid urban growth associated with industrial age factories and mills.[1] Society used its experiences in combating great fires to create a body of knowledge related to fire-protection and building-construction methods. This body of knowledge formed the foundation for a professional fire service. The paid fire service retained some of the volunteer fire culture and a fire suppression mentality. Had the U.S. fire service looked across the ocean to European fire departments, things today might be different.

Fire prevention is not a new concept. The fire service likes to talk about prevention but cannot seem to make it a top priority. This is partly a failure of leadership within the fire service, but also culpable are the numerous appointed and elected officials of town and city governments who fail to meet their own moral obligation to reduce fire losses in property and human life. This negligence is typical of American politics. The ideas of modern fire prevention date to seventeenth-century Europe, where various provisions were issued for the use of noncombustible building materials, the restriction of open fires, and the use of fire at night. In Amsterdam in particular, city leaders adopted a proactive stance toward fire prevention when they accepted the revolutionary ideas of Jan van der Heyden.

The city of Amsterdam was wealthy and had a population of roughly 200,000 inhabitants. Construction in the city was a mix of newer buildings using brick and older buildings of wood, including dwellings, trade shops, and warehouses. In such a congested and combustible area, the threat of fire was real. Fire service histories of U.S. origin rarely mention van der Heyden and his revolutionary ideas for fire prevention and protection. The artist and his brother Nicolaes would serve as fire master generals (fire chiefs) of Amsterdam for many years; they introduced new methods and new tools for combating fires, including fire hose, an improved fire pump, and aggressive firefighting methods, all of which were essential to fire protection in a built-up environment.[2]

A German, Otto von Guericke, first developed the vacuum pump, and borrowing on this idea, van der Heyden designed and built a series of portable fire pumps for use in Amsterdam. The Germans, French, and English, and later William Hunneman in the United States, improved on van der Heyden's pump design, building similar models. Interestingly, the British Royal Navy and the East India Company favored van der Heyden's lighter, portable pumps over those of their own English pump builder, Richard Newsham. Van der Heyden's contributions are significant, even if mostly forgotten. He analyzed building fires and the existing firefighting methods used in the city and reached a radical conclusion that there was a better way to fight fires. He convinced city leaders to replace the old fire engines of the city with his newer models and to use his new fire hose. Leather fire hose stitched together with thread was one of his inventions. An artist, he rendered fire scenes and drew fire attack plans, which led him to propose a radical reorganization of the city's firefighting force. He also had an engineer's mind and a knack for analysis, design, and organization. He developed novel approaches such as using suction pumps, pressure pumps, and crude fire hose to move water a distance from a source to a fire.[3]

In 1690 he documented his ideas, his work, and the results in the world's first known firefighting manual, the *Brandspuittenboek* (*Fire Engine Book*). Because he submitted fire incident reports after every serious building fire to the city's mayor and council, his claims are substantiated by their acceptance into the public record by the businessmen who held the political leadership in Amsterdam.[4] His new ideas and inventions replaced unorganized efforts, inefficient bucket brigades, and crude pressure pumps with fixed nozzles. In the narrow and crowded streets of Amsterdam, the old firefighting method involved getting close to the building on fire and attempting to hit the flames with water. Fires that were near windows were easier to extinguish than those in back rooms, especially the kitchen (where many fires started), which were impossible to reach with buckets and fixed nozzles. In these cases, the old method involved using hooks to pull apart the building's exterior sheathing. The building and fire were thus opened up to the air and frequently erupted into an even greater fire. Van der Heyden was the first to come up with a practical solution for transporting or relaying water to a fire using a hose. He observed that bucket brigades in a direct attack did little to help and proved effective in checking fires only in those cases when fire reached open space or double-sized walls between buildings. With his improved version of the suction pump, he could move water from one of the many canals in the city to a pressure engine up to a thousand feet away. If the suction proved inadequate owing to a high lift, organized bucket brigades made up of a dozen or so firemen could supply the source pump with water. At the fire building, pressure pumps supplying long fire hoses with attached nozzles allowed firemen to aggressively carry the attack forward inside to the heart of the fire. Attacks on the flames using fire hoses from adjacent buildings also helped control the fire. No longer did buildings have to be pulled apart with hooks.[5]

His fire hose (Dutch: *slang*) was made of stitched leather with the lengths coupled. Fire hose became critical to fire suppression because it made it possible to transfer water over a distance using pumps. The hose permitted firemen to advance inside buildings (close to the seat of the fire), to apply the water directly on the fire through a nozzle (also known as a branch pipe) attached to the end of the hose. Modern firefighters refer to this method or tactic as a *direct attack*. (The direct attack is in contrast to the *indirect attack* method, which uses a fog-nozzle to inject a fine spray into the super-heated atmosphere of a room to generate steam and smother the fire.)[6] Van der Heyden did not provide detailed construction drawings for his stitched leather hose. The experience of English and later U.S. firemen with stitched leather hose was not positive. The stitching tended to rot because the neat's-foot oil or tallow used to keep the leather pliable allowed hoses under pressure to burst at the seam. If van der Heyden's hose was truly practical in his time, he either knew something about making good hose, or the hoses were tended and maintained with great care by the firemen. The latter is probably true, given van der Heyden's conscientious approach to firefighting. The breakthrough in fire hose design came from two Philadelphia inventors, James Sellers and Abraham Penneck, in 1818, when they obtained a patent for riveted leather hose. In

1824 James Braidwood revolutionized Edinburgh's firefighting system by advocating that firemen with hoses enter burning enclosures to direct streams of water onto the seat of the fire.[7]

The second edition of *Fire Engine Book* included city ordinances for Amsterdam's fire service under the fire master generals, the van der Heyden brothers. The van der Heyden plan was composed of sixty districts, each with a firehouse, a fire engine, related equipment, two fire masters, and thirty-six firemen. Of the thirty-six men assigned, two served as assistants to the firehouse fire masters, who carried a baton with a municipal insignia to show their authority. The firemen each received a small brass disk with the municipal insignia stamped on one side and the opposite side stamped with a fire engine and a number from one to thirty-six, to serve as a badge of appointment. Upon arrival at a fire, the fireman handed over his badge to the fire master in command to prove his presence and entitlement to his premium for serving. Only six engines responded to an alarm of fire; this allowed other engines to be available for simultaneous fires in their respective districts (which occurred frequently in very cold weather). The fire master generals summoned additional engines from nearby districts, if required. Each of the fire masters, their assistants, and all appointees received a printed card with the streets of their assigned area, as well as the location of all fire buckets. The duty of the fire masters required that one go to the water source to direct that operation and the other go to the fire scene to direct that operation. Four firemen—selected for their skill with ladders, climbing to high places, and knowledge of building construction—advanced the hose line to the heart of the fire.[8] Since the nineteenth century, the fire service has employed similar principles. The concept of deploying fire forces in a logical manner, first developed in Amsterdam in the late 1700s, mostly withstood the test of time, at least in those places where decisions about placing fire stations and engines are not politically motivated.

The success of the factory mutual insurance companies of New England showed the value of fire prevention, fire-resistive construction, ample water supplies, and the installation of fire protection systems. Politicians responsible for leadership of U.S. towns and cities never grasped the concept of a comprehensive approach to preventing fires. Business and industrial leaders had a mixed response to fire protection, usually seeing the matter as one of suppressing fires only and less of preventing fires. Business leaders of nineteenth-century United States pressured politicians for paid fire departments equipped with steam-powered fire engines and the horses required to pull them. In the same era, European cities typically provided effective fire protection with fewer paid staff, relied heavily on portable pumps, and purchased fewer steam fire engines than comparable U.S. cities. This approach was effective and cost less money, conferring benefits owing in part to better construction methods, fire-resistive building materials, narrower streets, and a public that gave thought to fire-safe behavior.

Notification and passing of the alarm of fire to the fire brigade constituted the most critical shortfall of firefighting systems up to the mid-nineteenth century. Fires do not necessarily become raging blazes or grow to a conflagration. Even those with serious potential may be snuffed out in an early stage of development if proper action is taken. Beyond firefighting tools and a water supply, the key to fire control starts with prompt notification, a quick response, and a plan of attack. The early nineteenth-century fire brigade had the resources but lacked the means of communication over a distance. The solution to this problem came from another artist, an U.S. painter named Samuel F. B. Morse. While few know of Morse as a painter, more are familiar with his invention of the telegraph. His idea came to him from his experience in Paris, where the semaphore system of flags waved from atop hills permitted messages to be sent over a distance, provided one had a line of sight.[9] In 1844 Morse used his invention to send a message over wire. He thought of his invention, based on his experience in Paris, as something most likely to be used by the government or military. A Boston doctor, William Francis Channing, had another use for the telegraph—as a system to transmit fire alarms. In 1852, with the help of Moses Farmer, Channing built the first municipal fire alarm system and installed it in Boston.[10] From this point, the stage was set for rapid advances in the capability of fire departments to respond quickly.

The larger and heavily mechanized fire departments employed in the United States fit with the mentality and culture of nineteenth-century Americans. The idea that conditions in the United States were different and that Americans were a different people motivated them to shun or ignore European methods. The cities of New York and London looked at each other as competitors. London's fire brigade saw itself as the prototypical professional fire service, and indeed it was by all accounts. This was owing to the tangible efforts of the two great London fire chiefs, James Braidwood and Eyre Massey Shaw. Although not fully appreciated by the U.S. fire service, both men initiated radical improvements and wrote fundamental texts on fire protection concepts that have withstood the test of time. As the New York skyline climbed upward at the turn of the century, a succession of city fire chiefs finally took a stand and executed their professional duties with diligence by improving the city's fire department, not only addressing the suppression of fire but also putting the highest priority of saving lives.

Hugh Bonner, Edward Crocker, and John Kenlon proved to be extraordinary leaders and fire chiefs of the highest caliber in the FDNY. Bonner was an early advocate for standpipe systems and automatic sprinkler systems in New York's high-rise buildings. All three pushed for the high-pressure water system in lower Manhattan, a system that by 1908 allowed high-volume, master-stream attacks using hose wagons equipped with deck pipes, fed directly from hydrants, without the need for steam fire engines to add pressure. Crocker and Kenlon wrote on the subjects of fire prevention and protection. In 1910 Chief Kenlon asked for funds to create a Bureau of Fire Prevention, but building owners stood firm against paying for fire safety. It would take the tragedy of the 1911 Triangle Shirtwaist Factory fire in the Asch Building, in which 146 workers died, to persuade city politicians to approve Kenlon's request.[11]

While Kenlon paid tribute to the progressive European ideas of fire prevention orientation and formal education for firemen and fire officers, he still favored the traditional U.S. approach.[12] At the time, fire chiefs in the United States placed the emphasis on fire suppression, on-the-job training, and working one's way up the ranks. Even today, climbing the ranks to chief officer is the rule rather than the exception, a college degree in fire science notwithstanding. The argument went (and goes) that only a person who has worked in the ranks can acquire the necessary body of knowledge to lead a fire department effectively. This logic runs counter to the experience of urban fire services in England, France, and Germany, not to mention the experience of the military, with their academies for training officers to lead troops into combat and command ships in battles. It is more likely that the Americans were simply rejecting the social class structures of Europe, implied by having educated officers as commanders of fire departments, rather than men who moved up through an open system. Although departments in both London and New York shared a fire service mission to suppress fires and save lives, a difference in methods and practices existed because of inherent structural, geographic, and philosophical factors. Even in the twenty-first century, these factors continue to shape fire service delivery and result in various differences between departments and countries.

To his credit, Kenlon criticized the firefighting veterans' tired axiom that no two fires are the same, and thus rules and procedures for firefighting are useless. This adage is still bandied about today by a few old guards. Kenlon held to fundamental fire attack principles such as confinement of fire, exposure protection, and prevention of loss of life, as well as massing one's forces at the point of greatest danger.[13] He discussed at length the European ideas of minimizing fire damage caused directly by the application of water and of allowing fires in the upper levels and roofs of masonry buildings to burn of their own accord rather than suppressing them with water. He saw this method as something that U.S. fire chiefs could never condone.[14] In Kenlon's time, the problem of hotel fires in fireproof buildings was beginning to surface; he noted that at the time of his writing, a hotel fire occurred every thirty-three hours in North America.[15] It would take several decades of deadly hotel fires before firefighters and fire protection officials realized the dangers of unprotected vertical openings and rapid flame spread across highly combustible vertical surfaces in fireproof construction. They then used this knowledge to draft updated building and fire code provisions for hotels, as well as new technology to ensure the life safety of guests. Hotels became safer places, but not until hundreds died from fires in hotels.

The shortsighted attitudes and beliefs behind the creation of combustible cities and the perceived right to construct buildings as one pleased, as demonstrated in the nineteenth-century United States, remain entrenched today. Far too many property owners, architects, builders, developers, and planners wish to see buildings and cities built to their specifications for style or budget purposes. Architects and builders perfected the so-called fireproof building only to discover later that many hundreds of people died in fires in these buildings. The fear is that U.S. consumers will not willingly pay for their own safety. Perhaps there is some truth in that. The perception is that fires happen only to other people, and if by chance it ever happens to me, fire insurance exists to cover the loss. The model building codes and national fire safety standards contain provisions for fire and life safety. Yet, government officials, sensing political ramifications, resist efforts to adopt and enforce the safety requirements. In our largest cities, it is usually an enforcement issue; in our smaller cities and towns, it is an adoption issue. In either case, it is a public policy and political issue. Americans simply do not like others, especially the government, telling them what to do. They like to believe that government regulation is the problem and that the market will solve problems. When it comes to our safety, this model does not seem to work. The consumer seeks to pay only what they deem reasonable for their needs. If they do not believe they will have a fire, why pay for an automatic fire sprinkler system? Instead of assuming moral responsibility for fire safety, we transfer the duty for protecting life and preserving property to the fire service. If that is not enough, we routinely question the fire chief's request for adequate funding of the fire department or shun it totally and assume that local firefighters will fulfill their duties regardless. We have confidence in the fire service's ability to make do with what is available, and therein is the basis for the firefighter's "can do at any cost" attitude. This attitude exists because of the unique dedication and motivation of the people who are the fire service; firefighters can and do get it done, as best they can, with what they have, under any given circumstance. This is a level of commitment and service seen in only a few occupations.

The administrators of a small town or city will regularly replace its fleet of police vehicles but will question the need to replace a twenty- or twenty-five-year-old fire engine. The assumption is that the police need the latest model cruiser with the newest features, but firefighters can make do one or two more years with an old but serviceable fire engine, even if it is less safe than a more modern vehicle. Too often, the fire chief goes along because he or she likes having steady employment. The members of the fire department may not like decisions based on political expediency, but they have little choice in the matter. At the next fire, they will be there, with their outdated truck, doing their job. Because of their collective skill, knowledge, commitment, and dedication, they make the system work, in any circumstance, with whatever tools and equipment they have available. In large part, this is how they have earned the accolade of hero.

Given the public celebration of the firefighter as a hero, it is easy to see the firefighter coming to believe and possibly even thriving on the idea that the hero is invincible. Is this machismo the principal reason why women have found it difficult to penetrate the inner culture of the U.S. fire service? Women represent less than 4 percent of the total paid firefighter positions in the United States today.[16] This entrenched mind-set (call it a suppression culture) of the male-dominated U.S. fire service is rooted in the nineteenth century and remains powerful today. Efforts to transform the suppression culture with one that embraces occupational safety (call it a safety culture) is causing a rift among

U.S. firefighters. The rift is rooted in self-imagery, ego, and the nineteenth-century belief in the fireman as hero and firefighting as the epitome of manhood.[17] Popular culture in the nineteenth century held the fireman as a hero, even placing him higher than the soldier in terms of a moral masculinity; firemen saved lives while soldiers took lives.[18] This concept is the social contract between firefighters and the people they protect. The only way to reset the fundamental mind-set of the U.S. fire service is to change the job itself and change the mission of the fire department in a radical manner. Again, this is a public policy issue of the highest order. The fire service cannot do this of its own accord without a change in policy or lawmaking at the local, county, and state levels. The rules and tools to address the high cost of suppressing fires manually exist—they only need be adopted and diligently enforced. The key principles of change include education, engineering, and enforcement, and the fire service should be responsible for all three and supported by enforceable laws and regulations.

Overhaul the firefighting profession by building more fire prevention into the job. Give the firefighter more opportunity and responsibility to prevent fires through public education and occupancy inspection programs. Too often, these tasks receive only passing recognition; instead, make them fundamental duties. Instead of showing new firefighters how to extinguish a fire, have them study how fires start, teach them to determine the cause of fires, and teach them to educate the public in fire safety. Only after all of this experience should they attend an academy to learn the actual methods of firefighting. In the initial fire prevention and education phase, the new recruit might also receive emergency medical technician training, basic emergency management, disaster response, and related risk management skills. The introductory phase of training might also include basic wildland fire protection, limited hazmat incident response training, and the use of spatial mapping technology such as GPS and GIS software. Training recruits for fire attack embeds the fire suppression mind-set. The job of a firefighter is changing, continually evolving into a response to multiple hazards. It was slowly moving in this direction before the attacks of 9/11, and afterward the pace quickened. Federal emergency management policy dictates the use of local fire services in large-scale emergencies. The firefighter is on the front line, responding to everything that constitutes a public emergency.

The nineteenth- and twentieth-century firefighter fought fires. In the twenty-first century, the firefighter will be a multi-hazard emergency services technician, responding to various emergencies with a strong focus on risk management.

Urban areas will continue to need highly trained, aggressive firefighters, but the vast majority of the United States has everyday emergencies and problems of a different nature, which require multitalented responders. Firefighter training in the United States is front-loaded with fire suppression, when in fact fire suppression should come last and prevention first. The training should continue to broaden in scope to prepare recruits for response to many types of hazardous situations. The expected product of today's exhaustive training regime is a fully trained and certified firefighter/EMT. This is impractical for many reasons. New members will not retain even half of what they learn in recruit training unless they use the skills and knowledge frequently. This fact proves itself in the military, which uses a structured approach combining assignment to duty with periods of advanced training after basic seasons the warrior. This method allows soldiers to assimilate needed skills slowly under supervision. Law enforcement training follows a similar approach, with new officers receiving supervision and mentoring by an assigned training officer. We should restructure fire service training accordingly and prepare recruits with basic training followed in stages by advanced courses with mentoring. This will serve to help prepare and indoctrinate the new firefighter.

The fundamental issue regarding the fire service is the level of danger in fighting fires. What is the degree of risk involved and hazard mitigation available to reduce the odds of injury or death? A recent NFPA study, covering thirty years of firefighter fatality data, provides the trend in the numbers and hardly depicts a crisis in occupational safety and health within the fire services of the United States. Over thirty years, the number of firefighter deaths annually has dropped by one-third. Falls from apparatus (which are preventable) have declined significantly and rarely occur. Cardiac-related events—the number one cause of firefighter deaths—declined by one-third in thirty years. The second leading cause, motor vehicle accidents, indicated no discernable trend up or down in the total number. The victims in the accidents were mostly volunteers driving personal vehicles, water tankers, tenders. The only notable rise—and one for concern—is training-related deaths, which should be at zero. On average, we should expect just over a hundred volunteer and full-time firefighters to die on the job yearly. Given that many of these deaths are preventable (vehicle accidents and cardiac events), the prevention effort should focus in those areas. The basis for the new safety culture in firefighting rests, in part, on the fact that the number of actual fires is decreasing, so fewer firefighter should suffer injuries and fatalities. But, in fact, even though fires are in decline, the actual number of calls responded to is steadily increasing. If the cycle of emotional stress that induces cardiac events begins at the onset of the alarm, and the number of alarms increases steadily, then it stands to reason that cardiac events will continue to be high. Along the same line of reasoning, if the number of calls increases, then there will be more responses by volunteers in their private vehicles, meaning continued exposure to accident risk. There is no doubt that we can and should focus firefighter safety concerns on cardiac health and safer driving.[19]

What constitutes "safe" and what does occupational safety actually mean? Many jobs have higher on-the-job mortality and injuries than firefighting. Is a policy of zero tolerance for firefighter line-of-duty deaths practical or achievable? Is it possible to determine what number of deaths in an occupation is acceptable and thus how far safety regulations may be pushed? A starting point is research into the rates of occupational deaths and injuries among firefighters in other industrial countries, making adjustments as needed to maintain validity in the comparison. Making firefighting a safer occupation through occupational safety and health mandates is a public policy matter with moral and ethical components. These components are critical elements of fire service culture, and firefighters must not be excluded from the discussion, but they should not be allowed to thwart change. Lost in the push to make a risky job safer is the responsibility to the individual person whom a firefighter is committed to protecting and the expectations of that person for successful rescue. The social contract between Americans and their firefighters is the assumption that a firefighter will do everything necessary to save a life, even at great personal risk. Arbitrary revision of the social contract puts at risk the hard-earned image and standing of firefighters held by the public.[20] Is it time for Americans to stop assuming that firefighters will willingly risk death trying to save them?

There is an alternative to the culture war between the advocates of occupational safety and the advocates of aggressive fire attack. The idea is simple: keep the aggressive attack but apply practical rules of engagement and further reduce the number of serious fires through an emphasis on fire prevention coupled with adoption and enforcement of existing national standards for life safety. We have all the necessary rules and tools to create safer living and working environments. Make all firefighters responsible in some way for public fire safety education and occupancy inspections. Use the inherent respect for firefighters to enhance fire prevention efforts. The result will be fewer serious fires and fewer events in which firefighters may be injured or killed.[21]

The fire telegraph, the steam fire engine, and pressurized water systems were great and remarkable inventions that provided the technical pieces of fire defense for the combustible city. The virtue, courage, bravery, and sheer physical ability of firefighters, volunteer and paid, provided the essential human connection between these great inventions. The inhabitants of the nineteenth-century city envisioned their firemen as the epitome of immaculate manhood in an age when heroes were needed.[22] They needed a dependable hero in a time when everyday life seemed to be in perpetual transformation on societal and technological terms. The work of the fire department was labor-intensive, and the job of the fireman required knowledge of using technology to control physical forces. The art or craft of suppressing a fire at its heart has not really changed much since the time of van der Heyden and Braidwood. The fundamental rule of firefighting is to locate, confine, and extinguish the fire. The radical ideas of building safer buildings, preventing fires, and saving lives pushed forward by progressive fire chiefs such as Eyre Massey Shaw, John S. Damrell, Edward Crocker, and John Kenlon live on. The contribution of John R. Freeman to fire stream hydraulics and Lloyd Layman to the science of attacking interior fires formed the foundation of modern fire protection science. In time, the United States learned what Europe had learned about constructing fire-resistive buildings and developing building, life-safety, and fire prevention codes, which in turn reduced inherent risks and thus raised the level of safety for urban inhabitants, at least where the codes are adopted and enforced.

Those remarkable individuals who pushed forward the field of fire protection deserve far more recognition than they receive from the U.S. fire service. In too many places in the United States, the firefighter is more concerned with how many fires they attend than how many they prevent. The fire services in many developing countries put more emphasis on prevention than does the United States. The U.S. fixation with manual fire suppression is costly, deadly, deplorable, and shameful. The technology available today in the form of automatic life safety, quick-response sprinklers, sensitive fire detection, and alarm notification can help cut losses to fire, and yet we routinely shun them as too costly or unattractive.

Today the fireman is a firefighter. Female firefighters prove their capacity and capability daily in the occupation and earn promotions to the officer ranks and position of fire chief in our largest cities. The influence of the females in the profession will one day reach a tipping point, and history will have to acknowledge that the male-dominated firefighter culture has withered away.

The new fire threat is the wildland-interface fire that threatens life and property at the fringe of urban and suburban development. This form of fire erupted in Maine in 1947 and is now a threat where developed areas meet wildland and forest. Fighting these fires is akin to a military campaign involving ground and air forces that require planning, organization, and logistic support to attack multifaceted fire fronts, often extending over hundreds of miles. Setting broad public policy related to the environmental impact of such fires, developing a strategy of containment or full-control suppression, and determining the cost of the decision challenges the thinking of environmentalists, fire protection specialists, and politicians.

In the early twentieth century, the Municipal Grading Schedule of the NBFU almost defined the deployment of fire stations, types of apparatus, and the equipment used by local fire services in the United States. Its descendent, the ISO Fire Suppression Rating Schedule, influenced fire services in the later part of the same century and is mostly outdated and out of touch with the real needs of the twenty-first-century fire department. Fire department accreditation involving internal analysis and auditing by a third party is the trend of the future. Blanket acceptance of NFPA standards as the de facto model for the fire service nullifies local control and subverts representative government. For the fire services to reach true professionalism they need more than full-time, paid staffing; they also need self-analysis, self-regulation, and periodic third-party auditing and evaluation. The fire services must also become more proactive in prevention and risk management.

To maintain a viable volunteer fire service, individuals in such service must receive some form of financial consideration for the challenging work and dedication required to serve for extended periods of ten to twenty-five years. We need a quantitative economic model for the fair-market value of the services and sacrifices of being a volunteer emergency responder. The reward may be in the form of a length-of-service award, stipend, or per diem pay based on the hours they work. We need leaders for the volunteer service selected on merit and capability, not elected based on popularity or personal opinion. Similarly, advancement in the career fire service must also be by merit promotion. Communities should use a risk-based approach to strategic fire and emergency planning, not a standards-based, one-size-fits-all scheme. National standards have their proper place in codes and product development. In that manner, you achieve a universal standardization that can result in a general cost reduction.

The lesson of the nineteenth century, the urban United States' crucible of fire, is that we have not conquered fire and likely never will. The best defense involves education, engineering, and extinguishment through the dedication of educators, the technical knowledge of fire protection engineers, and the courage and eternal vigilance of firefighters.

"I have no ambition in this world but one, and that is to be a Fireman.
The position may, in the eyes of some, appear to be a lowly one; but those who know
the work which a Fireman has to do believe his is a noble calling."

—Edward F. Crocker, Chief of Department, FDNY, 1899–1911

Notes

Introduction

1. Adrian Tinniswood, *By Permission of Heaven: The True Story of the Great Fire of London* (New York: Penguin Group, Inc., 2004), 48–52. Prior to the Great Fire of 1666, organized fire protection planning at the local level was nearly nonexistent and consisted of a few fire pumps mounted on carriages purchased either by private companies or groups of individuals, with no enforceable plan to operate the equipment in event of fire. The assumption was that all upright citizens would volunteer for fire duty.

2. Eric L. Bird and Stanley J. Docking, *Fire in Buildings* (London: Adam & Charles Black, Ltd., 1949), 187.

3. Ibid., 187–189.

4. Momar D. Seck and David D. Evans, "Major U.S. Cities Using National Standard Fire Hydrants, One Century after the Great Baltimore Fire," National Institute of Standards and Technology, August 2004, 12, http://www.fire.nist.gov/bfrlpubs/fire04/PDF/f04095.pdf.

1. Origins of Organized Fire Service

1. Robert S. D'Intino, "Volunteer Firefighter Recruitment and Retention in Rural Pennsylvania," Center for Rural Pennsylvania, May 2006, 6–15, http://www.rural.palegislature.us/Volunteer_firefighters06.pdf.

2. Michael J. Karter Jr. and Gary P. Stein, "U.S. Fire Department Profile through 2007," National Fire Protection Association, November 2008, http://www.doi.idaho.gov/SFM/FDProfile_2007.pdf.

3. David Von Drehele, *Triangle: The Fire That Changed America* (New York: Atlantic Monthly Press, 2003), 154. A worker trapped in the Asch Building during the Triangle Shirtwaist Factory fire and waiting for the fire department ladders to reach her recalled her mother telling her, "In America they don't let you burn." This implies the belief that the firemen in New York City attempt to rescue people trapped by fire and smoke.

4. Charles R. Simpson, "A Fraternity of Danger: Volunteer Fire Companies and the Contradictions of Modernization," *American Journal of Economics and Sociology* 55, no. 1 (1996): 17–33. This research paper discusses the modern volunteer fire department and related issues, especially what motivates volunteers. Being a volunteer firefighter does not imply that one is somehow less capable or experienced than a paid member. A paid position staffed for tours of duty, twenty-four hours on and forty-eight hours off, may miss fires on days off and thus lose the working experience. On the other hand, volunteers may actually attend more fires because of their implied availability: twenty-four hours a day, seven days a week. Being paid or volunteer does not provide any distinction regarding firefighting knowledge, skills, and ability, though some would like to see it do so.

5. Robert Bruegman, *Sprawl: A Compact History* (Chicago: University of Chicago Press, 2005), 18–44.

6. James Braidwood, *Fire Prevention and Fire Extinction* (London: Bell and Daldy, 1866), 6–9 and 96–100.

7. James Braidwood, *On the Construction of Fire-Engines and Apparatus, the Training of Firemen, and the Method of Proceeding in Cases of Fire* (Edinburgh: Bell and Bradfute, and Oliver and Boyd, 1830), 88–90.

8. Ibid., 17–18.

9. Ibid., 135–140.

10. Ibid., 15–17.

2. Firefighter Culture

1. Dennis Smith, introduction to *Report from Engine Co. 82* (New York: Warner Books, 1999).

2. Lisa Snowden, "From Sweden, a Critical View of U.S. Firefighters," Firehouse.com, August 8, 2007, http://cms.firehouse.com/content/article/printer.jsp?id=56147; Brian A. Crawford, "To Die For," *Fire Chief*, 2007, 41–46; and Jamie Thompson, "FDNY Lt. Says Fire Service Needs Culture of 'Extinguishment Not Safety,'" FireRescue1, April 23, 2009, http://www.firerescue1.com/firefighter-safety/articles/483861-FDNY-Lt-says-fire-service-needs-culture-of-extinguishment-not-safety/.

3. Zac Unger, *Working Fire: The Making of an Accidental Fireman* (New York: Penguin Press, 2004), 47–55.

4. Neil Munro, "Our Heroes Turned Out to Be Cowboys in New York Attacks," *Oakland Press Online*, 2002, http://www.firehouse.com/news/2002/7/24_Ppaper_orig.html. This reporter was widely castigated for his comments. In truth, many people, including some veteran firefighters, thought this to be the case but withheld public comment.

5. William Pessemier, "Developing a Safety Culture in the Fire Service," *International Fire Service Journal of Leadership and Management* 2, no. 1 (2008). The writer of this article is a member of the Department of Political Science at Oklahoma State University and was the fire-EMS incident commander at the Columbine High School shootings in Littleton, Colorado.

6. Freeman Dyson, "Part I: A Failure of Intelligence," *Technology Review*, November 1, 2006, http://www.technologyreview.com/InfoTech/17724/?a=f; and Freeman Dyson, "Part II: A Failure of Intelligence," *Technology Review*, November 1, 2006, http://www.technologyreview.com/computing/17847/page1/?a=f.

7. National Fallen Firefighters Foundation, "The Firefighter Life Safety Initiatives Adoption and Implementation," Everyone Goes Home, 2008, 5, http://www.everyonegoeshome.com/kits/volume3/CD1/Final_IIW_Guidebook_v._5_for_PDF_4.24.08.2.pdf; and Pessemier, "Developing a Safety Culture."

8. Ibid.

9. Scott Ritter, "Fire Commentary: Picking up the Gauntlet," Fire Engineering, January 15, 2008, http://www.fireengineering.com/index/articles/display/317164/articles/fire-engineering/featured-content/2008/01/fire-commentary-picking-up-the-gauntlet.html.

3. Contemporary Firefighting

1. Paul Grimwood, *Euro Firefighter* (West Yorkshire, England: Jeremy Mills Publishing Limited, 2008), 2–4.

2. Ibid., 4.

3. Ibid., 8. In quantitative engineering, the definition of risk is Risk = Probability of Accident x Losses per Accident.

4. Ibid., 6–15.

5. Jean MacDougall-Tattan, "Firefighters Fear for their Safety," *Haverhill Gazette*, January 31, 2008, http://www.firehouse.com/news/news/massachusetts-firefighters-fear-their-safety.

6. J. Gordon Routley et al., "City of Charleston: Post Incident Assessment and Review Team: Phase II Report," City of Charleston, http://www.charlestoncity.info/shared/docs/0/sofa%20super%20store%20report%20may%2015%202008%20final.pdf.

7. Jim Knight and Lesia Kudelkja, "Report of S.C. OSHA: Findings in June 18, 2007 Charleston Sofa Super Store Fire," South Carolina Department of Labor, Licensing and Regulation, http://media.charleston.net/pdf/OSHAreport.pdf; Joseph P. Ripley, "Report to the City: Tragic Fire of June 18, 2007" (Charleston, SC: Mayor of the City of Charleston, 2007); Routley et al., "City of Charleston: Post Incident Assessment and Review Team: Phase 1 Report," City of Charleston, October 16, 2007, http://www.charlestoncity.info/shared/docs/0/charleston_fire_department_phase_one _report.pdf; and Routley et al., "City of Charleston: Post Incident Assessment and Review Team: Phase II Report."

8. Grimwood, *Euro Firefighter*, 25–32; and Randy Okray and Thomas Lubnau, *Crew Resource Management for the Fire Service* (Tulsa, OK: PennWell Corp., 2004), 65–83.

4. Great Fire in Pittsburgh

1. Franklin Toker, *Pittsburgh: A New Portrait* (Pittsburgh: University of Pittsburgh Press, 2009), 3–9; and Brian O'Neill, *The Paris of Appalachia: Pittsburgh in the Twenty-First Century* (Pittsburgh: Carnegie Mellon University Press, 2009), 11–13.

2. J. Heron Foster, *A Full Account of the Great Fire at Pittsburgh, on the Tenth Day of April, 1845; with Individual Losses and Contributions for Relief* (Pittsburgh: J.W. Cook, 1845), 18.

3. Donald E. Cook, "The Great Fire of Pittsburgh in 1845," *Western Pennsylvania Historical Magazine* 51 (1968): 127–129.

4. Ibid.

5. Foster, *A Full Account*, 3–10.

6. Ibid.; and Cook, "The Great Fire," 127–129.

7. Foster, *A Full Account*, 50.

5. Fire in the Built Environment

1. U.S. Fire Administration, "Fire Death Rate Trends: An International Perspective," Federal Emergency Management Agency, May 1997, http://www.usfa.dhs.gov/downloads/pdf/statistics/internat.pdf, fig. 1.

2. Rita F. Fahy et al., "Firefighter Fatalities in the United States—2009," National Fire Protection Association, June 2010, http://www.nfpa.org/assets/files/PDF/osfff.pdf; Marilyn Ridenour et al., "Leading Recommendations for Preventing Fire Fighter Fatalities, 1998–2005," National Institute for Occupational Safety and Health, November 2008, http://www.cdc.gov/niosh/docs/2009-100/pdfs/2009-100.pdf; and Lori Moore-Merrell et al., "Contributing Factors to Firefighter Line-of-Duty Injury in Metropolitan Fire Departments in the United States," International Association of Fire Fighters, August 2008, http://www.iaff.org/08News/PDF/InjuryReport.pdf.

3. U.S. Fire Administration and National Fire Data Center, "Fire in the United States 1995–2004, Fourteenth Edition," Federal Emergency Management Agency, August 2007, http://www.usfa.dhs.gov/downloads/pdf/publications/fa-311.pdf, tables 1, 27, and 39–48.

4. National Fire Protection Association, "Smoke Alarms in Reported U.S. Home Fires," http://www.nfpa.org/assets/files/PDF/SmokeAlarmsFactSheet.pdf.

6. Fire and Human Behavior

1. Public/Private Fire Safety Council, "White Paper: Home Smoke Alarms and Other Fire Detection and Alarm Equipment," U.S. Fire Administration, April 2006, http://www.usfa.dhs.gov/downloads/pdf/white-paper-alarms.pdf. The Public/Private Fire Safety Council is a sixteen-member council of federal agencies and nongovernment organizations created to develop a coordinated national effort to eliminate residential fire deaths by the year 2020.

2. David Canter, *Fires and Human Behavior* (Chichester, England: John Wiley & Sons, 1986), 2–7.

3. Larry Davis and Dominic Colletti, *The Rural Firefighting Handbook* (Royersford, PA: Lyons Publishing, 2002), 59.

4. International Association of Fire Chiefs and National Fire Protection Association, *Fundamentals of Fire Fighter Skills* (Sudbury, MA: Jones and Bartlett Publishers, 2004), 136–137.

5. Canter, *Fires and Human Behavior*, chap. 1, 5, and 6.

6. U.S. Fire Administration, "Socioeconomic Factors and the Incidence of Fire," Federal Emergency Management Agency, June 1997, http://www.usfa.dhs.gov/downloads/pdf/statistics/socio.pdf; U.S. Fire Administration, "The Rural Fire Problem in the U.S.," Federal Emergency Management Agency, August 1997, http://www.usfa.dhs.gov/downloads/pdf/statistics/rural.pdf; United States Fire Administration, "An NFIRS Analysis: Investigating City Characteristics and Residential Fire Rates," Federal Emergency Management Agency, April 1998, http://www.usfa.dhs.gov/downloads/pdf/statistics/city.pdf; and Paul Gunther, "Rural Fire Deaths: The Role of Climate and Poverty" (Washington, DC: U.S. Fire Administration 1981).

7. U.S. Fire Administration, "An NFIRS Analysis."

8. United States Fire Administration, "Socioeconomic Factors and the Incidence of Fire"; and United States Fire Administration, "An NFIRS Analysis: Investigating City Characteristics and Residential Fire Rates."

9. U.S. Fire Administration, "An NFIRS Analysis."

10. Kai Huang, "Population and Building Factors That Impact Residential Fire Rates in Large U.S. Cities," Texas State University–San Marcos, Spring 2009, http://ecommons.txstate.edu/cgi/viewcontent.cgi?article=1289&context=arp.

7. Fire in Rural Areas and Wildlands

1. U.S. Fire Administration, "The Rural Fire Problem in the United States," 3.

2. Ibid., table 2, fig. 1, and fig. 2.

3. Ibid., figs. 1–6.

4. Ibid., 19 and fig. 12.

5. Stephen J. Pyne, *Fire in America: A Cultural History of Wildland and Rural Fire* (Princeton, NJ: Princeton University Press, 1982), 5.

8. Transformative Forces to Make Firefighting Safer

1. Paul Peluso, "IAFF Responds to IAFC's Position on 'Two Hatter' Issue," Firehouse.com, November 6, 2008, http://www.firehouse.com/news/news/iaff-responds-iafcs-position-two-hatter-issue.

2. U.S. Department of Labor, "Fire Fighters' Two-in/Two-out Regulation," International Association of Fire Fighters, http://www.iaff.org/hs/PDF/2in2out.pdf.

3. The NFPA issues several hundred standards related to fire protection and the fire service. Three of the standards—1500, 1710, and 1720—are especially significant for the fire service in terms of occupational safety and deployment of resources. Though not mandatory unless adopted legally, the standards carry weight as industry practice. The full titles of the documents are: NFPA 1500: Standard on Fire Department Occupational Safety and Health Program; NFPA 1710: Standard for the Organization and Deployment of Fire Suppression Operations, Emergency Medical Operations, and Special Operations to the Public by Career Fire Departments; and NFPA 1720: Standard for the Organization and Deployment of Fire Suppression Operations, Emergency Medical Operations and Special Operations to the Public by Volunteer Fire Departments.

4. Richard Thompson Ford, "Bad Test: Sonia Sotomayor Rejected the New Haven Firefighters' Claim Because It Threatened to Burn Down Civil Rights Law," *Slate*, May 27, 2009, http://www.slate.com/id/2219062.

9. Cultural Change Needed to Improve Firefighter Safety

1. National Fallen Firefighters Foundation, "Firefighter Life Safety Summit Reports," Everyone Goes Home, http://www.everyonegoeshome.com/summit.html.

2. National Fallen Firefighters Foundation, "16 Firefighter Life Safety Initiatives," Everyone Goes Home, http://www.everyonegoeshome.com/initiatives.html.

3. Thompson, "FDNY Lt. Says Fire Service Needs Culture of 'Extinguishment Not Safety.'"

4. National Fallen Firefighters Foundation, "The Firefighter Life Safety Initiatives Adoption and Implementation," Everyone Goes Home, 2008, http://www.everyonegoeshome.comkits/volume3/CD1/Final_IIW_Guidebook_v_5_ for_pdf_4.24.08.2.pdf."

5. Moore-Merrell et al., "Contributing Factors to Firefighter Line-of-Duty Injury."

6. U.S. Fire Administration, "Special Report: Trends and Hazards in Firefighter Training," Department of Homeland Security, May 2003, http://www.usfa.dhs.gov/downloads/pdf/publications/tr-100.pdf.

7. Physical fitness and medical standards exist for the fire service, but they are voluntary. While most firefighters, volunteer and career, receive some form of medical screening, physical fitness standards are not as widespread. Career departments are increasingly adopting entrance tests to measure or ensure physical capacity for strenuous firefighting activities. Almost all entrance tests used by fire departments have been subjected to a legal review for applicability, appropriateness, and nondiscrimination factors in the testing of the wide range of people seeking to be firefighters in the United States.

10. Transitional Forces Create New Fire Service Model

1. Karter and Stein, "U.S. Fire Department Profile through 2007."

2. John Benoit and Kenneth B. Perkins, *Leading Career and Volunteer Firefighters: Searching for Buried Treasure* (Halifax, Nova Scotia, Canada: Henson College, Dalhousie University, 2001), 19–21.

3. Ibid.

4. Denise M. Hulett et al., "A National Report Card on Women in Firefighting," International Association of Women in Fire and Emergency Services, April 2008, http://www.i-women.org/images/pdf-files/35827WSP.pdf.

5. Bureau of Labor Statistics, "Occupational Outlook Handbook, 2010–11 Edition: Fire Fighters," U.S. Department of Labor, December 17, 2009, http://www.bls.gov/oco/ocos329.htm.

6. Lester W. Zartman, *Yale Readings in Insurance: Fire Insurance* (New Haven, CT: Yale University Press, 1909), 1.

7. Stephanie Schorow, *Boston on Fire: A History* (Beverly, MA: Commonwealth Editions, 2003), 2–12.

8. Harry Chase Brearley, *Fifty Years of a Civilizing Force: An Historical and Critical Study of the Work of the National Board of Fire Underwriters* (New York: Frederick A. Stokes Company, 1916), 9; and Benjamin L. Carp, "Fire of Liberty: Firefighters, Urban Voluntary Culture, and the Revolutionary Movement," *William and Mary Quarterly* 58, no. 4 (2001): 781–818.

9. Amy S. Greenberg, *Cause for Alarm: The Volunteer Fire Department in the Nineteenth-Century City* (Princeton, NJ: Princeton University Press, 1998), 1–17.

10. Ibid., chap. 1.

11. Ibid., chap. 3.

12. Lloyd Layman, *Fire Fighting Tactics* (Boston: National Fire Protection Association, 1953), 7–9; and James M. Bugbee, "Fires and Fire Departments," *North American Review* 117, no. 240 (1873): 108–41.

11. London and the Development of a Fire Service

1. Tinniswood, *By Permission of Heaven,* 48–53; and "The Way We Were: A History of London's Fire Fighters," (London: Public Relations Section, London Fire Brigade Headquarters), 3

2. Tinniswood, *By Permission of Heaven,* 48–53

3. Bird and Docking, *Fire in Buildings*, 33–34.

4. "The Way We Were," 8; and "Archives: The Royal Society for the Protection of Life from Fire," Society for the Protection of Life from Fire, 2008, http://www.splf.org.uk/archives.htm.

5. "The Way We Were," 8–9.

6. Bird and Docking, *Fire in Buildings*, 186–89.

7. Arthur E. Cote, ed., *Fire Protection Handbook*, 17th ed. (Quincy, MA: National Fire Protection Association, 1992), section 1, chapter 10. The NFPA uses the term "large loss" to describe serious fires.

8. Christine Meisner Rosen, *The Limits of Power: Great Fires and the Process of City Growth in America* (New York: Cambridge University Press, 1986), 92, 177–79, and 249–51; Joseph Kirkland, "The Chicago Fire," *New England Magazine* 12, no. 5 (1892): 740–41; Foster, *A Full Account of the Great Fire at Pittsburgh*, 3–10; Brearley, *Fifty Years of a Civilizing Force*, 22; Peter Charles Hoffer, *Seven Fires: The Urban Infernos That Reshaped America* (New York: PublicAffairs, 2006), 64–103; and John Neal, *Account of the Great Conflagration in Portland, July 4th & 5th, 1866* (Portland: Starbird & Twitchell, 1866), 1–22. In addition, numerous websites of public libraries and historical societies in the particular cities offer information about great fires.

12. Portland and the Board of Fire Underwriters

1. Brearley, *Fifty Years of a Civilizing Force,* 8.

2. A.L. Todd, *A Spark Lighted in Portland: The Record of the National Board of Fire Underwriters* (New York: McGraw-Hill Book Co., 1966), 7–14; and Bruce Hensler, "History and Analysis: MRSA Title 25—Chp. 313 'Municipal Inspection of Buildings,'" in *Maine Code Official's Institute* (Augusta, ME: Maine State Planning Office, 2002).

3. Todd, *A Spark Lighted in Portland*, 7–14.

4. Ibid.

5. Brearley, *Fifty Years of a Civilizing Force*, 11–14.

6. Todd, *A Spark Lighted in Portland*, 18–21; and Hensler.

7. Todd, *A Spark Lighted in Portland*, 24–26.

8. Ibid.

9. Ibid., 33–37.

10. Todd, *A Spark Lighted in Portland*, 33–44; and *Handbook of the Underwriter's Bureau of New England* (Boston: Standard Publishing Company, 1896), preface.

13. Boston and the Standardization of Fire Protection

1. Bugbee, "Fires and Fire Departments."

2. Bugbee, "Fires and Fire Departments," 110–11.

3. Ibid., 109–10.

4. Ibid., 111.

5. Rosen, *The Limits of Power*, 177–78.

6. Bugbee, "Fires and Fire Departments," 113–14.

7. Ibid., 114.

8. Bugbee, "Fires and Fire Departments," 116; and Eyre Massey Shaw, *Fire Surveys: Or, a Summary of the Principles to Be Observed in Estimating the Risk of Buildings* (London: Effingham Wilson, Royal Exchange, 1872).

9. William M. Shields, "Theory and Practice in the Study of Technological Systems," Virginia Polytechnic Institute and State University, 2007, 184–187, http://scholar.lib.vt.edu/theses/available/etd-04122007-085304/unrestricted/ShieldsETDDraft.pdf.

10. "Rules and Regulations Governing the Fire Department" (McKeesport, PA: City Council, 1909).

14. Fire Protection in Theory

1. Cote, *Fire Protection Handbook*, section 1, chapter 42 to section 1, chapter 55.

2. Ibid., sec. 5-127 to 5-163.

3. Ibid., sec. 6-13 to 6-19.

15. Deadly Fire in a Fireproof Hotel

1. James K. McElroy, "The Hotel Winecoff Disaster," *Quarterly of the National Fire Protection Association* 40, no. 3 (1947): 140; and Sam Heys and Allen B. Goodwin, *The Winecoff Fire: The Untold Story of America's Deadliest Hotel Fire* (Marietta, GA: Longstreet Press, Inc., 1993). The second worst hotel fire was the 1980 tragedy at the MGM Grand Hotel and Casino (now Bally's Las Vegas), during which eight-four people died, mostly from smoke inhalation.

2. McElroy, "The Hotel Winecoff Disaster," 140.

3. Maurice Webster, "What Is Fireproof?" *The Atlantic*, October 1946, 60.

4. Ibid., 60–61.

5. Ibid., 60.

6. Ibid., 61.

7. Ibid., 61–62.

8. Ibid.

9. National Institute for Occupational Safety and Health, "NIOSH Alert: Preventing Injuries and Deaths of Fire Fighters due to Truss System Failures," Centers for Disease Control and Prevention, April 2005, http://www.cdc.gov/niosh/docs/2005-132/pdfs/2005-132.pdf.

16. Firefighting, Building Codes, and Technology

1. Richard W. Bukowski, "Protection of Firefighters under the Building Codes," *Fire Engineering* (2002): 88–92.

2. John Watts, "Editorial: Codifying Firefighter Safety," *Fire Technology* 32, no. 4 (1996), 289–90.

3. National Institute for Occupational Safety and Health, "Six Career Fire Fighters Killed in Cold-Storage and Warehouse Building Fire—Massachusetts," Centers for Disease Control and Prevention, September 27, 2000, http://www.cdc.gov/niosh/fire/pdfs/face9947.pdf; U.S. Fire Administration, "Abandoned Cold Storage Warehouse Multi-Firefighter Fatality Fire, Worcester, Massachusetts," Department of Homeland Security, December 1999, http://www.usfa.dhs.gov/downloads/pdf/publications/tr-134.pdf; "Board of Inquiry: Worcester Cold Storage and Warehouse Fire" (Worcester, MA: Fire Department, City of Worcester, 1999); and Sean Flynn, "The Perfect Fire," *Esquire*, July 2000, http://www.esquire.com/features/perfect-fire-0700.

17. New England Mills and the Factory Mutual System

1. Sara E. Wermiel, *The Fireproof Building: Technology and Public Safety in the Nineteenth-Century American City* (Baltimore, MD: Johns Hopkins University Press, 2000), 37–44. The introduction also provides a general overview of the subject.

2. Ibid., 12–15, 37–44, 47, and 57.

3. Ibid., 43 and 79; Braidwood, *Fire Prevention and Fire Extinction*, 47–58, and Shaw; *Fire Surveys*, 2–4.

4. Braidwood, *Fire Prevention and Fire Extinction*, 47–58; and Wermiel, *The Fireproof Building*, 43.

5. Wermiel, *The Fireproof Building*, 37–44 and 57.

6. Ibid., 79; and Shaw, *Fire Surveys*, 2–4 and 9–10.

7. Wermiel, *The Fireproof Building*, 90–105 and 119–25.

8. Ibid., 105–6.

9. Ibid., 106–9.

10. Ibid., 110–12.

11. Ibid., 112.

12. Ibid., 112–13.

13. Ibid., 121–25.

14. Ibid., 134–37.

18. Fighting Fires: From Art to Science

1. Vannevar Bush, "Biographical Memoir of John Ripley Freeman 1855–1932," National Academies Press, 1935, http://books.nap.edu/html/biomems/jfreeman.pdf.

2. Cote, *Fire Protection Handbook*, sec. 5-40 to 5-46; John R. Freeman, "The Arrangement of Hydrants and Water Pipes for the Protection of a City against Fire," *Journal of the New England Water Works Association* 7 (1892); and John R. Freeman, "Experiments Relating to the Hydraulics of Fire Streams," *Transactions: American Society of Civil Engineers* 21 (1889).

3. Freeman, "The Arrangement of Hydrants and Water Pipes for the Protection of a City against Fire"; and Cote, *Fire Protection Handbook*, sec. 5-40 to 5-46.

4. Cote, *Fire Protection Handbook*, sec. 5-40 to 5-46.

5. National Fire Protection Association, "History of the NFPA Codes and Standards-Making System," *NFPA Journal* (May/June 1995): 97.

6. Casey Cavanaugh Grant, "The Birth of NFPA," National Fire Protection Association, 1996, http://www.nfpa.org/itemDetail.asp?categoryID=500&itemID=18020&URL=Abou t%20NFPA/Overview/History.

7. Schorow, *Boston on Fire*, 32.

8. Schorow, *Boston on Fire*, 36–41; and Robyn Cooper, "The Fireman: Immaculate Manhood," *Journal of Popular Culture* 28, no. 4 (1995): 139–70.

9. Schorow, *Boston on Fire*, 62.

10. Gerry Souter and Janet Souter, *The American Fire Station* (Osceola, WI: MBI Publishing Co., 1998), 37.

11. Schorow, *Boston on Fire*, 54–64.

19. Volunteers to Paid Firemen

1. Miriam Lee Kaprow, "Magical Work: Firefighters in New York," *Human Organization* 50, no. 1 (1991). In addition to the cultural element, there is a managerial element to the fire department realized in the need for formality and structure to address common workplace issues and everyday administrative tasks. For these aspects, see Mark Tebeau, *Eating Smoke: Fire in Urban America, 1800–1950* (Baltimore, MD: Johns Hopkins University Press, 2003).

2. Greenberg, *Cause for Alarm,* 3–17.

3. Ibid., 18–21.

4. Fahy et al., "Firefighter Fatalities in the United States—2009." The averages were calculated based on NFPA statistics.

5. Greenberg, *Cause for Alarm,* 18–40.

6. Ibid., 109–24.

7. Fred S. McChesney, "Government Prohibitions on Volunteer Fire Fighting in Nineteenth-Century America: A Property Rights Perspective," *Journal of Legal Studies* 15, no. 1 (1986): 85–92.

8. Greenberg, *Cause for Alarm,* 125–51.

20. Legacy of the Combustible City

1. Bird and Docking, *Fire in Buildings*, 26–30.

2. Jan van der Heyden, *A Description of Fire Engines with Water Hoses and the Method of Fighting Fires Now Used in Amsterdam (1690)*, 2nd ed., trans. Lettie Stibbe Multhauf (Canton, MA: Science History Publications, 1996).

3. Ibid., see the foreword written by Peter M. Molloy, Executive Director, National Historical Fire Foundation, for an analysis of seventeenth-century firefighting methods and equipment as used in Amsterdam.

4. Ibid., introduction; and Peter C. Sutton, *Jan van der Heyden (1637–1712)* (New Haven, CT: Yale University Press, 2006), 210.

5. van der Heyden, *A Description of Fire Engines*, 16–20.

6. Lloyd Layman, *Attacking and Extinguishing Interior Fires* (Boston: National Fire Protection Association, 1955), 31–53.

7. Van der Heyden, *A Description of Fire Engines*, x; and James Braidwood, *On the Construction of Fire-Engines*, 82.

8. Van der Heyden, *A Description of Fire Engines*, 87–94.

9. David McCullough, "The Story of Two Americans in Paris: Samuel F. B. Morse and James Fenimore Cooper in the Year 1832" (lecture, Strand Theatre, Rockland, ME, November 22, 2009).

10. Schorow, *Boston on Fire*, 48–66.

11. Terry Golway, *So Others Might Live: A History of New York's Bravest—The FDNY from 1700 to the Present* (New York: Basic Books, 2002), 169–74.

12. John Kenlon, *Fires and Fire-Fighters: A History of Modern Fire-Fighting with a Review of Its Development from Earliest Times* (New York: George H. Doran Company, 1913), 74–78.

13. Ibid., 1.

14. Ibid., 65–68.

15. Ibid., 170–71.

16. Hulett et al., "A National Report Card on Women in Firefighting."

17. Jacob A. Riis, "Heroes Who Fight Fires," *Century Magazine*, 1898, 483–97.

18. Cooper, "The Fireman," 163–65.

19. Fahy et al., "Firefighter Fatalities Studies 1977–2006: What's Changed over the Last Thirty Years?" *NFPA Journal* (2007): 49–67.

20. Thompson, "FDNY Lt. Says Fire Service Needs Culture of 'Extinguishment Not Safety.'"

21. Philip Schaenman, "Global Concepts in Residential Safety: Part 1—Best Practices from England, Scotland, Sweden, and Norway," System Planning Corporation, October 2007, http://www.sysplan.com/documents/tridata/international/global_concepts_1.2.pdf; TriData, "Global Concepts in Residential Safety: Part 2—Best Practices from Australia, New Zealand and Japan," System Planning Corporation, August 2008, http://www.sysplan.com/documents/tridata/international/Global_Concepts_Part%2 0II_2008.pdf; and TriData, "Global Concepts in Residential Safety: Part 3—Best Practices from Canada, Puerto Rico, Mexico, and Dominican Republic," System Planning Corporation, July 2009, http://www.sysplan.com/documents/tridata/international/Global_Concepts_Part_III_FINAL_8-11-2009.pdf.

22. Cooper, "The Fireman."

Bibliography

"Archives: The Royal Society for the Protection of Life from Fire." Society for the Protection of Life from Fire. 2008. http://www.splf.org.uk/archives.htm.

Benoit, John, and Kenneth B. Perkins. *Leading Career and Volunteer Firefighters: Searching for Buried Treasure*. Halifax, Nova Scotia, Canada: Henson College, Dalhousie University, 2001.

Bird, Eric L., and Stanley J. Docking. *Fire in Buildings*. London: Adam & Charles Black, Ltd., 1949.

"Board of Inquiry: Worcester Cold Storage and Warehouse Fire." Worcester, MA: Fire Department, City of Worcester, MA, 1999.

Braidwood, James. *Fire Prevention and Fire Extinction*. London: Bell and Daldy, 1866.

———. *On the Construction of Fire-Engines and Apparatus, the Training of Firemen, and the Method of Proceeding in Cases of Fire*. Edinburgh: Bell and Bradfute, and Oliver and Boyd, 1830.

Brearley, Harry Chase. *Fifty Years of a Civilizing Force: An Historical and Critical Study of the Work of the National Board of Fire Underwriters*. New York: Frederick A. Stokes Company, 1916.

Bruegman, Robert. *Sprawl: A Compact History*. Chicago: University of Chicago Press, 2005.

Bugbee, James M. "Fires and Fire Departments." *North American Review* 117, no. 240 (1873): 108–41.

Bukowski, Richard W. "Protection of Firefighters under the Building Codes." *Fire Engineering*, 2002.

Bureau of Labor Statistics. "Occupational Outlook Handbook, 2010–11 Edition: Fire Fighters." U.S. Department of Labor. December 17, 2009. http://www.bls.gov/oco/ocos329.htm.

Bush, Vannevar. "Biographical Memoir of John Ripley Freeman 1855–1932." National Academies Press. 1935. http://books.nap.edu/html/biomems/jfreeman.pdf.

Canter, David. *Fires and Human Behavior*. Chichester, England: John Wiley & Sons, 1986.

Carp, Benjamin L. "Fire of Liberty: Firefighters, Urban Voluntary Culture, and the Revolutionary Movement." *William and Mary Quarterly* 58, no. 4 (2001): 781–818.

Cook, Donald E. "The Great Fire of Pittsburgh in 1845." *Western Pennsylvania Historical Magazine* 51 (1968): 127–29.

Cooper, Robyn. "The Fireman: Immaculate Manhood." *Journal of Popular Culture* 28, no. 4 (1995): 139–70.

Cote, Arthur E., ed. *Fire Protection Handbook*. 17th ed. Quincy, MA: National Fire Protection Association, 1992.

Crawford, Brian A. "To Die For." *Fire Chief*, 2007.

Davis, Larry, and Dominic Colletti. *The Rural Firefighting Handbook*. Roycrsford, PA: Lyons Publishing, 2002.

Dawson, Charles T. *Our Firemen: The History of the Pittsburgh Fire Department, from the Village Period until the Present Time*. Pittsburgh, PA: Charles Fenno, 1889.

D'Intino, Robert S. "Volunteer Firefighter Recruitment and Retention in Rural Pennsylvania." Center for Rural Pennsylvania. May 2006. 6–15. http://www.rural.palegislature.us/Volunteer_firefighters06.pdf.

Dyson, Freeman. "Part I: A Failure of Intelligence." *Technology Review*. November 1, 2006. http://www.technologyreview.com/InfoTech/17724/?a=f.

———. "Part II: A Failure of Intelligence." *Technology Review*. November 1, 2006. http://www.technologyreview.com/computing/17847/page1/?a=f .

Fahy, Rita F., Paul R. LeBlanc, and Joseph L.Molis. "Firefighter Fatalities in the United States—2009." National Fire Protection Association. June 2010. http://www.nfpa.org/assets/files/PDF/osfff.pdf.

———. "Firefighter Fatalities Studies 1977–2006: What's Changed over the Last Thirty Years?" *NFPA Journal* (2007): 49–67.

"Final Report for LODD Project: Phases I–II." Stillwater, OK: Oklahoma State University—IFSTA/FPP, 2006.

Flanagan, Luke. *Science in Fire-Fighting.* New York: S.L. Parsons & Co., 1920.

Flynn, Sean. "The Perfect Fire." *Esquire,* July 2000.
http://www.esquire.com/features/perfect-fire-0700.

Ford, Richard Thompson. "Bad Test: Sonia Sotomayor Rejected the New Haven Firefighters' Claim Because It Threatened to Burn Down Civil Rights Law." *Slate,* May 27, 2009. http://www.slate.com/id/2219062/.

Foster, J. Heron. *A Full Account of the Great Fire at Pittsburgh, on the Tenth Day of April, 1845; with Individual Losses and Contributions for Relief.* Pittsburgh: J.W. Cook, 1845.

Freeman, John R. "The Arrangement of Hydrants and Water Pipes for the Protection of a City against Fire." *Journal of the New England Water Works Association* 7 (1892).

———. "Experiments Relating to the Hydraulics of Fire Streams." *Transactions: American Society of Civil Engineers* 21 (1889).

Golway, Terry. *So Others Might Live: A History of New York's Bravest—The FDNY from 1700 to the Present.* New York: Basic Books, 2002.

Grant, Casey Cavanaugh. "The Birth of NFPA." National Fire Protection Association. 1996.
http://www.nfpa.org/itemDetail.asp?categoryID=500&itemID=18020&URL=About%20NFPA/Overview/History.

Greenberg, Amy S. *Cause for Alarm: The Volunteer Fire Department in the Nineteenth-Century City.* Princeton, NJ: Princeton University Press, 1998.

Grimwood, Paul. *Euro Firefighter.* West Yorkshire, England: Jeremy Mills Publishing Limited, 2008.

Gunther, Paul. "Rural Fire Deaths: The Role of Climate and Poverty." Washington DC: U.S. Fire Administration, 1981.

Handbook of the Underwriter's Bureau of New England. Boston: Standard Publishing Company, 1896.

Hensler, Bruce. "History and Analysis: MRSA Title 25—Chp. 313 'Municipal Inspection of Buildings.'" In *Maine Code Official's Institute.* Augusta, ME: Maine State Planning Office, 2002.

Heys, Sam, and Allen B. Goodwin. *The Winecoff Fire: The Untold Story of America's Deadliest Hotel Fire.* Marietta, GA: Longstreet Press, Inc., 1993.

Hoffer, Peter Charles. *Seven Fires: The Urban Infernos That Reshaped America.* New York: PublicAffairs, 2006.

Huang, Kai. "Population and Building Factors That Impact Residential Fire Rates in Large U.S. Cities." Texas State University–San Marcos. Spring 2009. http://ecommons.txstate.edu/cgi/viewcontent.cgi?article=1289&context=arp.

Hulett, Denise M., Marc Bendick, Sheila Y. Thomas, and Francine Moccio. "A National Report Card on Women in Firefighting." International Association of Women in Fire and Emergency Services. April 2008. http://www.i-women.org/images/pdf-files/35827WSP.pdf.

International Association of Fire Chiefs and National Fire Protection Association. *Fundamentals of Fire Fighter Skills*. Sudbury, MA: Jones and Bartlett Publishers, 2004.

Kaprow, Miriam Lee. "Magical Work: Firefighters in New York." *Human Organization* 50, no. 1 (1991).

Karter Jr., Michael J., and Gary P. Stein. "U.S. Fire Department Profile through 2007." National Fire Protection Association. November 2008. http://www.doi.idaho.gov/SFM/FDProfile_2007.pdf.

Kenlon, John. *Fires and Fire-Fighters: A History of Modern Fire-Fighting with a Review of Its Development from Earliest Times*. New York: George H. Doran Company, 1913.

Kirkland, Joseph. "The Chicago Fire." *New England Magazine* 12, no. 5 (1892): 726–43.

Knight, Jim, and Lesia Kudelkja. "Report of S.C. OSHA: Findings in June 18, 2007 Charleston Sofa Super Store Fire." South Carolina Department of Labor, Licensing and Regulation. http://media.charleston.net/pdf/OSHAreport.pdf.

Layman, Lloyd. *Attacking and Extinguishing Interior Fires*. Boston: National Fire Protection Association, 1955.

———. *Fire Fighting Tactics*. Boston: National Fire Protection Association, 1953.

MacDougall-Tattan, Jean. "Firefighters Fear for Their Safety." *Haverhill Gazette*, January 31, 2008. http://www.firehouse.com/news/news/massachusetts-firefighters-fear-their-safety.

McChesney, Fred S. "Government Prohibitions on Volunteer Fire Fighting in Nineteenth-Century America: A Property Rights Perspective." *Journal of Legal Studies* 15, no. 1 (1986): 69–92.

McCullough, David. "The Story of Two Americans in Paris: Samuel F.B. Morse and James Fenimore Cooper in the Year 1832." Lecture at the Strand Theatre, Rockland, ME, November 22, 2009.

McElroy, James K. "The Hotel Winecoff Disaster." *Quarterly of the National Fire Protection Association* 40, no. 3 (1947): 140–59.

Moore-Merrell, Lori, Ainong Zhou, Sue McDonald-Valentine, Randy Goldstein, and Chloe Slocum. "Contributing Factors to Firefighter Line-of-Duty Injury in Metropolitan Fire Departments in the United States." International Association of Fire Fighters. August 2008. http://www.iaff.org/08News/PDF/InjuryReport.pdf.

Munro, Neil. "Our Heroes Turned Out to Be Cowboys in New York Attacks." *Oakland Press Online*, 2002. http://www.firehouse.com/news/2002/7/24_Ppaper_orig.html.

National Fallen Firefighters Foundation, The. "16 Firefighter Life Safety Initiatives." Everyone Goes Home. http://www.everyonegoeshome.com/initiatives.html.

————. "The Firefighter Life Safety Initiatives Adoption and Implementation." Everyone Goes Home. 2008. 5.http://www.everyonegoeshome.com/kits/volume3/CD1/Final_IIW_Guideboo k_v._5_for_PDF_4.24.08.2.pdf.

————. "Firefighter Life Safety Summit Reports." Everyone Goes Home. http://www.everyonegoeshome.com/summit.html.

National Fire Protection Association. "History of the NFPA Codes and Standards-Making System." *NFPA Journal* (May/June 1995): 97.

————. "Smoke Alarms in Reported U.S. Home Fires." http://www.nfpa.org/assets/files/PDF/SmokeAlarmsFactSheet.pdf.

National Institute for Occupational Safety and Health. "NIOSH Alert: Preventing Injuries and Deaths of Fire Fighters due to Truss System Failures." Centers for Disease Control and Prevention. April 2005. http://www.cdc.gov/niosh/docs/2005-132/pdfs/2005-132.pdf.

————. "Six Career Fire Fighters Killed in Cold-Storage and Warehouse Building Fire—Massachusetts." Centers for Disease Control and Prevention. September 27, 2000. http://www.cdc.gov/niosh/fire/pdfs/face9947.pdf.

Neal, John. *Account of the Great Conflagration in Portland, July 4th & 5th, 1866.* Portland: Starbird & Twitchell, 1866.

Okray, Randy, and Thomas Lubnau. *Crew Resource Management for the Fire Service.* Tulsa, OK: PennWell Corp., 2004.

O'Neill, Brian. *The Paris of Appalachia: Pittsburgh in the Twenty-First Century.* Pittsburgh: Carnegie Mellon University Press, 2009.

Peluso, Paul. "IAFF Responds to IAFC's Position on 'Two Hatter' Issue." Firehouse.com. November 6, 2008. http://www.firehouse.com/news/news/iaff-responds-iafcs-position-two-hatter-issue.

Pessemier, William. "Developing a Safety Culture in the Fire Service." *International Fire Service Journal of Leadership and Management* 2, no. 1 (2008).

Public/Private Fire Safety Council, "White Paper: Home Smoke Alarms and Other Fire Detection and Alarm Equipment." U.S. Fire Administration. April 2006. http://www.usfa.dhs.gov/downloads/pdf/white-paper-alarms.pdf.

Pyne, Stephen J. *Fire in America: A Cultural History of Wildland and Rural Fire.* Princeton, NJ: Princeton University Press, 1982.

Ridenour, Marilyn. "Leading Recommendations for Preventing Fire Fighter Fatalities, 1998–2005." National Institute for Occupational Safety and Health. November 2008. http://www.cdc.gov/niosh/docs/2009-100/pdfs/2009-100.pdf.

Riis, Jacob A. "Heroes Who Fight Fires." *Century Magazine,* 1898.

Ripley, Joseph P. "Report to the City: Tragic Fire of June 18, 2007." Charleston, SC: Mayor of the City of Charleston, 2007.

Ritter, Scott. "Fire Commentary: Picking up the Gauntlet." Fire Engineering. January 15, 2008. http://www.fireengineering.com/index/articles/display/317164/articles/fire-engineering/featured-content/2008/01/fire-commentary-picking-up-the-gauntlet.html.

Rosen, Christine Meisner. *The Limits of Power: Great Fires and the Process of City Growth in America.* New York: Cambridge University Press, 1986.

Routley, J. Gordon, Michael D. Chiaramonte, Brian A. Crawford, Peter A. Piringer, Kevin M. Roche, and Timothy E. Sendelbach. "City of Charleston: Post Incident Assessment and Review Team: Phase 1 Report." City of Charleston. October 16, 2007. http://www.charlestoncity.info/shared/docs/0/charleston_fire_department_phase_one_report.pdf.

———. "City of Charleston: Post Incident Assessment and Review Team: Phase II Report." City of Charleston. http://www.charlestoncity.info/shared/docs/0/sofa%20super%20store%20report%20may%2015%202008%20final.pdf.

"Rules and Regulations Governing the Fire Department." McKeesport, PA: City Council, 1909.

"Rules of Engagement for Structural Firefighting: Increasing Firefighter Survival (Draft)." Fairfax, VA: IAFC—Safety, Health and Survival Section, 2009.

Schaenman, Philip. "Global Concepts in Residential Safety: Part 1—Best Practices from England, Scotland, Sweden, and Norway." System Planning Corporation. October 2007. http://www.sysplan.com/documents/tridata/international/global_concepts_1.2.pdf.

Schorow, Stephanie. *Boston on Fire: A History.* Beverly, MA: Commonwealth Editions, 2003.

Seck, Momar D., and David D. Evans. "Major U.S. Cities Using National Standard Fire Hydrants, One Century after the Great Baltimore Fire." National Institute of Standards and Technology. August 2004. http://www.fire.nist.gov/bfrlpubs/fire04/PDF/f04095.pdf.

Shaw, Eyre Massey. *Fire Surveys: Or, a Summary of the Principles to Be Observed in Estimating the Risk of Buildings*. London: Effingham Wilson, Royal Exchange, 1872.

Shields, William M. "Theory and Practice in the Study of Technological Systems." Virginia Polytechnic Institute and State University. 2007. http://scholar.lib.vt.edu/theses/available/etd-04122007-085304/unrestricted/ShieldsETDDraft.pdf.

Simpson, Charles R. "A Fraternity of Danger: Volunteer Fire Companies and the Contradictions of Modernization." *American Journal of Economics and Sociology* 55, no. 1 (1996): 17–33.

Smith, Dennis. *Report from Engine Co. 82*. New York: Warner Books, 1999.

Snowden, Lisa. "From Sweden, a Critical View of U.S. Firefighters." Firehouse.com. August 8, 2007. http://cms.firehouse.com/content/article/printer.jsp?id=56147.

Souter, Gerry, and Janet Souter. *The American Fire Station*. Osceola, WI: MBI Publishing Co., 1998.

Sutton, Peter C. *Jan van der Heyden (1637–1712)*. New Haven, CT: Yale University Press, 2006.

Tebeau, Mark. *Eating Smoke: Fire in Urban America, 1800–1950*. Baltimore, MD: Johns Hopkins University Press, 2003.

Thompson, Jamie. "FDNY Lt. Says Fire Service Needs Culture of 'Extinguishment Not Safety.'" FireRescue1. April 23, 2009. http://www.firerescue1.com/firefighter-safety/articles/483861-FDNY-Lt-says-fire-service-needs-culture-of-extinguishment-not-safety/.

Tinniswood, Adrian. *By Permission of Heaven: The True Story of the Great Fire of London*. New York: Penguin Group (USA), Inc., 2004.

Todd, A.L. *A Spark Lighted in Portland: The Record of the National Board of Fire Underwriters*. New York: McGraw-Hill Book Co., 1966.

Toker, Franklin. *Pittsburgh: A New Portrait*. Pittsburgh: University of Pittsburgh Press, 2009.

TriData. "Global Concepts in Residential Safety: Part 2—Best Practices from Australia, New Zealand and Japan." System Planning Corporation. August 2008. http://www.sysplan.com/documents/tridata/international/Global_Concepts_Part%20II_2008.pdf.

————. "Global Concepts in Residential Safety: Part 3—Best Practices from Canada, Puerto Rico, Mexico, and Dominican Republic." System Planning Corporation. July 2009. http://www.sysplan.com/documents/tridata/international/Global_Concepts_Part_III_FINAL_8-11-2009.pdf.

Unger, Zac. *Working Fire: The Making of an Accidental Fireman.* New York: Penguin Press, 2004.

U.S. Department of Labor. "Fire Fighters' Two-in/Two-out Regulation." International Association of Fire Fighters. http://www.iaff.org/hs/PDF/2in2out.pdf.

U.S. Fire Administration. "Abandoned Cold Storage Warehouse Multi-Firefighter Fatality Fire, Worcester, Massachusetts." Department of Homeland Security. December 1999. http://www.usfa.dhs.gov/downloads/pdf/publications/tr-134.pdf.

————. "An NFIRS Analysis: Investigating City Characteristics and Residential Fire Rates." Federal Emergency Management Agency. April 1998. http://www.usfa.dhs.gov/downloads/pdf/statistics/city.pdf.

————. "The Rural Fire Problem in the United States." Federal Emergency Management Agency. August 1997. http://www.usfa.dhs.gov/downloads/pdf/statistics/rural.pdf.

————. "Socioeconomic Factors and the Incidence of Fire." Federal Emergency Management Agency. June 1997. http://www.usfa.dhs.gov/downloads/pdf/statistics/socio.pdf.

————. "Special Report: Trends and Hazards in Firefighter Training." Department of Homeland Security. May 2003. http://www.usfa.dhs.gov/downloads/pdf/publications/tr-100.pdf.

U.S. Fire Administration and National Fire Data Center. "Fire in the United States 1995–2004, Fourteenth Edition." Federal Emergency Management Agency. August 2007. http://www.usfa.dhs.gov/downloads/pdf/publications/fa-311.pdf.

Van der Heyden, Jan. *A Description of Fire Engines with Water Hoses and the Method of Fighting Fires Now Used in Amsterdam (1690).* 2nd ed. Translated by Lettie Stibbe Multhauf. Canton, MA: Science History Publications, 1996.

Von Drehele, David. *Triangle: The Fire That Changed America.* New York: Atlantic Monthly Press, 2003.

Watts, John. "Editorial: Codifying Firefighter Safety." *Fire Technology* 32, no. 4 (1996).

"The Way We Were: A History of London's Fire Fighters." London: Public Relations Section, London Fire Brigade Headquarters.

Webster, Maurice. "What Is Fireproof?" *The Atlantic*, October 1946.

Wermiel, Sara E. *The Fireproof Building: Technology and Public Safety in the Nineteenth-Century American City*. Baltimore, MD: Johns Hopkins University Press, 2000.

Zartman, Lester W. *Yale Readings in Insurance: Fire Insurance*. New Haven, CT: Yale University Press, 1909.

Index

About the Author

Bruce Hensler has served over thirty years in career and volunteer fire departments. He was born in McKeesport, Pennsylvania, and served in the U.S. Navy as a corpsman. He now lives in coastal Maine and serves as a paid-call fire officer in Rockport. He is a certified fire protection specialist and emergency medical technician, earned a master's degree in public administration, and attended the National Fire Academy. His website is www.brucehensler.com.